Enemies of the State

ENEMIES
OF THE
STATE

PERSONAL STORIES FROM THE GULAG

Edited with an Introduction by

Donald T. Critchlow

and

Agnieszka Critchlow

IVAN R. DEE

CHICAGO

The editors are grateful to the following publishers for permission to reprint
excerpts from copyrighted materials:

Eleven Years in Soviet Prison Camps by Elinor Lipper. Copyright © 1951 by Henry
Regnery Publishing. All rights reserved. Reprinted by special permission of
Regnery Publishing, Inc., Washington, D.C.

In God's Underground by Richard Wurmbrand. Copyright © 1968 by Richard
Wurmbrand. By permission of Random House, Inc.

Volunteers for the Gallows by Bela Szasz, published by Chatto & Windus.
Used by permission of The Random House Group Limited.

Four Years in a Red Hell: The Story of Father Rigney by Harold William Rigney.
Copyright © 1956 by Henry Regnery Publishing. All rights reserved. Reprinted
by special permission of Regnery Publishing, Inc., Washington, D.C.

The Vietnamese Gulag by Doan Van Toai and David Chanoff. Copyright © 1986
by Doan Van Toai and David Chanoff. By permission of the authors.

Life and Death in Shanghai by Nien Cheng. Copyright © 1986 by Nien Cheng.
Reprinted by permission of HarperCollins Publishers Ltd.

The editors and the publisher have made every effort to secure permissions from
appropriate rights holders. They will be glad to rectify any omissions in
subsequent printings.

Library of Congress Cataloging-in-Publication Data:
Enemies of the state : personal stories from the Gulag / edited with an
introduction by Donald T. Critchlow and Agnieszka Critchlow.
    p. cm.
    Includes index.
    ISBN 1-56663-456-3 (alk. paper)
    1. Prisoners—Communist countries—Biography. 2. Political persecution—
Communist countries. 3. Concentration camps—Communist countries. I.
Critchlow, Donald T., 1948– II. Critchlow, Agnieszka.

HV8964.C725 E54 2002
365'.45'0922—dc21
[B]   2002073555

In memory of those who suffered

and died for a dream misconceived;

and to Andrew Critchlow,

who embodies our dream for a better world to come

Contents

Acknowledgments

THE EDITORS wish to thank Bob Duplantier, John Korasich, and Patricia Critchlow for their help in making this a better book. Graduate students William Glankler, Michelle Rutledge, and Ahron Zorea helped with research. Vicki Hsu at Ivan R. Dee paid careful attention to the text. Also, we owe a special thanks to Ivan Dee, who took an interest in this project from the start and offered sound advice in keeping this book a manageable size.

We are also grateful to the following publishers and authors for permission to excerpt from copyrighted materials: Regnery Publishing, Inc.; Random House, Inc.; The Random House Group Limited; HarperCollins Publishers Ltd.; and Doan Van Toai and David Chanoff.

D. T. C.
A. C.

St. Louis and Prague
May 2002

Enemies of the State

Introduction

LONG BEFORE Alexander Solzhenitsyn's *One Day in the Life of Ivan Denisovich* (1962) shocked the Western world with its frightening tale of a typical day in the life of an inmate in a Soviet forced-labor camp during the Stalin era, there were those in the West who knew of prison life in the Soviet Union, the Eastern bloc, and other Communist countries. A powerful genre of "gulag" literature had emerged in the late 1930s and developed throughout the cold war. It told of prisons and slave labor camps, of prisoners tortured into false confessions and then sentenced to execution or to long terms in the camps, which just as often meant death. Books such as W. G. Krivitsky's *I Was Stalin's Agent* (1939) and Victor Kravchenko's *I Choose Freedom: A Personal and Political Life of a Soviet Official* (1946) revealed in graphic detail the systematic implementation of terror in a totalitarian police state through torture, imprisonment, and death.

Rumors of slave labor camps in the Soviet Union were heard in the West as early as the 1930s, but direct confirmation of these camps remained difficult. The USSR denied that such camps existed, and many intellectuals and journalists in the West were anxious to support these denials. Typical was the case of Victor Kravchenko—a former senior Soviet official—who described in shocking detail the nightmare of life under Stalin. His account told of mass starvation in the Ukraine during the forced collectivization of agriculture in the 1930s; of kulaks shot or sent "away" for refusing to give up their land; of a young girl caught for hiding a potato during the harvest to feed her starving family and sentenced to a labor camp for "stealing from the people"; and of the atmosphere within

3

the party during the Stalinist purges as comrades denounced other comrades to save their own necks—all to little avail.

Apologists for the Soviet Union denounced Kravchenko as an agent working for Western imperialism. For his revelations he was "tried" from January to April 1949 in the pages of the French Communist magazine *Les lettres française*, managed by the intellectual Louis Aragon. Another "trial" caused a sensation when *Les lettres française* savagely attacked David Rousset, a former Trotskyite who had received the prestigious Renaudot Prize for his book *The World of Concentration Camps*. Rousset had called for a commission of inquiry into the Soviet camp system, whereupon the Kremlin unleashed attacks on him. In this atmosphere Margaret Buber-Neumann came to Rousset's defense, recounting her experience of being in both a Nazi concentration camp and a Soviet labor camp in an article, "An Inquiry on Soviet Camps: Who Is Worse, Satan or Beelzebub?" published in *Figaro littéraire*. Elinor Lipper's *Eleven Years in a Soviet Labor Camp* (1951) offered a full indictment of these camps based on her own experience working in labor camps in Siberia. Nonetheless, intellectuals sympathetic to the Soviet Union continued to condemn such reports as "Western" propaganda. The French philosopher Jean-Paul Sartre, in his tract *Les Communistes et paix*, serialized in 1952, dismissed reports of a Soviet gulag system. Following a trip to the Soviet Union in 1954, he told Western journalists that "the freedom to criticize is total in the USSR."

In 1956, Soviet premier Nikita Khrushchev, in his famous "Secret Speech," which remained unpublished in the Soviet Union until the 1980s, denounced Stalin's crimes. He spoke only of those victims who were Communists loyal to the regime and had been caught up in the "abuses committed under Stalin" to maintain his power. Five years later in 1961, however, Khrushchev, speaking at the Twenty-second Congress of the Communist party, extended the list of victims of Stalin to include nonparty members.

The history of these revelations and denials reveals much about the nature of communism and its appeal to many Western intellectuals in the twentieth century. Of equal interest, however, is the influence of this "gulag" literature on anti-Communists in

Europe and the United States. Accounts of life in Communist prisons developed a wide audience among anti-Communist conservatives, especially in the West. Often published by conservative publishing houses such as Regnery and Devin-Adair, the books were avidly read by anti-Communists on the grassroots level as confirmations of the nature of communism. Indeed, books about prisons and work camps in Communist countries continued to appear from the outset of the cold war until well into the 1980s. They first reported on life in the Soviet Union and the Eastern bloc countries, but later included prison memoirs from Cuba, Vietnam, and China. One expects future accounts to be published telling of prison life in North Korea, China, North Vietnam, and Cuba—the remaining Communist countries in the twenty-first century.

Stories of life in Communist prisons and work camps were dramatic by nature. They depicted humanity at its heroic best as former prisoners escaped to tell of their experiences. While the literary qualities of these books are notable, their historical value is of prime interest. They provide ghastly accounts of Communist regimes but also explain why Western readers developed such a deep mistrust of "peaceful coexistence" with any Communist nation.

Memoirs of survivors of Communist prisons reinforced beliefs that the Communists could not be trusted. These books reaffirmed that Communist regimes operated through deception and denial, and that too often liberals such as Norman Davies and Henry Wallace, and later visitors to the Soviet Union, China, North Vietnam, and Cuba, had been misled by the carefully staged performances of Communist officials. In short, gulag literature presented American anti-Communists with a Manichean view of the world, an apocalyptic struggle between communism and Western Christendom. These stories are riveting, inspiring, and tell the reader much about the cold war mentality.

In the early years of the cold war, the grassroots anti-Communist movement was composed of disparate organizations operating through local organizations with little coordination among them. Fred Schwarz's Christian Anti-Communist Crusade, incorporated in 1953, offered a national focus for the movement, but it is worth noting that Schwarz's operation consisted primarily of himself and one assistant.[1] Operating with a small staff, Clarence Manion, the former dean of the law school at the University of Notre Dame, produced a nationally syndicated radio program and a newsletter that focused, though not exclusively, on what he perceived as the international and domestic Communist threat. Similarly, the Cardinal Mindszenty Foundation remained a family-run organization without a paid national membership. Billy Hargis's Christian Crusade, based in Tulsa, took in huge amounts of money through the sales of its publications but failed to organize local chapters. Other anti-Communist groups, including Kent and Phoebe Courtney's Conservative Society of America, Edgar Bundy's Illinois-based Church League of America, and the Life Line Foundation, sponsored by H. L. Hunt in Texas, produced publications but did not maintain memberships. Although occasional attempts were made by various anti-Communist leaders to bring these organizations together, they had little contact with one another.

Grassroots activists read the same authors and heard the same speakers.[2] The anti-Communist movement, however, remained organizationally fragmented. Both the anti-Communist movement and the larger conservative movement were, in effect, local movements that shared similar anxieties about the Communist threat. These groups differed in their organizational focus and often disagreed as to whether this threat was chiefly internal or external. The founding of the John Birch Society by candy manufacturer Robert Welch in 1958 provided the first anti-Communist organization with a nationally based membership and a centrally directed program. Still, many conservatives and grassroots anti-Communist activists shied away from the Birch Society after it was revealed that Robert Welch had accused President Eisenhower of being a conscious agent of the Soviet Union. Thus in the 1950s there was not a conservative movement per se but only conservative movements. The

1. Fred Schwarz, *Beating the Unbeatable Foe* (Washington, D.C., 1996).
2. Leading authors and speakers included Herbert Philbrick, W. Cleon Skousen, Louis Budenz, Anthony Bouscaren, Robert Morris, Clarence Manion, Rosalie Gordon, and John T. Flynn.

modern "conservative movement" came of age with the Goldwater presidential campaign of 1964.

In the 1950s anti-Communist activists offered political support for the investigations of Senator Joseph McCarthy and congressional investigations into Communist infiltration of the government, the movie industry, and the schools, but much of their time was given to the study of communism.[3] Through educational seminars and local reading groups, activists studied Marxist doctrine, the history of bolshevism, and Communist strategy and tactics. As one anti-Communist tract declared, "Brains and moral courage are needed to stop the Communist, not brawn and lung power. The remedies we suggest are undramatic. . . . First study Communism."[4] Another brochure advised, "Only an expert can tell who is a Communist." Avoid reckless charges and avoid racial, religious, social, and economic intolerance, it cautioned, because "it not only is unfair, but intolerance plays directly into the hands of the enemy."[5] The emphasis was on individual commitment in the battle against communism.[6] Self-education was touted in pamphlets, brochures, and newsletters as the first step in the confrontation with this global conspiracy. Study groups were organized to read government reports and books such as Schwarz's *You Can Always Trust the Communists (to be Communists)*, W. Cleon Skousen's *The Naked Communist*, Herbert Philbrick's *I Led Three Lives*, and a myriad of other anti-Communist books.[7]

As a result of their common reading, grassroots anti-Commu-

3. A useful summary of anti-communism in these years is found in M. J. Heale, *American Anticommunism: Combating the Enemy Within, 1830–1970* (Baltimore, 1990), 145–191.

4. Associated Industries of Missouri Newsletter, "The Manifesto," December 20, 1955.

5. American Coalition of Patriotic Societies, "Fight for Survival" (New York, 1962).

6. For example, see Freedom Bookshelf, "What Can I Do (Just One Person)" (Lombard, Ill., 1963), and Phyllis Schlafly, "Reading List for Americans" (Alton, Ill., 1957).

7. This genre of memoir literature needs further exploration by scholars. Along with the books excerpted in this volume, see for example, W. G. Krivitsky, *I Was Stalin's Agent* (London, 1939); Victor Kravchenko's moving account of life in Soviet factories and torture under the NKVD, *I Chose Freedom* (New York, 1946); Alexander Barmine's heroic account of Soviet life in the Ukraine before the German invasion, *One Who*

nist activists developed a unique subculture based on radically different assumptions about the nature of communism and the possibilities of negotiating with Communist regimes. Although this subculture remained in many ways insular, its outlook was not terribly different from Republican party statements about the domestic Communist threat.

Roman Catholics provided a major source of support for grassroots anti-communism. In 1958, after one of Fred Schwarz's schools on communism, Fred Schlafly, along with his wife Phyllis and his sister Eleanor, organized the Cardinal Mindszenty Foundation as a Catholic counterpart to the Christian Anti-Communist Crusade. The foundation, named after the Hungarian cardinal, brought a moral enthusiasm to its efforts to educate American Catholics about domestic communism and the oppression of Christians in Communist countries. Working with a small volunteer staff under Eleanor Schlafly, with most of the writing done by Phyllis, the foundation quickly emerged as a prominent anti-Communist organization in Catholic circles. Although not officially endorsed or formally affiliated with the Catholic church, the advisory board was composed only of priests with "direct" experience with communism—many of them had been imprisoned under Communist regimes before joining the Mindszenty Council.[8]

Survived: The Life Story of a Russian Under the Soviets, Introduction by Max Eastman (New York, 1946); Jerzy Glikksman's memoir of a Polish Communist in the Soviet Union during World War II, *Tell the West* (New York, 1946); Helena Sikorska's *Dark Side of the Moon*, Preface by T. S. Eliot (New York, 1946) and *Russia* (New York, 1960); Unto Parvilahti's story of a Finn sent to the gulag, *Beria's Gardens: A Slave Laborer's Experiences in the Soviet Union* (New York, 1960); and Walter J. Ciszek, S.J., *With God in Russia: My 23 Years as a Priest in Soviet Prisons* (New York, 1964). In addition, a comparable memoir literature developed out of Communist China, including Robert W. Greene, *Calvary in China* (New York, 1953).

8. Council members originally included C. Stephen Dunker, a former Chinese missionary; Father John A. Houle, assistant director of the American Jesuits in China; Father Harold W. Rigney, S.V.D., once imprisoned by the Chinese Communists, who later worked in a leper colony in the Philippines; Father John Kelley, who ran a Catholic boys school in Chile; Father Vincent Loeffler, who worked among black parishioners in Panama; and Bishop Rembert Kowalski, who had spent seventeen years in a Chinese prison. Joining the board in the next two years were Reverend Robert Crawford, who had been imprisoned for five years in China; Reverend Warren DiCharry, a missionary in China under Communist rule before he was expelled; and Reverend Ismael Teste, an exiled Cuban priest.

The foundation's message was that the struggle against communism was not simply a battle between two economic systems but between communism and Christianity.[9] To fulfill its mission the Mindszenty Foundation conducted seminars and organized local study groups to "safeguard our Church and our country."[10] The foundation offered a ten-week study program involving group discussion and individual homework based on an extensive reading list of government documents. Remember, the Mindszenty Foundation told its students, "To be an effective Freedom Fighter you must spread your knowledge with tact and with facts. Don't argue generalities, but calmly present specific facts."[11] At a time when Roman Catholic Masses ended with prayers for the conversion of Russia, this program attracted wide attention.

By 1961 the Cardinal Mindszenty Foundation was sponsoring more than 3,000 groups in 49 states, and in Canada, several Caribbean countries, and Mexico. Attendance at its seminars ranged from a hundred to several thousand. In Houston a four-day seminar in 1960 drew a total audience of 10,500; more than 20,000 pieces of free literature were distributed, and 1,600 books and pamphlets were sold. A monthly newsletter, *The Mindszenty Report*, written by Phyllis Schlafly, reached tens of thousands of subscribers. In 1961 alone the foundation distributed more than 125,000 copies of the American Bar Association's report, "Communist Tactics, Strategy, and Objectives." That same year the foundation began sponsoring a fifteen-minute radio talk program, "The Dangers of Apathy," which ran in 20 cities coast to coast and is still running.[12]

Phyllis Schlafly also took her anti-Communist message to a receptive audience at the Daughters of the American Revolution. Following a national resolution by the DAR urging its members to "take up the study of Communism for the protection of our country

9. Phyllis Schlafly to Vincent P. Ring, July 4, 1960, Schlafly Annual Correspondence, Box 1959–60, Schlafly Home Files.

10. Cardinal Mindszenty Foundation, "The Cardinal Mindszenty Foundation Invites You to Combat Communism with Knowledge and Facts" (brochure, 1957).

11. Mindszenty Foundation, "We Invite You to Join a Cardinal Mindszenty Speakers Club" (1960).

12. Duncan Stewart, "America's Freedom Fighters," *Priest Magazine*, August 1961, 1–5.

and our freedom," Schlafly, who had been appointed chairman of the DAR's national defense committee, organized DAR study groups. She told DAR members, "Our republic can be saved from the fires of Communism which have already destroyed or enslaved many Christian cities, if we can find ten patriotic women in each community."[13] She urged these DAR study groups to become involved in community activities by sponsoring writing contests in local high schools on American history and freedom; by donating anti-Communist books to local public and school libraries; and by hosting well-known anti-Communist speakers at public forums. Chapters were also encouraged to write letters to Congress.

Anti-Communist bulwarks such as the Mindszenty Foundation and elements of the Republican party fell within the general ambit of conservatism. The resolutions of state Republican grassroots organizations throughout the 1950s and early 1960s expressed equally intense anti-Communist sentiments and opposition to trade and cultural exchanges with Communist regimes, U.S. participation in the World Court, arms control treaties, and other policies perceived as being "soft" on communism.

In the late 1950s, dozens of books and magazine articles began to appear warning of the dangers of "right-wing extremism" in America. In these criticisms, anti-Communists of every type tended to be lumped together. The John Birch Society bore the brunt of these attacks, but other anti-Communist groups also came under heavy fire. More detrimental to the anti-Communist cause, however, was the release in early August 1961 of the so-called Fulbright Memorandum. It had been sent confidentially by Senator J. William Fulbright, Democrat of Arkansas, to President John F. Kennedy warning of anti-Communist educational programs in the U.S. armed services. Fulbright declared that "extremely radical right-wing speakers and/or materials" were being used to propagandize the troops into believing that "the primary, if not exclusive, danger to this country is internal Communist infiltration."

13. Speech, Phyllis Schlafly, "What Can One Individual Do for Freedom?" (1960), Schlafly Annual Correspondence, Box 1960, Schlafly Home Files.

This open attack on anti-Communists by a leading U.S. senator, as well as a subsequent change in the military's educational policies, placed anti-Communist organizations on the defensive. The dismissal and resignation of a number of military educational officers, and the dramatic resignation of General Edwin Walker (who became briefly a *cause célèbre* in right-wing circles), led many people to conclude that the anti-Communist movement had gone too far in its warnings about Communist subversion in the United States. While the anti-Communist schools and seminars of such groups as Fred Schwarz's Christian Anti-Communist Crusade and the Mindszenty Foundation continued to draw thousands of participants, the influence of these organizations beyond their hard-core followers was waning. The emergence of the campaign to draft Barry Goldwater for the Republican presidential nomination gave many anti-Communists an outlet for their activism.

Following Goldwater's defeat in the 1964 election, President Lyndon Johnson's escalation of the Vietnam War in 1965 marked a decisive turning point in the cold war. Agony over the war led to student protests on college campuses, anti-war demonstrations across America, polarization between the two major political parties as well as internal divisions within the parties, and deep alienation from and distrust of the U.S. government by large numbers of Americans. With American war casualties mounting even as the Johnson administration poured greater numbers of troops into what critics called the Vietnam quagmire, a growing distrust of America's war against communism emerged in the United States.

Anti-Communist conservatives supported the U.S. war effort, but with ambivalence and waning confidence as the war dragged on. Many conservatives saw this as "Johnson's War" and blamed liberal Democrats for the Vietnam debacle. Conservatives also saw in Vietnam a distraction from the massive Soviet arms build-up that was occurring at the time. The argument that the Soviets had deliberately lured the United States into the Vietnam conflict, or at the very least welcomed American stupidity for allowing itself to become bogged down in Vietnam, arose frequently in conservative circles. Right-wing groups such as the John Birch Society and Young Americans for Freedom called for support of the American war effort and held patriotic rallies across the country in support of the war, but they were fighting an uphill battle.

America's "longest war" and its "defeat" in Vietnam led to a serious reevaluation of U.S. foreign policy. The issue of communism became unsettled. The opening of relations with the People's Republic of China, and détente with the Soviet Union—both of which occurred as the United States was trying to extricate itself from Vietnam, suggested that just because a nation was Communist did not mean that we needed to make it our enemy. Foreign policy experts such as Henry Kissinger, Nixon's secretary of state, articulated a view that the real politics of the balance of power needed to replace abstract ideological foreign policy that rested on the assumption that Communist regimes could never be trusted under any circumstances or through any treaty.

Anti-communism continued as a force in American politics, but after Vietnam it took different forms. Only the most militant groups worried about Communist infiltration at home. Instead the American right came to focus on the Soviet defense buildup and its adventuristic foreign policy that had led to Soviet support of "liberation" movements in Latin America and Africa.

In the 1970s anti-communism concentrated increasingly on the hazards of arms control with the Soviet Union, under the initiatives of the Gerald Ford and Jimmy Carter administrations. Republican conservatives were joined in this fight by a group of former Democrats who became known as "neo-conservatives." Underlying their criticism of strategic arms control treaties, the decline of the U.S. military and Soviet adventurism in Africa and Latin America remained a continued anti-Communist perspective, though the rhetoric of anti-communism was tempered.

The ideology of anti-communism remained a potent force among conservative Republicans. The election of Ronald Reagan in 1980 reflected the power of the continuing anti-Communist ideology. Once in office, Reagan adopted anti-communism as a major theme of his administration's international outlook. Denouncing the Soviet Union as an "evil empire," he pursued an aggressive foreign policy characterized by a military arms buildup, military interventions in Grenada and Central America to prevent the spread of communism in the Western Hemisphere, and a tough stand on arms control negotiations with the Soviet Union. Scholars continue to debate the consequences of Reagan's foreign policy and its role in the collapse of the Soviet Union in the late 1980s, but anti-Communists saw this event as a triumph of their cause.

Even before the end of the cold war, only a few obscure groups remained devoted exclusively to anti-communism. Communism as a domestic threat in the United States had lost its urgency among even the most ardent anti-Communists by the late 1960s, though some organizations continued to promulgate the view that Communists were behind the New Left and the anti–Vietnam War movement. Yet most conservatives did not publicly espouse this view, even though they sharply criticized student radicals, black nationalists, and anti-war protesters. When the Soviet Union disappeared as American's major rival in the world, the international Communist threat ceased to exist.

This is not to say, however, that anti-communism as an ideology no longer existed in American politics. While the collapse of communism in the Soviet Union and Eastern Europe left only the remnants of the once-powerful political parties who now had to compete in multi-party systems, Communist regimes remained in China, North Korea, and Cuba. Anti-Communists in the United States criticized these undemocratic regimes, but they were not alone in their stance. Environmentalists, human rights activists, evangelical Christians, and leaders of organized labor joined in condemning these Communist regimes on various grounds. This made for an odd politics as uneasy coalitions were formed to condemn China's "occupation" of Tibet and to oppose trade with China, recognition of Cuba, and arms control treaties with North Korea.

Still, for nearly a half-century anti-communism in the United States had played an important role in American politics. The powerful grassroots movement that emerged in the 1950s and 1960s put liberals on the defensive, shaped Republican party politics, prevented recognition of China into the 1970s, and restrained Democratic and Republican administrations alike in their foreign policies toward Communist regimes.

Gulag literature fed this opposition to communism by revealing the brutality of Communist regimes. In making the selections in this book, the editors chose from some of the most widely read books of their day, though arguments could be made for any number of other memoirs. These readings include prison memoirs from the Soviet Union, Ukraine, Romania, Hungary, Cuba, North Vietnam, and China. In order to provide the reader with a sense of the history of anti-communism in the United States, as well as the development of this genre, the selections proceed chronologically from the early 1950s through the early 1980s. Although the authors of these memoirs differ in nationality, background, and political perspective, they present common themes about the nature of Communist regimes. The brutal suppression of their people suggested that, if given a chance (and proper encouragement from the West), these people would throw off the yoke of communism. It seemed too that communism was an ineffective economic system which survived only through forced labor; in the long run these Communist regimes would collapse of their own weight. Thus trade with Communist countries only helped bolster these regimes and allowed tyrants to maintain their power. Communism could be resisted, as the authors of these memoirs showed, but resistance took courageous determination. Thus anti-Communist activists in the West must remain determined in their actions and ask the same of their leaders.

These memoirs also revealed the deceptive nature of Communist leaders, who simply could not be trusted. Many of the memoirs told of disillusionment among party followers, young idealists who had supported the cause of "revolutionary socialism." Communists had a beguiling message, and too often liberals in the West were taken in by it, either by ignoring or apologizing for the brutality of these regimes or by believing that détente, arms control, or even appeasement would ease international tensions and eventually "liberalize" Communist dictatorships.

Finally, many of these memoirs told of valiant resistance by

Christians persecuted for their beliefs. The memoirs cast a world in war between civilization and savagery, freedom and totalitarianism, a God-centered universe and a man-centered universe. In this struggle there could be no compromise but only one victor.

· 1 ·

ELINOR LIPPER

The God That Failed in Siberia:
A Tale of a Disillusioned Woman

ELINOR LIPPER'S *Eleven Years in a Soviet Prison Camp* (1951), published by the newly formed publishing house of Henry Regnery Company, became a classic in "gulag" literature. The book had literary merit in its own right and set the standard for other prison memoirs that followed. Lipper's moving account of her travails in prison reached a wide audience of general readers. Gracefully written, unflinchingly detailed, and compelling in its stories of human courage and human fragility, *Eleven Years* revealed to Western readers the extent and brutal nature of labor camps in the Soviet Union. As a consequence, the book exerted a powerful influence that extended well beyond conservative anti-Communist circles.

Lipper was a young Belgian Communist who voluntarily entered the Soviet Union in 1937 in order to work toward building a better society, only to be imprisoned as a spy a year later. Her memoir emerges as a Christian confession in the meaning of salvation. Sixteen hundred years earlier, St. Augustine (354–430 A.D.) in his *Confessions* told of his life of sin before he became a confirmed Christian. Lipper's memoir similarly follows the path of her disillusionment as a young German medical student who naively seeks redemption in the false religion of the Soviet Union, only to suffer for her sins of error, before finding salvation in God.

Two years before the U.S. publication of Lipper's revelations, *The God That Failed* (1949), edited by Richard Crossman, had

17

appeared. In this collection of essays, leading writers and intellectuals, including the African-American novelist Richard Wright, the Italian author Ignazio Silone, the poet Stephen Spender, the novelist Arthur Koestler, and others confessed how they had been led astray by a false god. The year after Lipper's *Eleven Years in a Soviet Prison Camp*, arguably the best book within this genre appeared, Whittaker Chambers's *Witness* (1952).

Lipper opens her story with her arrest by Soviet officials in 1937, shortly after she had arrived in Russia to work in a foreign-language publishing house. At first she thinks that a mistake has been made and that she will be released. She writes, "My only fault was my boundless naiveté in imagining that the Soviet Union was the realization of my ideals." (Her initial belief that she had been falsely arrested is a common response in this gulag literature. She is typical in this regard.) Sentenced to Kolyma in northern Siberia, she realizes that the secret police had not made a mistake. Any foreigner in Moscow at the time was suspected of being a foreign spy.

Sentenced for "counterrevolutionary" activity, Lipper was given five years in prison. She was not released until 1948, after spending eleven years in work camps in Siberia. She writes: "The machinery of injustice, once it has begun moving, behaves illogically and wantonly. It is not for nothing that we speak of 'blind' terror. . . . For when the day of arrest comes, nothing counts, neither work nor merit, neither heroism nor submissiveness, neither wisdom nor silence. There are many who die in the camps, and the gaps must be filled."

As the author of one of the first memoirs from a former prisoner of the work camps, Lipper is anxious to convince her readers that such camps exist and are brutal. Keep in mind that the French existential philosopher Jean-Paul Sartre had proclaimed publicly following his visit to the Soviet Union that same year, 1951, that no such work camps existed in the Soviet Union and that talk of them was anti-Communist propaganda. To capture how prisoners "even forgot how to despair over this sinking down into a dull, brutish indifference," Lipper centers her memoir on the tragic stories of prisoners—men, women, and children—who lost everything, often their lives, in these camps. Because she spent most of her time in women's work camps, she pays special attention to the lives of women in these camps. Interlaced with these stories, Lipper suggests the extent of these camps by relating her experiences at the women's camp at Balagannoye, the Talon women's camp, the prisoners' hospital nearby, the Magadan women's camp, the "regimen" camp at Elgen, and the prisoners' hospital in the northern mining district.

Anti-Communists in the West found in Lipper an affirmation of what they had been saying all along, that the Soviet economic system was based on slave labor, and that it would collapse without it. And the Soviet political system was based on terror. As Lipper declared, "Speaking out [in the Soviet Union] is courting death; objectors will be liquidated in absolute secrecy and can be certain that scarcely anyone will hear about their resistance." In short, fascism in Germany and communism in the Soviet Union were two sides of the same beast—the totalitarianism of centralized government.

Lipper also touches in her memoir (not recounted in the excerpt below) on how American liberals were easily duped by Soviet officials. She devotes an entire chapter recounting Vice President Henry Wallace's visit to Kolyma during World War II, when the Soviet Union was allied with the United States. In preparation for Wallace's visit, the secret police built an elaborate performance to show how Soviet citizens were developing the Siberian frontier, much in the same spirit as American pioneers had done a half century before in the West. All watchtowers were torn down. A theatre for showing movies was built, a volleyball court constructed. Prisoners were given more rations to fatten them up.

Before his arrival, when word began to leak that Wallace would be visiting Kolyma, a wild rumor began to circulate that the Soviet Union would cede this region to the United States. "Even the soberest and most reasonable of the prisoners," she observes, "conceded the possibility." They quickly realized that they were to be part of a grand performance. During his visit, the inmates were gathered together to greet him. Suddenly, when Wallace appeared

before them, one woman broke ranks and threw herself at
Wallace's feet, sobbing in Russian, "Please, please help us." The
guards quickly removed the woman as Wallace's translator
explained that she was mentally deranged. Lipper sarcastically
concludes, "Every prisoner who was there owes Mr. Wallace a debt
of gratitude. For it was owing to his visit for the first and last time
the prisoners had three successive holidays." The day after he left,
the volleyball court was blown up by the guards.

American readers concluded that liberal politicians like
Wallace (as well as others less naive) underestimated the Soviet
threat. Soviet Communists simply could not be trusted, whether it
came to trade agreements or arms treaties. As the saying went, "You
can always trust a Communist (to be a Communist)."

Eleven Years became standard reading in anti-Communist
study groups in the 1950s and 1960s. While the book was read to
reinforce common perceptions of the Soviet Union, its literary
quality helped it gain an audience beyond a narrow readership of
anti-Communists.

In 1955, while attending an anti-Communist conference in
Berlin, Lipper disappeared. Rumors were that the Soviets had
kidnapped her, or worse. The only trace of her in history remained
her frightening revelations of the reality behind the illusion of
socialist equality in the Soviet Union.

🔲 In this book I have described my personal experiences only to
the extent that they were the characteristic experiences of a prisoner
in the Soviet Union. For my concern is not primarily with the for-
eigners in Soviet camps; it is rather with the fate of all the peoples
who have been subjugated by the Soviet regime, who were born in
a Soviet Republic and cannot escape from it.

The Russian people, and the other peoples of the Soviet
Union, cannot be equated with the Soviet government. Though

From *Eleven Years in Soviet Prison Camps* (Chicago, 1951), pp. v–viii, 90–95,
98–116, 142–151, 162–174, 197–199, 259.

they may have brought it into being, they are now the helpless victims of a ruling caste whose arbitrariness they must endure in silence. They have not the slightest chance to control their rulers. It is easy to condemn "the Russians"—but to do so is to do the Russian people a great injustice. For only would-be suicides and heroes can raise their voice against the decisions of their government in Russia. There are few such people in Russia, as there are few everywhere in the world. And it is not only that speaking out is courting death; objectors will be liquidated in absolute secrecy and can be certain that scarcely anyone will ever hear about their resistance.

Let us therefore avoid passing judgment on the Russian people. They are already condemned to the most horrible kind of existence: living in perpetual fear.

Who are the so-called counterrevolutionaries who make up the majority of the prisoners in Soviet camps? Are they guilty, are they innocent? There can be only one answer. From the standpoint of objective, non-Soviet justice, and from the standpoint of the strictest kind of class justice as well, these people are innocent. Of all the millions of persons in Soviet prisons and camps, very few have consciously taken action against the government in speech or in writing, by demonstrating or by attempting to escape from the Soviet Union. Their number is so small that they are insignificant in the great mass of prisoners. Only after spending many years in camp is one likely, with luck, to meet up with a "genuine" counterrevolutionary.

It is courting error to suggest hard and fast rules about the reasons for imprisonment. The machinery of injustice, once it has begun moving, behaves illogically and wantonly. It is not for nothing that we speak of "blind" terror. Nevertheless, the so-called counterrevolutionaries fall into two main categories.

1) Those who by reason of their origin, their education, their nationality, their past political behavior or their general cultural level are or could be potential opponents of the regime. This need not mean that they have ever committed the slightest offense. On the contrary, though as members of Soviet society they could not help feeling discomfort, most of them were not even conscious of any such feeling until the moment they were arrested. They did not

want to be conscious of it. That is especially true of the members of the Communist Party and the Young Communist League, whose eyes were opened to the results of their own work only after they were imprisoned.

2) The second, and by far the largest group, consists of "counterrevolutionaries" who were politically and socially neutral and who had obviously been arrested solely to increase the supply of slave labor.

One consequence of all these arrests has been complete intimidation of the people. No one knows what group will be struck tomorrow, whether it will be "undisciplined" workers, or peasants whose harvest proved too small, or national minorities, or "insubordinate" Russians, or government officials, or army officers, or members of the intelligentsia who today are proud of being "proletarian intellectuals" and who tomorrow may be denounced as corrupt cosmopolitans. There is no security for anyone in the Soviet Union, just as the word "security" does not exist in the Russian language— the only word covering that concept means "lack of danger."

And so a generation of children is growing up there whose first word is "Talin" (Stalin), and who speedily learn that there are questions which must never be asked, answers which can never be given. Throughout life all the members of a great nation are forced to mask their faces. Millions of human beings struggle to prove their guiltlessness anew every day, without ever being able to prove it completely. For when the day of arrest comes, nothing counts, neither work nor merit, neither heroism nor submissiveness, neither wisdom nor silence. There are so many who die in the camps, and the gaps must be filled. I have not based this book on any notes I took during my imprisonment. Taking notes is suicidal in the Soviet Union. But during eleven years of imprisonment everything that happens in the world beyond the barbed wire becomes as intangible and unreal as a dream. The only reality is the land of wooden watchtowers—our land, the land of prisoners. Reality is the one white highway along the ridge of the white ravine where the frozen river flows, a highway of loneliness and howling snowstorms which leads straight into the silence of the white forests. If you have shoveled the endless snow upon that road, you never forget it. If you have jolted mile after mile over that road in a jammed truck, incapable of moving your numbed limbs from under your neighbor's numbed limbs, you will not forget that road.

Everything we once knew—lines from our favorite poems, foreign languages, history—more and more vanished from our minds. At last we even forgot how to despair over this sinking down into a dull, brutish indifference. The number of ounces in the bread ration became more important than all the dates in world history. We can no more forget how many ounces were distributed where and when than we can forget those places which often had no names, just a number in kilometers, but which meant life or death to us.

The events I describe are the daily experiences of thousands of people in the Soviet Union. They are the findings of an involuntary expedition into an unknown land: the land of Soviet prisoners, of the guiltless damned. From that region I have brought back with me the silence of the Siberian graveyards, the deathly silence of those who have frozen, starved, or been beaten to death. This book is an attempt to make that silence speak.

＊   ＊   ＊

Everyone in the transit camp of Vladivostok had to resign himself to being shipped off to Kolyma sooner or later. Nobody knew anything about the place. "The end of the world," some said, "completely cut off from everything." Then one day a geography book found its way into our barrack and was passed from hand to hand. We skipped over the material on fisheries and the fur-bearing animals in which the Kolyma district was rich, and we paid little attention to the fact that there were gold and silver mines in the area. What was impressed upon our minds forever were the three sentences about the cold. "Even in summer the earth here thaws out only to a depth of eight and a half inches. The lowest temperatures on earth have been recorded in this region. In winter the temperature drops to minus seventy degrees centigrade (-94° F.) and even lower."

We became very quiet and thoughtful after reading that. Next morning I saw the girl [Lillian] who slept next to me, a young pianist from Moscow, busily searching through her suitcase. After a while she came up with a pair of thick woolen stockings which she offered to me. "You must take them," she said. "Last night I had a dream about you with frozen feet."

The following winter, when I tramped through the snow in Kolyma, I returned again and again to the gratifying thought that I still had Lillian's woolen stockings. I kept routinely putting off the day for wearing them on the theory that I could still endure the present cold and it might get still colder. The presence of those stockings, the mere possibility of wearing them, comforted and warmed me. Finally the day came when I opened my knapsack— improvised out of a piece of blanket—to get the stockings. The stockings were gone; they had been stolen long ago. From that day on I felt the cold worse than before.

Lillian and I were separated in Vladivostok. One of her legs was shorter than the other, and she was among the group of invalids and cripples who were to be sent back to Mariinsk in Central Siberia, an invalid camp where such prisoners were permitted to die slowly. There is no camp drearier and more hopeless than an invalid camp, as I heard later on from many eyewitnesses. A medically certified invalid does not have to work, but he receives only fourteen ounces of bread a day. Mad with hunger, the cripples will battle over a fishhead in the garbage heap of the camp kitchen. Unlike all other prisoners whose only thought is how to get a day off from work, the invalids report to work again and again, hoping in this way to receive a little more bread. But they are always sent back by the foremen on the grounds that they are unable to do the work.

Transfer to an invalid camp does not mean that a prisoner serves the rest of his term there. Medical commissions regularly comb the invalid camps, declare some of the inmates fit for work, and send them to the general camps. These in their turn send their waste human material to the invalid camps, so that there is a constant interchange between the two types of camp.

I do not know what became of Lillian. She had an eight-year sentence for "counterrevolutionary Trotskyist activity" because she had been briefly acquainted with a young cellist, a German exile who had spent three years in Nazi camps for illegal Communist activity and had then escaped to the Soviet Union in 1936. In 1937 he was arrested and convicted as a Trotskyist. Lillian's husband, a resident of Moscow, had repudiated her. Nevertheless, she never doubted for a moment that he still loved her and she bore him no ill will for the repudiation. She knew what it would have meant had he refused to do it: the sacrifice of his artistic career as a composer and teacher of music at best, prison at worst. Lillian was one of the few prisoners who received a package from home during the winter of 1938 in Vladivostok. Among all the wonderful things her mother had solicitously packed was a tiny package wrapped in letter paper and marked "Vitamin C." That was all. But this tiny notation in her husband's handwriting, on his letter paper, meant as much to her as a long, ardent letter; it was a silent message from a suffering man that he still loved her.

Early in May 1939 the first rumors of a ship waiting for us at the port trickled through. It was the steam freighter *Dalstroi*, and one bright, warm day we vanished into its hold. There were seven thousand prisoners, among them five hundred women in a separate, partitioned-off section.

During the entire voyage, which lasted a week, no member of the guard or the ship's crew ever entered the prisoners' hold. They were afraid to, especially when a large number of murderers and bandits were being transported, since they were an insignificant, though heavily armed, minority compared to the number of prisoners. They stood with raised guns, ready to fire, when the prisoners were let out on deck in small groups to use the toilet. None of them took any account of what went on below decks. As a result, during all such voyages the criminals put across a reign of terror. If they want the clothing of any of the counterrevolutionaries, they take it from him. If the counterrevolutionary offers any resistance, he is beaten up. The old and weak are robbed of their bread. On every transport ship a number of prisoners die as a result of such treatment.

In the course of every voyage some counterrevolutionaries attempt suicide by jumping overboard. Usually they drown quietly. Some of them attempt the leap while the ship is passing through the narrow Strait of Tartary, a few miles from Sakhalin Island. Here they may manage to swim to shore or be rescued by a fishing vessel.

In such cases the ship is stopped, and if the fugitive cannot be picked up, he is shot. . . .

In 1944 several hundred young girls came to Kolyma. They were the so-called *ukazniki*, sent out here for unauthorized absences from a war factory, or for some similar minor offense. During the war the number of guards was cut down everywhere, and on the ships as well; moreover, the guards had to put on civilian clothes during the passage through Japanese waters, since the Japanese would allow no military personnel to pass. The criminals, who formed the greater part of the human freight aboard this ship, had an absolutely free hand in the hold. They broke through the wall into the room where the female prisoners were kept and raped all the women who took their fancy. A few male prisoners who tried to protect the women were stabbed to death. Several old men had their bread snatched from them day after day, and died of starvation. One of the criminals, who appropriated a woman whom the leader of the band had marked for his own, had his eyes put out with a needle. When the ship arrived in Magadan and the prisoners were driven out of the hold, fifteen were missing; they had been murdered by the criminals during the voyage and the guards had not lifted a finger. The upshot of this particularly glaring scandal was that after the facts became known in Magadan, the commander of the ship's guard was called on the carpet and arrested.

We lay squeezed together on the tarred floor of the hold because the criminals had taken possession of the plank platform. If one of us dared to raise her head, she was greeted by a rain of fishheads and entrails from above. When any of the seasick criminals threw up, the vomit came down upon us. At night, the men criminals bribed the guard, who was posted on the stairs to the hold, to send over a few women for them. They paid the guard in bread that they had stolen from their fellow prisoners.

*   *   *

Kolyma, a region in the northeastern part of Siberia, is named after the Kolyma River. It is bounded on the north by the Arctic Ocean, on the east by the Sea of Okhotsk, an arm of the Pacific, on the south and west by impenetrable virgin forests *(taiga)*. There is no railroad into the area. Administratively, it belongs to the Khabarovsk district. On Russian maps it is marked as being directly under the jurisdiction of the Executive Committee of the Ministry of the Interior (NKVD). There is no civil authority; there are no local elections. The region's candidate for the Supreme Soviet, however, is confirmed by a general election. . . .

In this country the geologists found immeasurable wealth in gold. To mine the vast treasure would require hordes of workers. But who would go voluntarily to this inaccessible, inhospitable country? The solution was found swiftly, for there is an inexhaustible supply of one kind of human material in the Soviet Union—prisoners.

In 1934 for the first time they were loaded by the thousands into the holds of freighters at Vladivostok and unloaded at the place on the shore of the Sea of Okhotsk where the port of Magadan now stands. The bay there bears the pretty name of Bukhta Vesyolaya or "Cheerful Bay." Another bay which forms part of the port of Magadan is called Bukhta Nogayevo. At the time of the arrival of the first prisoners, three tiny wooden huts amid the forest were all there was to see.

A member of the People's Commissariat of the Interior (NKVD) was placed in charge of Kolyma. He was a Latvian by birth and an old-time Communist named Benin. His task was to produce gold out of the void, out of the virgin forest and the ice. The early years took a frightful toll of life, and he realized that the army of prisoners—at that time it consisted mainly of criminals—could do productive work only if it were well fed, warmly dressed, and adequately paid. During the last years of his administration Benin managed to establish the necessary preconditions, in spite of being cut off entirely from all sources of supplies during six months of the year.

Woods were cleared and an excellent broad highway was begun; it now runs for hundreds of miles through the entire country. This highway, which is called a *tros*, was built upon the bones of thousands of prisoners. It runs from Magadan across the northwestern gold territory to the gold mines further west in Indigirka; from there it runs southwest across the Aldan, a tributary of the Lena, to Yakutsk on the Lena, the capital of the Yakut Soviet Socialist Republic. As yet it is passable only in winter. A railroad is also planned which will rescue the country from its utter isolation. Magadan, the capital of the area, was built, and all through the region, in the vicinity of the large gold mines, there sprang up small settlements of free citizens in addition to the large prison camps. The forest was cleared for five large state farms with pasture and tillage. . . .

Because of the shortage of free labor, hunting and fishing are largely left to the native population, who cannot approach anything like full exploitation of the tremendous wealth of fish that abounds in the country. There are, however, five large fisheries; the fish are caught by men and cleaned, salted, and packed mostly by women prisoners. These fish factories are in Nogayevo, near Magadan, Ola, Balagannoye, a hundred and ten miles south of Magadan, Yana, sixty miles south of Magadan in the Yana Government, and Armany, thirty-seven miles south of Magadan.

Most of the gold mining in Kolyma is done underground. But some of it is done by a simple panning process, each man working by himself or with a single partner. The average production is twenty grams (.7 oz.) of pure gold per man per day. The season for panning gold is about a hundred days. But months before, the preliminary work is done; this consists in removing the layers of peat which cover the ground everywhere in Kolyma. In the underground mines machine drills and explosive cartridges filled with ammonal are used. The pace of the work is so furious that the use of explosives occasions frequent accidents and prisoners are crippled or killed. There are also many tales of despairing workers who blow themselves up.

At the end of each day's labor the workers, free men as well as prisoners, are searched with extreme care, although there would be little point in smuggling out gold, since there is nowhere to sell it. All the gold that is dug belongs to the state and anyone who offered it for sale would be convicting himself of theft. It is somewhat amusing that in this rich gold country there is not a single individual who is allowed to have a cap for his teeth made of gold. In the Soviet Union steel is used instead.

During the hundred-day season for panning gold some two hundred thousand men are employed and the extraction of gold amounts to about four hundred tons annually, in value some $460,000,000.

The 1937 wave of terror also overwhelmed the rulers of the Kolyma gold mines. When Yagoda, head of the NKVD, fell, his whole organization fell with him. Benin was arrested, taken to Moscow and shot, although he had achieved great triumphs in gold mining and laid the foundation for his successors' work. His wife also was arrested; she was a pale, fragile woman with whom I shared a collective cell in Butyrka Prison in 1938. Yagoda's successor, Yeshov, in collaboration with the then Chief Prosecutor of the Soviet Union, ground down millions of human beings in his thousands of prisons. It was the first flush of the NKVD purge which Stalin had inaugurated.

During the years 1937 and 1938 the elite of Russian intellectual life were annihilated. All who were still capable of independent thinking and independent decisions, all those who still knew what the word socialism meant, who still had some idealism, all those whose vision of freedom was not yet distorted, were to be robbed of their influence and liquidated.

The penal code was made far more stringent in 1937. Hitherto the longest sentence had been ten years; it was now raised to twenty-five years. The death penalty was retained—until 1948. The former practice of curtailing prison terms as a reward for good work was now rescinded. The treatment, diet, and clothing of the prisoners deteriorated immeasurably.

[His] successor in Kolyma was Garanin, a worthy associate of the men now in authority in Moscow. At that time the Kolyma "population" rose tremendously; about a hundred thousand prisoners were now brought in annually. These new prisoners were preponderantly counterrevolutionary elements; that is, mostly people who had never done any physical work. Scientists, artists, politicians, educators, leaders of industry, trade, and government, set out every morning on the horror march to the gold mines.

In 1938 Garanin undertook to liquidate thousands of intellectuals. Henceforth there was no more fur clothing for the prisoners.

The standard equipment became wadded jackets and trousers which soon hung like torn rags upon the bodies of the gaunt prisoners. The felt boots were replaced by shoes made of canvas, and practically every mine worker suffered from frozen feet. But as the Russian proverb puts it: If you lose your head, you don't weep over your hair. And here the head was at stake. The wretched rations of the prisoners were deficient in fats; the major component was bread. But the quantity of bread in all Soviet camps is governed by the amount of work the prisoner performs. He gets more bread or less according to whether he fulfills, over-fulfills, or fails to meet his quota. Each worker's performance is listed by free "brigadiers" (foremen) or by criminals, who are favored for such supervisory posts. It is common practice for the brigadiers to assign part of the work performed by counterrevolutionaries to the criminals who "grease" the brigadiers in various ways, while the counterrevolutionaries are without the means to practice bribery. But even if the work performed is listed honestly, it is impossible for a person unaccustomed to physical labor to fulfill the quota. He quickly falls into a vicious circle. Since he cannot do his full quota of work, he does not receive the full bread ration; his undernourished body is still less able to meet the demands, and so he gets less and less bread, and in the end is so weakened that only clubbings can force him to drag himself from camp to gold mine. Once he reaches the shaft he is too weak to hold the wheelbarrow, let alone to run the drill; he is too weak to defend himself when a criminal punches him in the face and takes away his day's ration of bread. He employs his last remaining strength to creep off to an out-of-the-way corner where neither the curses of the guards, the fists of the brigadiers, nor their eternal cry of, "*Davai, davai!*" (Get going!) can reach him. Only the fearful cold finds him out and mercifully gives him his sole desire: peace, sleep, death.

But Garanin was not satisfied with this sort of liquidation of the "enemies of the people." It was too slow for him. Therefore he traveled about from camp to camp examining the list of counterrevolutionaries. He took special note of those who were convicted of KRTD (counterrevolutionary Trotskyist activity).

"Which of these have not met their quota?" he would ask.

Most had not, could not. At evening roll call, when they returned from the mines, he would call out these unfortunates, revile them as saboteurs who were trying to continue their criminal counterrevolutionary Trotskyist activities even in camp, and he would have them driven in a herd out of the gate. At a short distance from the camp they would be shot en masse under his personal supervision.

This was still not enough. At night he would have thousands of enemies of the people taken out of all the Kolyma camps, loaded on to trucks and driven off to a prison. This prison, called Serpantinka, is about three hundred and seventy-five miles west of Magadan, in the midst of the forest, and it is probably one of the most ghastly institutions in the Soviet Union. Only ice and snow, mountains and forests, were the witnesses of the death-rattle of those tortured men who uttered their last scream of terror before they were shot. Only a few fortunate prisoners, who were sentenced merely to a ten-year addition to their term, came back from this prison to the labor camps. Years later they were so gripped by the horror of it that they did not dare to tell their fellow prisoners of the inhumanity they had seen and experienced. When they at last brought themselves to speak of it, they looked anxiously around to make sure that no informer was near by. In terse whispers they told of how Garanin, the Communist, had ordered thousands of innocent persons to be tortured and shot to death at Serpantinka during 1938.

It was estimated that Garanin had the deaths of some twenty-six thousand persons on his conscience. Twenty-six thousand people were killed in one year before the alarming reports of some of Garanin's assistants forced Moscow to intervene. He was finally recalled. According to one rumor, he was given fifteen years of penal labor; according to another, he was shot. Most of the additional sentences he had imposed were rescinded, but a certain percentage of the prisoners—in spite of all their written protests and petitions—were held without explanation to the extra ten-year sentence—if they could survive it.

*   *   *

Article I.24 of the Constitution of the USSR

"For the purpose of assuring freedom of conscience to the citizens of the USSR the church is separated from the state and the schools from the church. The freedom to practice religious rituals and the freedom of antireligious propaganda is extended to all citizens."

During the war, in the hour of need, the rulers of the USSR bethought themselves of God. Everything had to be done to inspire the very least of Soviet citizens with absolute devotion to his country. In spite of all the Communist propaganda the Russian villages, and not alone the villages, had remained religious. That was true even of a generation who were born and educated after the Revolution.

In the ten different Soviet prisons and the fourteen Soviet camps in which I was confined, I met a great many people. During the eleven years of my imprisonment constant streams of new people poured into the camps. Only an infinitesimal minority of these people were convicted of a "religious crime." But contrary to my original conception, I learned that the majority of my fellow prisoners, apart from former Party members and Young Communists, had not lost their faith, although they scarcely ever practiced the rituals of religion. And many former Party members who had lost faith in their ideal because of their unjust imprisonment sought to fill the void within them with something else—and that something was God.

During the war high church dignitaries—those who were still alive—were released from their camps in the far north and restored to office. They were by then willing to do anything, for decades of imprisonment had not failed to leave a mark upon their souls. They prayed for the Little Father Stalin as they had formerly prayed for the Tsar. They uttered prayers of thanksgiving to God for His goodness in sending the nation Stalin, the "leader of the peoples, the genius of the twentieth century, the benefactor and liberator of the Soviet people." The rulers of the Soviet state, with a great show of sincerity, pinned the Order of the Red Flag to the breasts of these church dignitaries.

But all the lesser people who were rotting in the forced labor camps on account of their religion were not affected by this religious renaissance. Not one of them had his term shortened. And they continued to cling to their view that everything done by the Soviets was "an act of the Antichrist." They were the hardiest and most stoical people in camp. Among them were members of sects whose forefathers had been persecuted under the Tsar, but who still adhered steadfastly to their customs and beliefs.

Among them were nuns whose convents had been destroyed thirty years before, but who still felt themselves and called themselves nuns. The prisoners in the women's camps called all those who were serving a sentence for religious reasons *monashki*, little nuns.

On all Sundays and church holy days they would go to the lockup. Neither persuasion, threats, mockery nor physical punishment could force them to work on the Lord's days. They ate their slender punishment rations and sang their songs. They were beaten. Their skirts were tied over their heads, and sometimes they were tied together by the hair. It did not help. On the following Sunday they allowed themselves to be pushed into the lockup as patiently, submissively, and unflinchingly as ever.

There were sectaries whose religion forbade them even to give their names to the Antichrist. Matushka Seizeva was one of these. Every night when she passed through the guardroom she looked with silent contempt at the commander of the guard, who had to register each prisoner in his book. Other prisoners who knew her quickly called over her shoulder, "Seizeva," and she was allowed to pass. If no one else was there at the time the commander roared once or twice, "Name?" and when he received no answer, Matushka was promptly sent to the lockup without her supper, to spend the night there.

In many sects there were tenets against accepting any official documents. Contact with any such devices of the Antichrist was sin. Lack of papers was the cause of the arrest and conviction of many sectarians. After serving their five years they were taken to the camp office to receive their discharge papers. But they refused to accept them. Without papers no one can live in the Soviet Union. Therefore they were soon brought to trial again, and vanished once more into the camps.

Nadya, a dark-complexioned, dark-eyed peasant woman with

shining black hair, who always radiated cheerfulness and kindness, whose strong, beautiful body not even camp life could afflict, came from some sect in the Ukraine. She was about thirty-eight years old.

Her release and her husband's occurred during the war. It had been a rare piece of good fortune that the two had met again, for usually husband and wife are not only sent to different camps, but also to regions very far from each other.

It was impossible at this time, of course, to return to the Ukraine where their orphaned children had been left behind. And so they went to work on the Elgen state farm, she as a field worker and her bearded husband—for shaving too is sinful to this sect—as a cabinetmaker. At forty-eight he was a broken old man. But they were at last together after so many painful years of separation.

Then came the Easter holidays. Nadya did not go to work. Absence from work without a medical certificate is punishable, and during the war there were few days of rest even for free Soviet citizens. There was always some "shock-troop work" that was urgent and had to be done on Sundays. And the rare official rest days did not coincide with the church holidays.

Her husband submitted to the state power, but Nadya remained at home and spent the holidays in praying and singing hymns. This first time she got away with a public rebuke. Then came Ascension Day. Again Nadya stayed at home in their tiny room and prayed and sang. Her husband pleaded in vain with her to go to work and not to bring fresh misfortunes down upon them. This second time she was rebuked sharply and told that a third such absence from work would be punished to the full extent of the law.

Then came Pentecost. Sobbing, her husband went on his knees and pleaded with her. "Nadya, I implore you, Nadya, give in. This sin cannot be counted against us because we are not committing it voluntarily; we do it only out of bitter necessity. Nadya, have mercy on yourself, on me. Nadya, I no longer have the strength to go through all that horror again. Nadya, listen to me, Nadya. . . ."

But Nadya would not listen.

"You do what God has given you the strength to do," she said softly in her melodious Ukrainian dialect, "as I must do what my conscience tells me to do."

And she stayed home for the third time, devoting herself to prayer, accepting martyrdom.

Three weeks later we were sitting, hungry and exhausted, around the stove with its dying fire. A woman entered and softly closed the barrack door behind her.

"Nadya, where have you come from? Greetings, Nadya."

Her powerful arms embraced us; her large eyes examined our wasted faces with sorrowful affection.

"Nadya, what did you get?"

"Five years," she said in a calm, indifferent voice, putting her bundle down on the boards of a bedstead.

*   *   *

Katorga was the severest form of forced labor in Siberian mines under the Tsars. It was abolished by the victorious Revolution, but reintroduced during the war, along with death by hanging for war criminals and collaborators with the Germans. Those who were spared death were sentenced to from twenty to twenty-five years katorga.

Katorga convicts, both men and women, were shipped to Kolyma to serve their sentences. The differences between ordinary prisoners and katorga prisoners are as follows:

Katorga prisoners are transported in chains.

They have no names, but only numbers which they wear on their backs.

They live in barracks on bare boards in three tiers, without straw mattresses or blankets, so that they never dare to take off any of their wet work clothes. They are granted a blanket only after three years of good conduct.

Their camp is totally isolated from all other prison camps.

All contact with the outside world, all correspondence, is forbidden to them.

In 1944 three thousand Katorga prisoners were delivered to the Maxim Gorky gold-mine camp. Sickness became such a problem that a special hospital had to be set up at the camp, for these prisoners could not be sent to an ordinary camp hospital. Since Katorga prisoners may be used only for the hardest physical labor and there were not enough free citizens on hand to staff the hospital, the hospital personnel was drawn from ordinary prisoners. With the help of one of the hospital attendants a Katorga prisoner contrived to smuggle out a letter to his family, who foolishly sent him an answer addressed to the Maxim Gorky Gold Mine. When it was discovered that the addressee was a Katorga convict, there was a grand investigation and it was decided to send these prisoners to an even more remote mine called Laso, where total isolation would be easier. The transfer took place in 1945. Of the three thousand convicts, five hundred were healthy enough to be shipped; another eight hundred were in the hospital with dysentery, in a hopeless condition; the other seventeen hundred had died. (I was given these details by the head of the medical division who was in charge of both the Maxim Gorky hospital and the camp hospital where I was working as a nurse.)

*   *   *

Camp Rations
It is impossible to live on the camp ration for prisoners, for more than two years, at any rate. By the third year—whoever tries it is a physical wreck; by the fourth he has become incapable of work; and by the fifth year he bites the dust, or more often the snow.

Daily Bread Ration for Prisoners in Kolyma

FULFILLMENT OF LABOR QUOTA	WOMEN	MEN
100% or better	21.0 ozs.	28.5–32 ozs.
70% to 99%	17.5 ozs.	25.0 ozs.
50% to 69%	14.0 ozs.	17.5 ozs.
Disciplinary ration	10.5 ozs.	10.5 ozs.

The higher bread ration for men applies to miners. As soon as a male prisoner is sent to lighter work in the woods or on construction, he receives the meager women's ration.

For all prisoners, per day: 3.5 ounces of salted fish; 2.1 ounces of cereals—barley, barley-groats, millet, or oats—0.17 ounce of meal or starch; 0.5 ounce of vegetable oil; 0.34 ounce of sugar; 0.106 ounce of herb tea; 10.5 ounces of cabbage leaves, brined.

Menu for Prisoners

BREAKFAST: Half a herring or 1.75 ounces of salt fish; sweetened tea; one-third of the bread ration.
LUNCH: Cabbage leaf soup, one pint. Groats. One-third of the bread ration.
SUPPER: Cabbage leaf soup, with a few grains of some cereal and boiled-down fishheads floating in it. One-third of the bread ration.

Year in and year out, on weekdays and on holidays, the diet is the same. Its monotony alone, aside from its lack of vitamin C, tends to bring on scurvy. To combat the disease the prisoners are given a dose of "concentrate" in the camp dining rooms. If you don't drink your glass of concentrate, you don't receive a wooden spoon for eating. This concentrate is an extract of pine; it is a beverage bitter as gall, but it has actually proved to be effective against scurvy and is manufactured in the local vitamin factory of Taskan, on the Taskan River, a tributary of the Kolyma.

The lack of vitamin B has resulted in mass cases of pellagra. A prisoner with a serious case of pellagra must give up 1.75 ounces of his bread ration and is given instead a brew made of flour and yeast, which is supposed to restore the missing vitamin B.

In spite of these measures, one of the most frequent diagnoses of the cause of death in prisoners is polyavitaminosis—lack of vitamins. Another frequent cause of death is dystrophia alimentaris, that is, starvation.

In evaluating the prison rations it must be kept in mind that these rations are for people who perform the heaviest kind of physical labor twelve, fourteen, and sixteen hours a day in a country which during the eight months of winter has the lowest temperatures of any inhabited country on the face of the earth.

*   *   *

The last way out is suicide. This is a way never chosen by the criminals, though it is occasionally taken by male counterrevolutionaries and less frequently by female counterrevolutionaries. The chief reason for the relatively low rate of suicides is the fact that prisoners are never alone. In the barracks and at work they are constantly surrounded by other prisoners or by guards. The very fact that thousands of others are enduring the same fate tends to suppress the thought of suicide.

There is an incessant flow of rumors to the effect that revision of cases, amnesty, relaxation of the rules, or improvement in the rations are "on the way." No one believes these rumors; they are laughed at, but they nevertheless leave a lingering spark of hope.

Women are far more enduring than men. A man can reach a point of exhaustion where he no longer recognizes anything but food and sleep. A woman will still try to preserve a remnant of her humanity. And women are also more adaptable to unaccustomed physical labor. Strictly speaking, wood chopping is lighter than the work in the gold mines, from which women are exempt. But the transition from working as a stenographer, housewife, or teacher to wood chopping is no easier than the transformation of an intellectual into a gold miner. In almost every case it was the intellectual who chose voluntary death by freezing, hanging, or plunging from the tower of the refinery into the depths of the mine, rather than endure the slow, deadly torture of the camp.

Members of the family are not informed, no matter whether death is "natural" or violent. The fact is entered into the statistics, and the prisoners' documents are transferred to another file which bears the identifying mark: "File Number 3". . . .

Aside from criminals, peasants formed the main body of so-called counterrevolutionary prisoners during the thirties. After the assassination of Kirov* in 1934, large contingents of workers and intellectuals were sent to the camps. At the end of 1936 and in 1937 and 1938 there began an endless stream of counterrevolutionaries

---

*Sergei Kirov was a young rising star in the Communist party who opposed many of Stalin's policies. His murder in December 1934 triggered show trials, purges, and the ultimate demise of thousands of people living in the Soviet Union under Joseph Stalin.

from all classes of the population and from all the towns and villages of the Union republics. In 1939 and 1940 came the Poles who were arrested in large numbers after the partition of their country. In 1941 they enjoyed an amnesty, since they were to be formed into a Polish army of liberation to fight Hitler.

People from the Balkan countries, many of them Jews, who had fled before Hitler's armies, were arrested immediately after they crossed the borders of the Soviet Union and were sentenced to either three years as border violators or to eight years as suspected spies. Both groups had to do time for eight years, since the border violators were not released during the war. In 1940 a ship arrived in Kolyma with six hundred such refugees. At the end of the war sixty returned to their native lands; in the gold mines of Kolyma the others had given up the lives they had hoped to save by fleeing to the Soviet Union.

In 1941 a new category of prisoners came in, the *ukazniki*. A ukase was issued which provided that any worker who left his job in a war plant, no matter for what reasons, was subject to from six to eight years of imprisonment. Hundreds of young girls between the ages of eighteen and twenty were sent to Kolyma for running away to their villages because they could no longer endure the starvation in the cities where they had been forced to work. Some had only gone back home for a few days to visit a sick mother, but the factory manager would not give them any days off and when they returned they were arrested. They came as adolescents and were instantly transformed by Kolyma into full-fledged prostitutes. Thousands of workers were sent into the Kolyma camps as ukazniki, for some petty misdemeanor. These prisoners were given amnesties when the war ended in 1945, but those who had not been physically wrecked were morally shattered.

In 1944 and 1945, when the Soviet armies were advancing westward, prisoners came from the liberated areas. Thousands of young Latvians and Lithuanians were first kept prisoner in Kolyma and then forced to become colonists under the name of "special contingents."

Thousands of people who had unwillingly endured the German occupation were convicted of treason and sent to Kolyma on

ten-year sentences solely for this reason, or because they were victims of the flourishing practice of denunciation.

At this time other hundreds of young girls between the ages of
seventeen and twenty-two were sent to Kolyma on charges of treason. These were western Ukrainians—after the war Poland ceded
western Ukraine to the Soviet Union—who had belonged to the
bandyerovtsi organization. Polish partisans later told me that this organization had committed the most frightful and inhuman crimes
against both Polish and Soviet citizens, and that it had carried out
many pogroms, urged on by the Germans. They had been arrested
and were being punished. But why had Soviet officers, interrogating
seventeen-year-old girls, broken the girls' collarbones and kicked in
their ribs with heavy military boots, so that they lay spitting blood in
the prison hospitals of Kolyma? Certainly such treatment had not
convinced any of them that what they had done was evil. They died
with tin medallions of the Virgin on their shattered chests, and with
hatred in their eyes.

And then, in 1946, the homecomers came to Kolyma. These
were women and girls whom the Germans had carried off from the
Ukraine to Germany, where they had been put to work in Nazi mu-
nitions plants. The war had ended and the slave laborers, homesick
and eager, at last boarded the trains for the Soviet Union. The same
fate was reserved for them as for the unfortunates who had been
taken prisoner by the Germans—for a soldier of the Soviet Army
was not supposed to have been taken prisoner; he should have
fought to the death.

There were no prisoner-of-war camps for Germans in Kolyma,
but there were such camps for Japanese prisoners. Their camps
were isolated from the Russian penal camps. The inmates worked
only eight hours a day, and their own former officers, who did not
have to do any physical work, functioned as brigadiers. Usually they
were employed in road building. They received a fixed rice ration
which was independent of the amount of work they did. Later, however, they shifted to bread—apparently bread was more satisfying
under the climatic conditions, which the Japanese found very hard
to adjust to.

Before the war, during the war, and after the war, continuous new hordes of prisoners were ground to dust. The snows of Kolyma covered the graves; the gold mines along the Indigirka swallowed more and more prisoners; the vast Arctic peninsula of Chukotsk, rich in coal, uranium, and other metals, demanded more and more laborers.

No one knows their names. No one can count the dead.

But the Soviet Union is rich and mighty, and the Soviet people stand united behind their Leader. So it is said, so written. United? Who then are these twelve million prisoners—a figure the NKVD officials repeatedly confirm—who are constantly filling the prisons and camps of the Soviet Union? If they are really opponents of the regime, then the government can rule only by suppressing with brute force twelve millions of the people in whose name it rules. On the other hand, if they are innocent victims, as in fact they are, who can assert that this regime and its leaders are what they say they are, the liberators of the people?

· 2 ·

JOHN H. NOBLE

An American's Tale

JOHN NOBLE'S *I Was a Slave in Russia: An American Tells His Story* appeared in 1960 and quickly became a favorite in anti-Communist circles in the United States. Noble's story reinforced what other prison memoirs had told the West about the brutal nature of labor camps in Siberia, but this book drew special attention because Noble was a native-born American. He had first been interred by the Germans, only to be arrested by the Soviets and sent to a work camp.

Noble's account went beyond other accounts in important respects. First, he confirmed that following the death of Stalin in 1953, major revolts had broken out in labor camps in the region surrounding Vorkuta, a Siberian city above the Arctic Circle where Noble had been sent. News of this revolt reinforced a general belief among anti-Communists in America that the people behind the Iron Curtain would rise up if given an opportunity. Second, Noble spent considerable time in his book outlining the diversity of people found in these camps—loyal Communists, priests, workers, peasants, men and women, and people from every region in the Soviet Union and every nation under Soviet control. It was a cardinal tenet of American anti-Communists that the people in the Soviet Union and the Eastern bloc wanted freedom but had been subjugated and terrorized into submission by a totalitarian government. This belief made America's failure to come to the aid of the Hungarians in their revolt against the Soviet Union all too tragic.

I Was a Slave impressed its readers with the profound importance of Christian spirituality as essential to surviving the dehumanizing brutality of communism. Throughout his memoir, Noble attributes his capacity to resist his captors and overcome the animal-like conditions in which he had been placed because of his faith in God. In the memoir he writes, "I was alone in my cell, with no one to talk to, no one to turn to for help, except God, perhaps. Would He hear a prayer from me? Would He persuade those creatures in the prison corridors to open the door and bring me food, or even freedom? I spoke my prayers, asking God in heaven to comfort my body and soul." Noble's message was clear: Christianity offered literal salvation—to the prisoners in the labor camps, to the peoples behind the Iron Curtain, and, ultimately, to all humankind. The cold war was a spiritual war between the forces of light and darkness.

Noble's account is important in another respect as well—his reports of English and American soldiers being held captive in the Soviet Union. In the selection that follows he mentions an English soldier named Chapman, but elsewhere he remarks that a Yugoslav national at Camp 3 reported seeing eight survivors of a U.S. Navy spy plane shot down on April 8, 1950, by the Soviets over the Baltic Sea. He tells of rumors of other Westerners being held in Soviet camps throughout northern Siberia.

Isolated rumors and reports of American prisoners in the gulag persisted throughout the cold war. A Soviet veteran claimed to have seen an American fighter pilot in June 1953, after the pilot's plane had been shot down over North Korea; a Polish prisoner reported sharing a cell with a captured U.S. Army sergeant in the infamous Lubyanka Prison in 1948; and most intriguing was the allegation that following the collapse of the Soviet Union, a female prisoner in Siberia provided investigators with twenty-two names of American prisoners she had met in the labor camps in 1951–1952. She claimed to have copied their names and buried them in a bottle. Supposedly many of the names proved to be Korean War MIAs, including Chan Jay Park Kim, a soldier of Korean descent from Hawaii. Both American and Russian officials dismissed these reports as isolated and unfounded.

Nonetheless these rumors gave new life to Noble's report of American prisoners, even though he makes it clear in his memoir that these reports were based only on hearsay. Reports of captive Americans in the Soviet Union, North Korea, and later North Vietnam became a common theme in anti-Communist literature. Most readers of these memoirs were not shocked by such allegations.

卐 Dresden, crumbled by the giant blows of American air raids, moved restlessly and expectantly in its ruins. It was the first week of May, 1945. War sounds of a new sort had been heard from east and west. On May 6, just sixty-five miles to the west, American soldiers were pushing against the last lines of German resistance. To the east, Russian troops were moving toward the city.

For my family, in our house high above Dresden on Bergbahn Strasse (the Street of the Mountain Railway), the sounds meant something far different from what they meant to any of our neighbors.

Throughout the war we had been locally interned by Hitler's forces. We were not permitted to leave the city, and every third day we had to register with the police. We were under constant observation by the Gestapo. Yet we were treated well, even courteously.

For we were enemy aliens, American citizens. I was born in the United States. My father and mother, born in Germany, and my brother, born in Switzerland, were naturalized Americans and remain so to this day. The war sounds of May 6, therefore, meant that our countrymen were coming—and peace. Peace, at long, weary last.

Perhaps, though, we were listening more closely to the west than to the east, where the Soviet cannonading was. Dresdeners knew that the war was really ending. The only question was which side would reach Dresden first, the east or the west. Many hoped it

From *I Was A Slave in Russia: An American Tells His Story* (New York, 1960), pp. 3–12, 18–23, 112–120.

would be the east, the Russians; the horrors of American bombing raids were fresh in their minds.

There had been rumors of Russian outrages in other parts of the country, but these were only rumors. Few people believed them. . . .

The occupying forces flooded in. The highway from Bautzen was lined for miles with the horse carts in which the Red army traveled through Germany. Drunken soldiers roistered along the road. The fighting was over, and there was no discipline. Permission had been given the soldiers to pillage and rape. Marshal Zhukov had issued the order: full liberty for the Red army to do as it pleased for three days. But the horror was to go on unendingly for three weeks.

On that first day in Dresden we saw soldiers pulling mattresses out of houses, and we knew they would be put to one of two uses: for drunken sleep or for rape. Rape was the sport of the day, and it was not done in private. The soldiers didn't care about privacy; the screaming victims couldn't.

One might hurry down a residential street and hear screams also from houses which one might have visited socially the week before.

Red flags now replaced the white. Swastikas had been carefully unstitched, leaving only a red field on which greetings to the conquerors had been scrawled: "WE THANK THE RED ARMY FOR FREE-DOM, WORK, AND BREAD."

Before I left the house to look at "liberated" Dresden, George and I had taken a precaution which to some might have looked foolish. We had hung on the gate a sign that read "U.S. PROP-ERTY." To the Russians it must have seemed potent. Not one unauthorized Red soldier set foot on the property, even though drunken soldiers later in the month set fire to the Loisenhof, Dresden's best restaurant, across the street from us. And routed 300 persons out of a bomb shelter nearby and raped every woman there, regardless of age or condition. But the sign on our gate seemed to throw a circle of exemption around our house. It was easy to infer that the friendship of Russia and the United States was the reason.

I was 21 then. Before my next birthday I was to learn a lot more about that friendship. . . .

The nightmare had begun. And it was to rule us for nine years. [Noble and his father were arrested as American spies shortly after the arrival of Soviet troops.—ED.]

*   *   *

It was several days before I realized the most important fact of prison life. This paramount concern, riding the days and nights like a monkey perched on the head, is food, the belly-craving that fills one like a cancer and crowds out everything else. On the first morning, it was the scenes and sounds of violence that preoccupied. Screams could be heard almost constantly from the questioning room. I learned, though, that the mind can erect barriers against such sounds, so that unless one tries one cannot hear them. Prisoners who couldn't shut them out didn't last long. They went mad. I was told that one of the many prisoners who attempted suicide tried to kill himself in his madness by crashing his head against the wall of his cell.

When food was first brought in to me, I still hadn't learned about the domination of the stomach when men are made to live like animals. The meal was a bowl of coffee-colored soup with a fishy taste. I threw it out without a second thought.

The day went easily and without incident. The cell was swarming with bugs, and I occupied myself by catching them and flipping them into the toilet bowl. At noon and in the evening, watery, fishy soup was again distributed, and again I poured it out. I told myself I didn't need it.

Within a very few days I realized how mistaken I was. Inexplicably, the food stopped coming. It didn't stop just for me; it stopped throughout the prison. There was no food for anyone. There was no explanation from the guards. "There will be food tomorrow," they said. There wasn't. Warm water with a coffee taste was passed out instead. Later in the day, the guards brought twenty-quart buckets from which they served, as solemnly as if it were food, plain warm water, yellowish and without taste.

Slowly, the stomach took over body and mind. There was no

food the next morning, only more of the warm water. I had never really been hungry before. . . .

But now I began to know about hunger, and it was frightening. It was not just an emptiness; it was a positive, driving force, urgent and constantly on the mind—like the urgency of a schoolboy's body as he dreams his first pulsing dreams of sex.

I had to face the situation. I was alone in my cell, with no one to talk to, no one to turn to for help, except God, perhaps. Would He hear a prayer from me? Would He persuade those creatures in the prison corridors to open the door and bring me food, or even freedom? I spoke my prayers, asking God in heaven to comfort my body and soul.

I am sure many others in those prison walls were asking divine help too. And many outside the walls, for even the "free" people of Germany had had to pull in their belts a notch or two. Food was scarce. Everywhere, the Soviet troops had been trampling down stock rooms, looting. The stock room in Münchenerplatz prison had been full when the Russians arrived, but they had nearly emptied it, so that they might trade food for vodka or schnapps. Other food reserves had been carried away by the soldiers to feed the women they were using day and night. I found out later that, at the time we were starving in our cells, the guard and officers in my house were forcing my mother to cook our food for the girls whom the Russians brought into the house.

Three days passed and no food was distributed to us. At last, on the fourth day—which was July 31, 1945—a few ounces of bread and some thin soup were handed to me; on the fifth day, more of the same, but as I lay down that evening I had no idea that on the following morning would begin a twelve-day starvation period.

When it became apparent on the first of those days that there was to be no food, loud protests, uncontrolled curses and screaming were let loose. They became louder as the second, third, and fourth days went by. Men went out of their minds, woman prisoners became hysterical. Some Moslem prisoners chanted their prayers. Then death struck, right and left. Cell doors were opened and dead bodies pulled out by an arm or a leg. I wondered when it would be my father's turn and mine. I no longer was strong enough to lift my feet off the floor, I put myself into the hands of God.

Some seven hundred prisoners had entered that starvation period. I was one of twenty-two or twenty-three that survived, along with my father.

Each day, as the guards brought the warm water around, they roused the prisoners with a cry of "breakfast" or "coffee." If the cry was "breakfast," there would be a tense silence as the prisoners waited to see if food was meant, or more water. And during those twelve days it was always the water.

On the thirteenth day my cell door opened and a guard, as indifferent as if he had been supervising a delivery of water, stepped into the cell. From a large container he took a tiny mound of bread crumbs wrapped in a piece of crumpled paper. The crumbs weighed two ounces.

I stared at the crumbs for twenty minutes, then ate them one at a time. They did little for the aching emptiness, but their dry, tasteless texture started the saliva flowing, and each crumb was an almost unbearable pleasure.

At noon, the usual buckets were brought to the cells. It was again warm water, mainly, that was ladled out, but also it had the aroma of soup. And the bottom of the bucket could not be seen through the liquid. It was that thick.

With bread and soup on the menu again, at least some of the prisoners who had survived the twelve days of starvation began to feel normal again. They could be seen standing and moving in their cells. Others were dying, however, from the lasting effects of hunger. As new prisoners were brought in, it was very evident that the "old-timers" had built a mental refuge for themselves. Compared to the horrors of the twelve days, to have a couple of cups of weak broth and a piece of bread meant a good life. [Later, Noble was sent to a prison in East Germany. —ED.]

*   *   *

There was also the matter of filth. It preoccupied everyone. To our Soviet guards, cleanliness was of little concern. A guard to whom it was, stood out as an oddity. For the most part, the guards were like the soldiers who had streamed into Dresden to rape and burn and steal. They were dirty, ill clad, and untroubled by their condition. Few showed any familiarity with modern plumbing. In the prison toilets they scattered filthy toilet paper about the floor. Often they laughed at the toilets, like children seeing a strange, impractical toy for the first time.

For practically all the prisoners, however, the chance to take a bath once a week was very important. My father and I, along with the few others who had survived the starvation regime, had waited six months or more for that day, December 28, 1945, when for the first time soap was distributed, a bath was made available, and we had shaves and haircuts. For the first time we could wash the bundle of stained and rotten rags which we called underclothes.

Bathing was so important to us that we could even manage to live with the typically Soviet bathing regulations. No matter how many men were confined in a cell, from the luxurious three or four in my case to the ten to twenty in some others, only one tubful of water was permitted for each cell. For the last man in the tub, this meant stepping into mildly tepid mud that reeked of body dirt. A prisoner not hardened to the system sometimes became ill as he stepped into the tub—and this usually put an end to bathing for the members of his cell.

To me, using the filthy tub water for bathing was as absurd as it was repulsive. The drinking water we got in our cells was the best for "spot cleaning." The water of the tub was more suitable for washing clothes.

We were permitted now to have our long, matted hair cut. Barbering was one of the miscellaneous skills my father had picked up when he first came to America as a Seventh Day Adventist missionary during the Depression. He practiced it before he took up his highly successful camera business.

When he told the guards of his skill he was quickly appointed to the prison barbering staff. This gave us a perfect chance to meet and talk regularly. My father became an encyclopedia of prison information.

One thing we learned through him was the interchangeability

of guards and guarded in the Soviet world. My father had met the man who had been in charge of our arrest, the MVD officer Stepanenko. He was no longer an MVD officer. Now he was a prisoner, like us, in Münchenerplatz prison. He had been jailed as a direct result of his role in our arrest. From our home, where we kept a reserve stock, protected from possible air raids, Stepanenko had confiscated six hundred cameras. Then, as he explained freely, he had put the cameras on the black market. He was performing, after all, a simple equation in black-market economics. But he had been caught at it—possibly by a superior who felt *he* should have had the black-market concession for the cameras.

Stepanenko was not the only MVD officer on the prisoner list. The former chief of the prison was now a prisoner himself.

It was a mark of how complete a world our prison was that when a former prison chief or MVD officer became a prisoner there was no feeling of vengeance toward him. The prisoners accepted him as they would any prisoner, realizing, perhaps, that Communists are all captives of a system more rigid even than prison. When they in turn were imprisoned, they moved from one world to another with singular good feelings, it seemed. They showed an earthy, peasant indifference to their state.

While this was true of those who were jailed for graft or theft, crimes that meant little to their superiors, I was later to see that Russians imprisoned for political crimes quaked with terror. Stepanenko accepted with a shrug his seven-year sentence for black-market activities; had he passed an indiscreet remark about the regime, he would have been put to death. [Noble was transferred to a prison in Muhlberg, then to a work camp in Siberia, Vorkuta. — ED.]

*   *   *

"Johnny, everything in Vorkuta depends on who you know," Vaska, a Ukrainian in my barracks, told me. "With enough *blat* the guards and brigadiers will give you the right job. There are few Russians that can't be bribed. You need friends in the kitchen for a little extra food, and a contact in the hospital will also never hurt you. If you

are part of a tight-knit group, not even the blatnois will bother you."
He was right.

Learning Russian was my first survival project. My teacher was
a barracks mate, Ivan, a former student at Moscow University, one
of the many disgruntled Soviet intellectuals. Without realizing it, I
had already picked up a few words on the slate job—"pull," "stop,"
and others from the guards' commands. In no time I was making
excellent progress. "Soon you will speak better than many of the
Ukrainians," Ivan said. I worked at it every spare minute, and in a
short time could speak halting, grammatically poor Russian.

Now that I was out of my cocoon, my circle of friends grew
rapidly. Three prisoners, Vaska, Ivan, and Alexia, became my closest friends. Vaska, a twenty-five-year-old, short, dark-haired Ukrainian peasant, worked the electropulley that hauled my slate to the
top of the heap. A fervent Ukrainian nationalist, Vaska fought with
the Ukrainian Banders army during World War II against both the
Nazis and Communists. Ivan, a thirty-year-old Ukrainian, had some
secondary education—somewhat of a rarity in the rural areas. He
hated the Communists with a passion reserved for Ukrainians.
Three million of his people died of famine in 1932 during the severe
drought. Red troops closed the Russian-Ukrainian border to keep
the starving people from leaving, and stole whatever grain existed.
Both Ivan's parents had been deported to Siberia.

"Millions were sent to Siberia or killed in the thirties when the
Communists forced us to collectivize our farms," another Ukrainian
told me. "When Hitler invaded Russia it was a chance to fight back
against the Kremlin. We had millions of soldiers ready to destroy
Stalin. But when we saw that Hitler was no better—he kidnapped
thousands of our people to work in his factories and had no intention of giving us independence—we had to fight on both fronts. We
died on the west against the Nazis and on the east against the Communists. It was hopeless."

Alexia was a Russian from Smolensk. He had been arrested in
1946 while a senior high school student, charged with the ubiqui-
tous Paragraph 58–10, Agitation, the standard charge for anything
from telling jokes about Stalin to intellectual deviationism.

My new friends made life a little more bearable. I shared in

their meager food packages sent from home. Sometimes a friend in
the kitchen could find a little extra cabbage soup or fat to help protect my 95 pounds against the cold. When I went to the camp hospital later, my friends brought me bread saved from their own
rations, and other favors for which I'll always be grateful.

Learning Russian dispelled another fear. The language is so
harsh I always thought everyone was screaming at me. Later I realized it was just a way of speaking. Actually the Russians are far from
firm. They are masters of bluff—but when you stand up to them ag-
gressively, they invariably back down.

Through my triumvirate and my new command of the language, I came to know the more than one hundred other slaves in
my barracks, and others throughout Vorkuta. Vorkuta was a verita-
ble League of Nations, and it contained many notables of the Communist world. The former First Secretary of the Communist Party
of Estonia, who had labored to turn his country over to the Soviet,
was handing out food in the *stolovaya* of Mine 29.

There were slaves who had been deputy ministers of East Germany and satellite countries, and regional leaders of the Communist Party itself. Gureyvich, a Russian Jew and former Soviet
diplomat, was in Camp 3 just a few barracks from me. He had been
recalled from France by the Kremlin shortly after World War II
(when the "cold war" policy developed) and arrested by MVD
agents as he stepped off the plane in Moscow. We had a colleague
of Trotsky, who had been in dozens of slave camps for the last nine-
teen years; a former Professor of History at the University of
Leningrad, and many former university students. A barracks mate,
Dmitri Bespalo, an active member of the Young Communist
League (Komsomol) at the University of Kiev, was serving fifteen
years for "agitation."

We had many former CP members from East Germany, who
were arrested in periodic purges from 1946 to 1950. There were even
two Spanish Communists who had been in Odessa in the thirties
expediting war materials to the Spanish Loyalists during the Civil
War. They stayed on in Russia after Franco won, and a year later
were arrested for "espionage." Most of the ex-Communists were dis-

illusioned with what they consider the Kremlin's perversion of Marxism.

Not everyone in Vorkuta was an ex-Red. We were a polyglot army of slaves from every walk of life and almost every nation in the world. In Camp 3 we had Poles who had served with the Allies in General Anders's army during World War II and were arrested back in Poland when the Communists took full control in 1947. There were hundreds of Baltic people—Lithuanians, Latvians and Estonians, whose nations had been gobbled up in 1940 and made into Soviet republics.

"When the Russians realized they couldn't really communize us," a Latvian, a former resident of Riga, told me, "they started to bring hundreds of thousands of Russians in to live in our country. They sent our people in exile to Siberia. Those of us who fought the deportation are here in Vorkuta, or in Karaganda or Irkutsk, or other slave camps instead of living in collectives in Siberia. Well, maybe there isn't much difference anyway."

Another Latvian had been a student at the University of Riga before his arrest. A prominent athlete, he had often visited Moscow with various sports groups. He confided to me that a good part of the Russian Olympic teams are actually made up of closely guarded, blond-haired anti-Communist athletes from the Baltic nations.

There were slaves from Iraq, Iran, Italy, Mongolia, China, and Czechoslovakia and later two North Koreans accused of disloyalty to their regime. There were a number of Russian and Ukrainian Jews, victims of Stalin's anti-Semitic pogroms of 1949–1953. In Camp 3 alone there were ten Greeks who had been taken prisoner by the Communists during their civil war. One of my barracks mates was a young Hungarian, James, a former university student in Budapest. He had been arrested as a "Western agent," allegedly for spreading Colorado potato bugs, thus causing the bad potato crop in Hungary. There were hundreds of Germans, both Communists and Nazis, and some former SS troopers. We had representation from France in one prisoner, Rene (his wife was in the women's compound), who had been attached to the French government unit in West Berlin; an Englishman named Chapman (in Camp 10), a British army man who had been captured by the Germans in Holland. He was liberated in 1945 by the Russians from a Nazi PW camp, then promptly rearrested by the Reds and sent to Vorkuta. When I met him in mid-1954, his mind had been almost completely destroyed.

A number of my fellow prisoners were clergymen, Catholic priests from Lithuania, Protestant ministers from Latvia and Germany, and Russian Orthodox priests who were the only ones allowed to keep their long beards. Religion was one of the most serious crimes in Vorkuta. Possession of a Bible meant at least a month in jail.

But, despite all controls, religion flourished. Some groups held services at an altar in an unused hallway of the mine. A group of Baptists sat together at the evening meal in the *stalavaya* and prayed. When an MVD guard came over, they said: "There is nothing wrong, *Chort* [devil]. We are just praying." (The guards in Vorkuta took the slaves' imprecations philosophically.)

On free days I sometimes attended Protestant services given by a Latvian minister. It was in a different barracks each time. It was dangerous, but only if two or more guards came along. Individual guards made believe they saw nothing and walked away. A Lithuanian priest in my barracks was arrested regularly. But after two months in the *bar* [solitary confinement in a box] he would return each time to minister to his flock.

I was the only American in Camp 3, but I had contact with a few men who claimed to be Americans. In Camp 10, where I lived in 1953 and 1954, there was a William Vlasilefsky, an English-speaking, Russian-born prisoner who claimed to be an American citizen. He said that he lived most of his early life in the Western states and that part of his family was still living in Seattle. According to Vlasilefsky, he was in the United States army in the early thirties, then migrated to China, where he started a successful business. In 1949, the Chinese Reds called him to Peiping, where he was arrested and sent to the Soviet Union as a slave laborer.

Then there was Roy Linder, in Vorkuta called Adolf Eichenbaum, a prominent Vorkuta citizen. I met him in the hospital in

1950. Later he would come over to my barracks once in a while to talk. He spoke perfect English and, for that matter, equally good Russian, German, Swedish, and Chinese. We reminisced about Detroit (he had been a stunt flier at the Michigan State Fair) and about the States in general. Linder was very tall and balding and had a scarred chin that was twisted to one side, the result, he said, of a plane crash. According to his story, he was born in Vancouver, British Columbia, was an American citizen and a colonel in the United States Air Force, one of our commanding officers at Templehof Airport in West Berlin. During World War II he had been a U.S. army pilot in China, and prior to the war had flown as a "neutral" observer in the Spanish war.

According to Linder's version of his arrest, he had been kidnapped by the Communists in West Berlin in 1949 and dragged over to the eastern sector. After a year in Lubianka prison in Moscow, he had been shipped to Vorkuta as a slave laborer.

His story seemed convincing (except for occasional references to himself as major instead of colonel), but his short sentence of five years for Paragraph 58–6, "Espionage," made everyone suspicious. An American officer (unless he was trusted by the MVD) would undoubtedly have been tagged with a fifteen-to-twenty-five-year sentence. He had a local reputation as a person who might be pro-Communist. He seemed to have more freedom of action than the other slaves, more to eat, and more respect from the guards and MVD officers. My friends warned me not to trust him—that he was probably an MVD *stuckachey*—an informer.

"Don't worry, Johnny. I won't make any trouble for you," Linder once told me in an unguarded moment.

The last time I saw Linder was just before he was released by pardon. He sent me a note a few weeks later, saying that he was in Vorkuta working in the village powerhouse as a free worker. He had a girl friend in Rostov in South Russia and hoped to go and meet her. I have no idea whether he was ever allowed to leave the Vorkuta area, or what has since become of him.

Many other Americans are still in the Soviet, working as slave laborers. I heard that an American engineer, seized while working for the Reds in Vladivostok, is still in Lubianka prison in Moscow.

According to newly arrived slaves coming from Moscow, so is
Stalin's son, Lt. Gen. Vassily Stalin. But a Yugoslav who had been
imprisoned only a hundred miles from Vorkuta told me more star-
tling news.

"I spoke with eight of your countrymen," the Yugoslav told me.
"They said they were American fliers who had been shot down by
the Russians over the Baltic Sea. The Air Force has, of course, acknowledged that several B-29s and B-50s on routine missions were
downed over the Baltic. One of them told me he was afraid they
would never get back to America. The Russians had reported them
dead, saying there were no survivors of the crash."

Prisoners being funneled into Vorkuta from camps in Tadzhik
and Irkutsk in Soviet Asia, Omsk in Siberia, and Magadan in the
Far East said there were many Americans, including veterans of the
Korean War, both GIs and officers, and South Korean soldiers,
working as slave laborers in their camps. From what I heard, they
were PWs captured by the Communist Chinese and North Koreans
who had been shipped to the Soviet for safe-keeping.

Some of the Ukrainians in our camp literally fell over every
newcomer, questioning him on what prison camp he had come
from and how many prisoners were there. Through adding, cross-
checking, and striking averages, it was possible to establish a fair ap-
proximation to the number of people interned in Russia. The total
population of the Vorkuta complex lay between four and five hundred thousand working in mines, brick factories, power plants, railroad lines, streets, city and village construction, food transportation,
prison help, and hospitals. According to records we were able to
piece together, throughout the entire Soviet Union in mid-1954 a
total of twenty-five to twenty-eight million people were held in
slave-labor camps, concentration camps, secret camps for foreign-
ers, PW camps, repatriation camps, MVD prisons, investigation
centers, MGB prisons, juvenile labor camps, and juvenile detention homes. An additional twelve million not in custody were interned in restricted areas. All told, a monstrous mass of slaves and
persecuted peoples.

[Noble was to spend eleven years in a Soviet labor camp. In his
story he tells of the dramatic rebellion that broke out among the

100,000 prisoners in the arctic slave camps in the spring of 1953, following Stalin's death. The rebellion was brutally crushed. Through the efforts of Congressman Alvin Bentley and Bohlen, then the ambassador to the Soviet Union, Noble was freed in early 1955. He learned that his father had been freed earlier. When he crossed the border into the West, he recalls thinking, "I had crossed a border that separated two worlds. The world of fear, terror, deceit, Godlessness, and slavery was behind me in the east. I was returning to the west to a world of busy people developing their lives according to their abilities, a world of freedom and of moral standards unknown to the people of the Communist realm. . . . I had been a slave in Russia; now I was free!" — ED.]

· 3 ·

NICHOLAS PRYCHODKO

A Professor's Tale from Ukraine

IN 1959, Nicholas Prychodko, a Ukrainian immigrant living in Canada, appeared before the House Committee on Un-American Activities to testify against the crimes of Soviet premier Nikita Khrushchev. Seven years earlier, Little, Brown, and Company had published his book, *One of the Fifteen Million* (1952), recounting his life in Soviet slave labor camps. Shortly before the publication of Prychodko's book, Elinor Lipper had published her book revealing the extent of labor camps in the Soviet Union.

At the committee hearings, Prychodko told of his twenty-one months in a Kiev prison, when he was arrested on false charges of being a member of a nationalist Ukrainian underground organization. He told committee members of how he had been "humiliated" and tortured. "The investigators," he said, "spit in my mouth and hit me with the leg of a chair. To this date, I have pains in my back from those beatings." At other times, he continued, "I was beaten by a small plank from which protruded about 20 small nails. They have just blunt points and you do not bleed, but you have blue marks after you are hit by that."

Prychodko went on to tell the congressional committee that he was sentenced to a slave labor camp in Ivdel. In the entire complex, he said, there were "350,000 slaves." In his particular camp were 3,000 slaves laborers, of whom 15 died each day he was there.

The committee was especially anxious to hear if Khrushchev bore any responsibility for these camps. President Eisenhower had sought a rapprochement with the Soviet Union, and while Khrushchev continued to display remarkable belligerence toward the United States, he also spoke of peace. Khrushchev's speech in 1956 denouncing Stalin had been widely reported in the Western press and had led some Western leaders to believe that U.S.-Soviet relations had entered a new, more productive stage. The committee was anxious to know of Khrushchev's sincerity—though the presence of Prychodko, the author of a book widely read by anti-Communists, suggested that they already knew the answer.

When asked about Khrushchev, Prychodko did not mince words. He recalled that in 1937 Khrushchev had stood just to the right of Stalin in the May Day parade, and that in 1938 he had been sent to the Ukraine as a "dictator." Shortly after Khrushchev's arrival there, the head of the Ukrainian People's Commissariat had been sent home, where he shot his wife and himself. There followed a "tremendous purge all over Ukraine." Prychodko reported that under Khrushchev the Ukraine experienced mass starvation of between six and seven million people, a deliberate consequence of the collectivization of farms. Prychodko spoke with great emotion of how the famine had led to cannibalism, with parents eating the corpses of their own dead children.

Prychodko concluded his testimony with this warning: Khrushchev has been invited to the United States and will soon arrive to be wined and dined. But do not mistake the enemy, he declared. "As today, many were hoodwinked then as to the realities in the Soviet Union."

"Hoodwinked" was exactly what American anti-Communists feared was happening to the American people and the Eisenhower administration. While Khrushchev might speak the words of "peaceful coexistence," anti-Communists knew that the Soviets remained treacherous. They were "masters of deceit" who had lured people and nations into false promises of a better life, only to impose a ruthless dictatorship. Anti-Communists continued to warn that the Soviet Union's propaganda was designed to "brainwash" the American people into believing that communism no longer posed a threat to the United States. Critical to this propaganda effort was a "peace" initiative to establish trade and cultural exchanges with the West. More ominous was the Soviets' call for nuclear arms control and a ban against the atmospheric testing of atomic bombs.

Prychodko's *One of the Fifteen Million* received wide attention in the West and became a standard book recommended by anti-Communist study groups. It confirmed that an Iron Curtain had been erected in Eastern Europe by the Soviets. Prychodko wrote with authority. He had been a professor at Kiev University who had direct experience with Communist prisons and the techniques of communism. Behind their sweet words, he warned, the Communists were ruthless barbarians who watched as fifteen million Ukrainians had starved to death.

Prychodko's message had great appeal in the United States among the many ethnic groups from nations within the Soviet bloc. Most of these Poles, Hungarians, Romanians, and Czechs were Roman Catholics, so it was not surprising to find that Roman Catholics composed a significant constituency in the anti-Communist movement in the United States. Masses often ended with prayers for the liberation of people behind the Iron Curtain. In 1959 a grassroots movement among Catholics called for President Eisenhower to declare a "Captive Nations Week," in which local communities, churches, and civic organizations would speak out against the Soviet dictatorships imposed on the peoples of Eastern Europe. Congress passed just such a resolution that year, followed by a presidential proclamation. This week became part of the American cold war ritual. Without doubt, Prychodko's book played a significant role in the grassroots campaign.

🈯 During the reign of the Czars a huge, three-story prison was built on Shevchenko Boulevard, one of the busiest streets in Kiev. It was the third largest prison in Kiev and seemed to serve as a sort of warning from Moscow to the residents of the Ukrainian capital,

From *One of the Fifteen Million* (Toronto, 1952), pp. 5–6, 17–18, 31–37, 57–59, 62–64, 112–118.

purposely built in a crowded section. Its drab gray facade, with heavy bars over the windows, stretched for about five hundred feet along the boulevard.

Night and day two guards with fixed bayonets paced up and down in front of this massive building. From time to time the pale, tired faces of inmates peered out through the bars.

Twenty years later, before the outbreak of one of the worst Soviet purges and waves of terror, the "Yeshov terror" of 1937–1938, the political prisoners of the Communist regime were all taken out of this prison. The bars were removed and through the large, freshly-cleaned windows one could see a neat row of dining-tables, each covered with a white cloth and decorated with a bouquet of artificial flowers. White curtains appeared on all the windows of the upper stories and trucks were seen bringing in material for workshops, to be set up in the inner courtyard.

When the renovation was completed, new prisoners were brought in, not political prisoners, but men who were serving short-term sentences for minor crimes. They spent their time at constructive work in the workshops.

This show prison, on Shevchenko Boulevard in Kiev, was shown to foreign delegates and other visitors to convince them of Russia's "great humanitarianism."

From this prison it was only ten minutes' ride to the real Soviet prison where I was held for twenty-one months. From there I was taken away to slave labour in a Siberian concentration camp.

*   *   *

The city of Kiev, capital of the Ukraine, was shrouded in a veil of ominous foreboding. Throughout that metropolis, and through the whole of the Ukraine, swept a merciless wave of terror. Each day, groups of people nervously approached the factory bulletin boards to scan the long lists of laid-off workmen. Each one expected to find his or her name on a list. Today, perhaps, there was no such name. But there remained the incessant fear that it would be there tomorrow.

And that would be the end. Relieved of work today and

snatched away tomorrow, in the black of the night. Or perhaps they would come tonight, and the name would appear tomorrow. There was no avenue of escape, for the NKVD was omnipresent and its sleepless eye saw everything, everybody, everywhere.

Life was unreal and terrible. Christianity had disappeared from the minds of the oppressors who had seized power.

In the streets the threat of death became more menacing. With the approach of the evening when people left their work for their homes, and continuing until dawn when they returned to their jobs, the ever-active "Black Crows" were allowed to proceed without stopping at intersections. Mostly these secret scourges pursued their course on the main street which leads from the Lukianiwska Prison to the Central and Regional Headquarters of the NKVD. In the dead of night they were seen on the Great Vasylkivska Avenue on their way to Kossy Kapanir, an old Czarist fortress where soldiers awaiting court-martial were held, under the old regime. Its thick walls completely deaden the reports of the incessant shots in the nape of the victim's neck which are the order of the day there now.

From Kossy Kapanir it is not far to the Mysholovka ravines where it is easy to conceal any evidence of foul play and the bloody corpses of the citizens of this "happiest country on earth."

There was no peace, either on the street or at home. In the middle of the night one woke up trembling, chilled by the screech of the siren or the grating of suddenly opened entrance doors, holding one's breath, intently listening for the direction of the footsteps. And in the morning terrorized neighbours haltingly related the incident and whispered about who was taken away.

It was difficult to name a single dwelling place in Kiev where there had not been an arrest. Not only in Kiev, but throughout the whole Ukraine, from the largest cities to the most remote villages, the Kremlin's emissaries in their cranberry-red and blue caps, faithful stooges of Stalin and his "beloved *Narkom*" Yezhov, [Stalin's chief in Ukraine] carried on their work of ferreting out victims. Periodic terrorization had ensued of all those who believed in freedom of thought and speech and who might become potential enemies. Especially was this true within the spheres of their "defensive interest" in Finland, or their interest in the "liberation" of the West

Ukraine and Poland. All those who might have introduced a suggestion of discord or implied the slightest suspicion of the Kremlin had to be removed. At the same time millions of serfs had to be recruited for the slave camps at Kolyma and in Siberia.

*   *   *

It was long past midnight. I woke with a start and sat up in bed. I listened intently. The sound of distant footsteps, coming closer and closer, reached my ears. The veins in my temples began to throb more and more violently as the steps drew nearer.

They stopped near my doorway. There was a short pause. Perhaps they were looking for the bell. Then there was a ring. Strangely, a load seemed to fall from my soul. The unbearable tension of constant anticipation lessened.

I calmly asked, "Who's there?"

"This is I, the janitor—for examination of passports."

Now I had not the slightest doubt. The janitor entered the room somewhat reluctantly, accompanied by two men in NKVD uniforms. One of them asked me with simulated politeness to produce my passport. After examining it he ordered me to be searched.

My wife, evidently perplexed, began to dress, meanwhile consoling our sobbing son who was awakened by the entrance of these strange men in uniform. Presently I regained some semblance of self-control, and when they began to search me I was on the lookout for any surreptitious planting of false evidence, such as proclamations or fire-arms. This was a routine device practised quite extensively by the Yezhov "heroes." Their search lasted over two hours, although our home contained only one little room which served as dining room, bedroom, kitchen and study.

I recollect that the attention of one of these NKVD men was drawn to a bottle of wine which he found on a shelf. He kept turning it around in his hands against the light so long that I finally suggested that they take some. This they did, guzzling down the contents to the very bottom. They then gathered up all the correspondence and papers they could find and told me to get dressed, issuing no order for arrest in the meantime.

"Come with us; we wish to ask you for some explanations."

When my wife asked them excitedly where they were taking me, one of them answered, "Don't worry. I hope this is a misunderstanding."

[Prychodko was arrested and detained in Kiev. — ED.]

*   *   *

In the evening the doors opened and a group of railroad men from Fastov were driven into the cell. One glance was enough to suggest that some railroad catastrophe was the reason for their incarceration. Their faces were literally covered with black and blue marks and some bore signs of freshly inflicted bloody gashes. We all rushed forward to question them about the accident but they were reluctant to explain, no doubt because of their strange surroundings and for fear of causing provocation. But one of them finally became communicative.

"This catastrophe took place at the Fastov NKVD office during interrogation," he said.

We asked them such questions as: "Were you actually beaten while you were being questioned? How was that possible? We thought such a thing was only practiced in capitalist countries!"

Of course not all of us were so naive about it, but those who were became disillusioned when he said: "Impossible, you say; well, take a look at me! If and when you get a few clouts with a chair leg you'll know different."

This episode had a depressing effect on the uninitiated, which was deepened by the memory of the brutal behaviour of the guards during the search, and by the fact that we had received neither food nor water during the whole day.

About one o'clock at night we were ordered outside into the inner court of the prison. . . . We were led across the yard to the washroom, where they cut off our hair. This operation was performed with unnecessary brutality by young degenerates from the criminal division. They abused us with the most vulgar and obscene epithets. We learned later that these same youngsters did the women-prisoners' haircuts as well. All our clothing was taken to be disinfected, and later returned in a badly scorched condition. They then turned on alternately hot and cold water for our bath. After this satisfaction they took us out into the yard at about three o'clock in the morning, keeping us there about an hour in the cold. Some-one timidly tried to protest against this treatment but was rewarded with a resounding blow delivered by a guard.

An hour later the guards began to herd us in groups of twenty into the prison. My group was taken up into one of the corridors on the second floor. We were halted at the end of this corridor and then marshalled in twos and threes into various cells. Another pris-oner and I came to an iron-braced door which had a peep-hole in the centre and on which the number "109" was painted in white. The door opened and we entered. We could hear the grating of an iron bar behind us; and before us there appeared one of the most unbelievable sights that the most imaginative person enjoying free-dom could conjure up. In this brilliantly lighted cell, about fifteen feet by twenty, fourteen iron cots were set up in tiers of threes, one on top of the other, reaching almost to the ceiling. On each of the cots four people were lying sideways, the end persons being tied to the cot with towels, to prevent them from falling off in their sleep.

Against the back wall there stood a long cupboard, a foot in depth, with shelves for dishes. On the top of it lay a man who as-sumed the proud demeanour of a king. He had, comparatively, so much more room than the others. The whole cement floor under the cots was covered with human forms, packed like herrings in a barrel. All were lying on their sides and, as I was to learn afterwards, one could only turn over if everyone else was willing to turn at the same time. We had standing room only near the door and could not move, for fear of trampling on somebody's head. On our appear-ance many sleepy, dirty heads were raised; but seeing nothing out of the ordinary, were soon lowered again. The orderly told us to re-main standing in the same position until morning. Cursing the prison administration for letting more people into the cell, he said:

"What the devil are they thinking about; we already have one hundred and sixteen persons here!"

There was not only no freedom of movement in the cell, but one could hardly breathe, especially while standing up. The awful stench of human perspiration and of the barrel-like urinal took one's breath away. We had to bend down low in order to breathe at all. From time to time some sleepy looking scarecrow in human form would make his way from some part of the room to the urinal. This was extremely difficult, as it had to be done over many closely packed bodies. Some of them took it with good grace; but others cursed or else dealt the "prowler" a blow. Those who passed by us stopped to ask questions such as where we came from; what was going on in the free outside world; whether there was any talk of an amnesty; and after they had completed their toilet they threaded their way over the protesting forms back to their places.

We did not ask them any questions for fear of annoying the inmates; but we observed much. If we had not found ourselves in the same fix, we would not only have regarded their plight with compassion, but it would have appeared comical as well. Later, when I was liberated, I often wished that I possessed a snapshot of this scene because mere words are inadequate to describe it.

On one of the top cots a large, black-bearded man was snoring vociferously. He looked like one of those fantastic highwaymen who had somehow managed to survive from the seventeenth or eighteenth century. But he turned out to be Professor B.I., one of the leading astronomers at the Kiev Observatory, a person of great learning and of a genial and optimistic nature. When I told him later, after making his acquaintance, that I mistook him for a medieval outlaw, he laughed heartily. He never lost his sense of humour. Even when he was being subjected to the third degree and forced to admit guilt as a mythical spy on the German payroll, Professor B.I., ostensibly unable to endure any further torture, wrote out a legendary confession, admitting to a series of systematic meetings with the German Schopenhauer in the library of the Ukrainian Academy of Sciences.

The young prosecutor, on hearing the name Schopenhauer, felt highly elated at being able to force these admissions, and with the exuberance of youth he hurried to his chief with the evidence and to ask for further instructions. But it was not long before he and the chief of the division returned in great anger.

"Do you think," yelled the officer, "that we are so stupid that we have never heard of Schopenhauer?"

Professor B.I. was given a vigorous beating for his facetious joke.

*   *   *

I rather unexpectedly met one of my old acquaintances in the cell—Professor L., formerly a district school inspector in Kiev. I had heard before that he had been arrested as an "enemy of the people," and this had seemed somewhat strange to me. He had always appeared to be a modest and hardworking sort of person and it was hard to conceive him guilty of any crime or subversive action. But when he was arrested I began to wonder whether there really was something wrong, for surely the NKVD would not do this to an innocent man! The more the terror raged, the greater grew the propagandistic eulogies about the justice of Soviet jurisprudence.

This man finally came over to me and shook hands. If he had not told me his name I would not have recognized him. It was hard to believe that this was the same person, so greatly had he changed in the two months since his arrest. His features were heavily furrowed and tired-looking and his face was covered with a thick stubble. The right eye was completely closed by a reddish-blue swelling.

"What happened to you?" I asked.

He replied, "I think you ought to have some inkling of what is going on by now. I don't know why they arrested me, and yet I have been questioned six times already. The day before yesterday I received these mementoes for refusing to sign a false statement. Look at my eye; but don't think that is all," he said, pulling up his shirt with trembling hands to disclose the black and blue welts on his chest and spine.

"What happened to you?" I asked with horror and on the verge of tears.

"My prosecutor," he continued, "has an oak board armed with the points of twenty nails. While he is questioning me he makes me take off my shirt and he conducts his investigation with the aid of this instrument. I can't stand much more of this. Perhaps I'll have to give in and confess to something."

It gradually became clear to me that these people were no more "enemies of the people" than I was; but as yet I could not see any sense in this mass persecution of wholly innocent people. It was not until later on in my prison term that it all became obvious, especially when I encountered a group being sent to the dark and limitless forests of Siberia. There was wealth in those forests in the form of foreign exchange. But who would want to go there of his own free will, to freeze in the intense cold, or feed with his blood the myriads of mosquitoes at the price of a crust of bread and a pint of sloppy soup made from decayed fish? In those parts millions of men were needed. That explained the double purpose they had in mind: first, to forestall any danger of rebellion among the people who might get ideas about the hypocrisy of the Stalin Constitution and expose the humbug to others; and secondly, to secure cheap slave labour which could be utilized without cost even within the Arctic Circle. There they can squeeze the last ounce of energy out of the prisoners and then bury them without leaving any trace in the silence of the inaccessible *taiga* [permafrost soil].

And why the interrogations, the false evidence and the trumped-up charges? This was all to justify the existence of the millions of loyal brutes comprising the NKVD. And then there was the propaganda aspect, as much as to say: "You see how the sleepless eye of the NKVD is guarding your welfare. You are hungry and without clothes because of these wreckers and diversionists. Read for yourself their own admissions."

I well remember them reading out the fantastic evidence of one of my fellow-workers at one of the meetings, touching on his alleged sabotage and spying activities.

Insulted and enraged, somebody shouted, "Well! Who would have thought that such a type could be so deceiving? The NKVD is really on the job; it sees and knows everything."

But when I saw the bloody welts on Professor L.'s spine I knew how and under what circumstances this "evidence" was signed and secured.

The former NKVD officials incarcerated along with us in the cells admitted that this was the case.

*   *   *

The inmates of our cell ranged from learned academicians to stupid beggars, from sublime characters to ridiculous buffoons. They were a polyglot conglomeration of nationalities: once we counted thirteen. But the Ukrainians were in the majority—a nation most "beloved by the older Muscovite brother." There were even high officials and military leaders. The Kremlin was always in constant dread of any person exerting real influence in military circles. Often the only reason for their arrest was the recitation of an anecdote or some picayune reference to government policy.

One day the commander of the Bila Tserkva Division was brought into our cell. He wore the Order of Lenin on his chest, the "Red Flag," and the "Red Star." It seemed strange they had not been ripped off before he entered the prison, but perhaps it was done with a view to impressing upon the prisoners the mighty reach of the penalizing hand.

At first the attitude of this commander was one of contemptuous haughtiness towards the other inmates. He evidently took the view, like ourselves earlier, that his arrest was just a misunderstanding, and that the other prisoners were actually "enemies of the people," such as he, not so long ago, had been denouncing in his speeches. He looked down his nose at us when we asked him questions.

In the evening of that same day he was taken out, along with his insignia, for questioning. He returned at dawn, or rather he was dragged back and thrown into the cell. He was splattered with blood, and the cloth where his insignia had been fastened was torn to shreds.

Choking with blood, which he kept spitting out, he found it hard to talk. His wounds were washed, and he was laid down in a quiet corner on two coats which were spread out to make his rest easier.

When he came to after a short nap, he began to relate how the investigator, prior to the interrogation, rushed over to him and tore off the insignia, calling them "rattle-toys," and ripped his shirt to pieces. Unable to stand such degradation, this commander of a division who had won his awards on the Spanish front, threw caution to the winds, picked up a chair and knocked the investigator off his feet. Hearing his cry for help, some guards hurried in from the corridor and flung themselves at the prisoner. They all gave full vent to their natures with the help of oak chair legs.

Forgotten were his services as an active commander in their passion to give him "the works." When he fainted, they revived him again, and the torture was renewed. Once more the same day, the commander was recalled for questioning, but he never returned to our cell again. Notwithstanding our efforts to find out more about him, we found no trace of his whereabouts or what was done with him.

In this manner prison life continued, the inmates slowly accustoming themselves to its hard and cruel routine. Human adaptability seems limitless; and in normal times the human mind can hardly conceive of the amount of pain and suffering it can endure.

There was little rest in the NKVD prison at night. The judicial investigation would begin about 11 p.m. and continue till 2 a.m. Some prisoners were interrogated, others simply disappeared. In such a strained atmosphere, sleep was out of the question except in snatches of fitful semi-consciousness. Whenever the door bar squeaked, most of us, as if electrified, lifted our heads and waited. Into the prison cell would move a guard with a list of names and call, for instance:

"With K?"

Then all prisoners whose surname began with that letter had to give their names. When the surname was given, the Christian name was asked.

Then the order followed: "Dress quickly!"

Sometimes the fatal words "with belongings" were added. The victim would dress with trembling hands and walk out of the cell into the corridor; his fellow inmates bade their farewells in silence.

Ten or twenty minutes later the door would open again and the guard would ask for names beginning with some other letter. Thus four to six men from each cell would be called. The torture chamber was working at full speed. Hardly a night passed without such visits.

At daybreak or even later, some of the victims would return from the investigation room to our cell, their faces unrecognizable from wounds and bloodstains. Often the victim was no longer able to walk, so the guards would pull him by the legs or the arms along the prison corridors, and throw him into our cell as if he were an inanimate bundle. Some individuals would be called to the investigation room night after night for weeks in succession. These victims would drop into a coma or become insane after so many nights of sleeplessness and suffering. In such a stupefied frame of mind they would sign any imaginary statement fabricated by the investigator.

Some victims never came back. Whether they were tortured to death or shot in the nape of the neck we could not find out. On the following day the guard would come to our cell and take away the belongings of the victim who had not returned.

Practically every night there would be an additional horror-drama enacted—a shrill, unearthly female shriek would come from the investigation chambers where some woman was being tortured. The interrogation of women was often conducted at night in order to further demoralize the men. The investigation chambers were in the basement between the sixth and eleventh corridors.

In moments like these we would sink to the bottomless pit of despair. We would listen breathlessly, apprehensively. Perhaps we would hear the voice of a sister, a mother, a wife, or a daughter. Those who could not stand these shrieks soon became hysterical, giving vent to blood-curdling yells like the cries of a wounded beast. The person guilty of such yelling would soon be discovered, pulled out into the corridor, and silenced with kicks.

One scene still rises before me like a bad dream. An inmate of our cell, a Red Army major, committed suicide by striking his head with all his might against the sharp corner of a brick chimney. With blood gushing from the wound, he fell down unconscious. He was instantly removed from the cell. Later we found that he had died the same night.

Along the sixth corridor of the prison, special cells were allocated for those who had been condemned to die. Terrible cries of agony often emanated from them. They were frequently interrupted as if the victims were being gagged; then there would be one more redoubled yell that dwindled down to an inaudible gurgle.

In moments like these, we resembled the inmates of an insane asylum more than ordinary prisoners in a jail. It was not until these heartrending cries had subsided that sleep of any kind was possible. Even what little snatches we did get were often broken by the shrill scream of a victim.

Under these conditions I pondered over my forthcoming interrogation, although I had committed no crime. It finally dawned on me that the guilt need not be genuine. It was all predetermined by Yezhov, who declared before a meeting of top NKVD officials in Kiev:

"What kind of NKVDists are you that you cannot produce confessions? So long as there is a man, a crime can be found!"

To the firm denial of a prisoner, the investigator would often reply with a repetition of these famous words:

"All the same you'll write. So long as there is a man, we will find the crime!"

And in most cases they did find the crime: by means of a chair leg, a rubber hose; by closing a door on the victim's fingers, by pumping air into the prisoner's stomach; and other Soviet investigation methods. Many of those who at first resolutely refused to sign ended up by doing so when they realized how hopeless their position was.

Such prisoners would usually return to their prison cells unharmed. In fact they would be rewarded by the investigator with two or three cigarettes for their legendary crimes. These individuals were spontaneously boycotted by the prisoners at large, despite the fact that open boycotts of a fellow-prisoner were strictly punished and were also dangerous because the boycotted inmate could revenge himself by provocation. But we all showed the deepest respect and sympathy towards those prisoners who steadfastly suffered persecution and refused to submit to giving false evidence.

One of the most remarkable figures I met in the prison was Mikhailo Savchuk, a member of the Ukrainian Academy of Sciences.

For sixteen successive nights he was led out for questioning and dreadfully beaten, because he refused to admit that a group of his colleagues were guilty of membership in a nationalist organization. The admission of this membership, imaginary, of course, was needed by the NKVD police to create a formal basis for the arrest of the other members of the Ukrainian Academy of Sciences.

Mikhailo Savchuk categorically refused to yield to this type of provocation, and consequently was tormented every night. At first he used to return from the torture chamber all alone and covered with bruises and bloodstains, pretending the while that everything was all right with him. Later on he could not walk at all, so the jailers threw him in like a sack on the floor of our cell. Even then he did not show any sign of pain except for an occasional shudder of agony.

Once I approached him, asking whether there was anything I could do for him. Actually, there was nothing I could do, yet I felt like saying some kind word to him. He understood and thanked me warmly.

"How can you stand all these tortures without losing your mental balance?" I asked him.

"I shall disclose to you," he said, "the secret of my tenacity. When they torture me, I imagine I see in the corner of the cell my sick wife standing there and holding my little daughter in her arms. Realizing fully the burden of their solitude and utter poverty, I feel it so keenly and so painfully that my physical suffering becomes less excruciating. I know that if I falsely sign the paper they demand, my loved ones will be bereft of their last shelter, and that none of my friends, who would take me then for a most contemptible wretch, would ever condescend to speak a kind word to them. Let me die in vain, but with a clear conscience. You follow my example and do likewise."

This conversation had a profound effect on me. My soul was greatly relieved. My friend's noble example strengthened me to endure all the tortures of which I, too, received my full share.

Three days after my conversation with Mikhailo Savchuk, he was dragged into the cell half dead.

We applied poultices to the sorest spots on his body and made room for him under a cot in the corner of our cell. He hardly moaned. We only heard him move from time to time from one wounded side to the other. Later we thought we heard him snore once rather noisily, perhaps in a nightmare. Then he was quiet. Everybody was glad that he was resting so nobody disturbed him. This time he slept longer than usual. We did not wake him up even when our jail dinner was brought in. But in the evening we decided to waken him. We called him by name, but he didn't move. We immediately understood that there was something wrong. We tilted the cot under which he was lying and saw what had happened. There he lay, all huddled up with his hands pressed against his heart. His hands and an overcoat that was spread under him were bloodstained. One hand firmly grasped a sharp cot spring, which he had used to pierce his own heart.

Now we knew why a few days ago he had begged us to help him detach a spring from the cot. He had not enough energy left in him to do it himself. Then he had sharpened one end of the spring against the cement floor, explaining that he was making an awl with which to repair his hopelessly worn-out footwear.

We called the guards. We all rose to attention, tearfully and with profound deference, as we sent him on his final journey to an unknown grave.

On the following day we refused to touch any food. Two days later the cots were removed from all the cells. This obviously was done in order to prevent any similar occurrences; for even prior to the Savchuk incident several inmates in other cells had committed suicide by hanging themselves from the uppermost cot by means of a rope made of strands from old socks or strips from shirts or towels.

*   *   *

Months passed, and Yezhov kept on destroying countless victims. Countless sealed trains wended their way without a trace to the far north, carrying millions of serfs for the slave camps. In the cellars and silent ravines tens of thousands fell victim to shots in the nape of the neck from the NKVD bandits. And within the prison walls the old preliminary work went on incessantly. New prisoners kept pouring in to replace those sent away.

At the beginning of summer there were one hundred and thirty-two prisoners in our small cell. There was hardly standing room, let alone a place to sit or sleep. It was stuffy beyond endurance, with the sun beating down on the roof and the window shutters closed. We stripped our clothes off, but even that didn't help much. We sweated profusely, using rags to wipe ourselves, and then wringing them out into bowls at our feet. These bowls were handed from one person to another and emptied into the urinal. Our bodies were covered with red itchy spots which bothered us all day long. Even when fresh air did blow in at night, myriads of bedbugs came out of invisible crevices and prevented sleep.

To slake the thirst of one hundred and thirty-two persons, all we got was a six-gallon iron bucket of water in the evening. It is hard to picture the state of mind with which we awaited this small dole of water. We poured it carefully into cups as if it were some priceless nectar. The water, of course, was locked all day long in the wash rooms. We had to go there in our bare feet across a lot of stinking filth to bring it with us to the cell, thus befouling the air still more.

When we were out for our exercise I glanced at my fellow-prisoners. They looked like illusory, skinny, wax skeletons. I was afraid to ask anybody what I looked like.

Some of the inmates did not have the strength to endure this sort of life, so they were taken away, we knew not where, and their places filled with others. Any protest against this order of things was punished with a sound beating, for the superintendents had full power of control to use us as they saw fit.

One day two peasants were brought into our cell directly following an investigation at Brovari near Kiev. They told us about a terrible "death combine" operating in the Darnitsky forest behind a barbed-wire enclosure. In damp cellars of about forty square yards in area, two hundred and fifty prisoners were incarcerated, with standing room only, in the stench of their own sweating bodies, and with hardly any water to drink or anything to eat.

Near these cells the torture chambers worked day and night, and the cries of the tortured victims kept on incessantly. Their feet were seared with hot irons, air was pumped into their stomachs with motorcycle pumps, needles were shoved under their fingernails, and they were beaten over the most delicate parts of their body with an oak ruler. This in the twentieth century, in the "most happy country in the world!" Several corpses were carried out from the cells every day, and in the dead of night many more were taken away to the Darnitsky forest to eternal peace. . . .

Their places in the cells were soon filled with other prisoners.

In the outside courtyard of the torture chamber there was a deep well. One day when they were marching a group of prisoners by this well, two of them broke out of line and dived into it head first. Following this incident, the well was covered over with boards.

When the Nazis invaded the Ukraine, they uncovered a mass burial place at Vynnytza, where thousands of corpses had been thrown. The same evidence was discovered in Darnitsky forest near Brovari, although here they had no time to disinter the bodies, since they had already begun to retreat from the Ukraine; and they had to cover up all traces of their own atrocities.

And so at Brovari thousands of unknown persons lay dead without benefit of decent burial or a cross to mark their graves. Somewhere in the night many bereft mothers and orphaned children must have been waiting in vain and shedding bitter tears.

*   *   *

We first learned about Yezhov's disappearance when we noticed the box for complaints to Yezhov missing from the courtyard wall. The prison inmates viewed this news very optimistically, hoping that the wave of terror was receding.

And that is exactly what happened. The purge had run its course. There were now enough victims and so it was time for a pause. The main instigator of this purge had been the goblin-like Yezhov, formerly Stalin's personal secretary. As Stalin's direct appointee he must have received his instructions from his chief. If results were the criterion, Stalin must have been satisfied with his choice; for in a short time hundreds of thousands had been shot, and millions mobilized for the Siberian slave camps and the mines of Kolyma. When this horrible orgy ended, the Kremlin must have felt secure. In order to sanctify himself and establish his "infallibility" among the people, Stalin then started a "Purge of the Purgers" by announcing at one of the meetings of the party that the policy of the party had been "twisted" by certain officials of the NKVD who were "enemies of the people."

And thus it happened that the man who not so long ago was called the "beloved *Narkom* of Stalin" perished in one of the undisclosed cellars as a twister of Stalin's directions. But the great father lived on as the infallible chief.

In order to conceal the real facts from the people, one tenth of one per cent of the prisoners incarcerated prior to the liquidation of Yezhov were liberated, and even a few hundred returned from Siberia. This was all done for propaganda purposes, as if to say: "The innocent ones are freed, but the real enemies are left in prison. You have been rescued from them by the most wise Stalin."

As a further propaganda measure, a few NKVD officials were thrust into prison on the pretext that they were "twisters of the party's policy," but thousands of others were awarded decorations of honour. I met two of these masterful "twisters" in the prison. One of them was a chief of the Chrystynivska NKVD area during Yezhov's reign, but I do not remember his name. The other was Hulakov, a chief of the 5th Division of the Kiev Regional NKVD. Fearing revenge, they tried desperately to ingratiate themselves with the more influential inmates in the cell, and they frequently divulged many secrets of the service. The Chrystynivska chief related that at the beginning of the Yezhov period he had been ordered to arrest 3,800 people in the area. He had arrested all those who at one time or another had been imprisoned for political crimes and then freed; and also those who were under suspicion on information supplied by the *seksots*. But he still did not have the required number and it was necessary to exceed the quota in order to make a good showing. He then proposed to the heads of the village councils that they supply him with lists of those who should be arrested. The quota was over-subscribed; and then the usual "confession" was extracted with the aid of an oak chair-leg. The Chrystynivska chief expected to be re-warded for his "service," but he wound up by being included in the quota desired by the regional chief!

Hulakov was a bigger fish. Formerly he had been a responsible member of a spy ring in Iran, where he masqueraded as a small offi-cial of the Soviet Embassy. Later on he was one of the eleven who kidnapped General Koutepov in Paris. For this "service" he had re-ceived the military order of the "Red Flag." The award was recorded in the usual phraseology: "For performance of especially important tasks for the party and the government." Now the investigators re-warded him with a few bloody decorations on his back and made him sign a confession about his sabotage within the NKVD organi-zation, and so he disclosed to us many secrets of the operation of the NKVD.

For instance, he told us about a garage in the court regional NKVD on Rosa Luxembourg Street in Kiev, into which Black Crows, loaded with prisoners, were driven at night. The back door of the Black Crow opened on to a stairway leading down into a cel-lar, where, from a dark there came the notorious shot in the neck. This shot cannot be heard by any passing pedestrian, for the sound is drowned out by the Crow's motor running at full blast. In this and in other ways, in Kiev alone, from November 1937 to February 1938, over ten thousand "enemies of the people" were liquidated.

[Prychodko tells of his cruel experiences in many camps, be-fore being transferred to another Siberia camp, Tansha—ED.]

*   *   *

Early in February of the year 1940 two hundred of us were trans-ferred from Yuriko to another camp called Tansha. At that time this was one of the most remote Ivdel camps, hidden away back in the taiga. Tansha had no barracks. Instead there were large tents on raised wooden foundations. We had to spend an intensely cold winter in these monstrosities. In the middle of each tent there was a small iron stove. We fired it until it got red-hot, but we could not warm the place. The canvas walls were still covered with hoarfrost.

We were given one ragged blanket each. For two months we had to sleep with all our clothes on, and we were always chilled to the bone. Many of the prisoners contracted lung trouble and rheumatism as well. The seriously sick were hauled on sleighs to the "hospital" at Camp Prystan. Usually that was the last we ever heard of them. It is safe to assume that they were buried in the graves which we noticed later by the roadside.

When the spring thaws came in April a proclamation from the Ivdel Camp Chief was read to us which stated that prisoners were to work only in the camp grounds in fifty below zero weather. For this benevolence we returned him some silent curses, but these would not bother him. He was too comfortably ensconced in his warm quarters to be concerned about the rest of us, half frozen and half dead from overwork, seemingly forgotten by God and man.

It was a most distressing sight to see those scarecrows of prisoners trudging back from work with heavy feet and bowed heads, dirty, tattered and deathly pale, a dull, grey and beggarly looking mass of hopeless human beings. They were a grotesque group of individuals, much alike in their degraded mien, walking more like robots than men. Under these terrible conditions of slave labour many thousands of people of high cultural standing lost their individuality, their hope for the future, and all semblance of normal human beings. All they could look forward to, and this was a wretched thing at best, was to be able to drag themselves back from work and warm their damp, rheumatic feet, eat a little *balanda* [slop] and try to forget themselves in fitful sleep on the dirty bunks.

Actual freedom was impossible, and dreaming of it in the abstract was too distressing, so we forgot about it completely. Our souls were empty voids, for there was no end to this grey uniformity, the unbearable monotony of this beastly life. We were silent slaves with desolate souls. We neither smiled nor sang, except once in a while when a prisoner from Poltava would break into the melancholy song: "The Cossacks weep in Turkish bondage."

In the spring we were hit by another misfortune. Because of

the lack of vitamins, many prisoners became ill with scurvy. At first our gums began to bleed, then our teeth began to fall out, then our muscles started to rot, especially around the joints. Fortunately during the first spring most of us got over this dread disease, while it was in its earlier stages. The following winter they soaked fir needles in barrels filled with warm water, and before entering the dining room each prisoner drank a cupful of this bitter concoction. But since some of them avoided the drink, this medicine was mixed with the *balanda*, giving it a highly unpalatable taste. We all had to eat this meal whether we liked it or not, even though a pig would have turned away from it in disgust. Who were we to be fussy about food; and hungry people have to eat!

Because of the lack of fats many of the prisoners contracted "chicken blindness," that is, after twilight they could not see anything, and so they had to be led around like blind people.

*   *   *

At the beginning of winter of the year 1940 new prisoners arrived in our camp from the "liberated lands" of Western Ukraine and Poland. They were from various walks of life and of diverse social standing. For the most part, they were peasants and small officials, who, as usual, were charged with Ukrainian or Polish nationalism, and were thus considered "enemies of the people." This mark was employed universally. It could easily be stamped on anyone, however innocent. This was one method the USSR employed to recruit the slaves for the Siberian camps. But not all of them were able to live through the "preliminary stages" in prison as we had.

The great majority of these prisoners were sent directly to Siberia; and on the way other cars, loaded with their fellow-countrymen, who had already undergone the chair-leg examination in the Kiev prison, were attached to their train.

Mr. J. B., one of the Polish prisoners, told us the history of his arrest. Not long after the installation of the Soviet civil government, or to be more exact, the NKVD, a general meeting was called in his county town. It was announced there that the Stalin constitution guaranteed to every citizen of the USSR and the liberated countries the right of personal freedom, and the other democratic liberties. Those who did not wish to remain in the "liberated countries" under those conditions were to have the right of unhindered departure beyond the borders. The next day at nine o'clock a train would be waiting at the station for those who wished to depart for Germany. An unlimited quantity of clothing and personal items could be taken along, but furniture would have to be forwarded later on by their relatives or friends. All packages must have the names of the owners written on them in large letters, so that they could be easily distinguished. All documents and papers that might be useful in the evacuees' new homes must be taken along. The train would depart at two o'clock in the afternoon. For lack of available passenger cars, the deportees would have to ride in cattle cars, but the journey would not be long.

When someone present suggested that the train be delayed two or three days to enable those going away to prepare themselves better for the journey, the speaker informed him that this would not be possible, since there was an urgent need for cars to ship various goods from the USSR to Poland, and that there would be no more trains for the emigrants to Germany. Even this train would not have been available, except that the Soviet Government wished to give them the opportunity to emigrate, since it did not intend to hold anybody in the country if he preferred to leave.

The next day at nine o'clock there really was a train at the station. All the cars were marked with chalk, designating the travel route to Germany. There were a few cars at the front which were intended for carrying heavy, bulky articles.

People began to arrive on foot and by vehicle. Some, more cautious than the others, and more suspicious of the proposition, now began to feel a little more optimistic when they failed to notice any guards around, and saw the people quietly unloading their bags into the cars, receiving receipts for them, and sitting down on benches and chairs in the cars reserved for passengers.

On the railway platform there were only two officials dressed in civilian clothes in attendance. They answered all questions put to them by the prospective emigrants politely and pleasantly. Noticing this idyllic scene, the suspicious ones hurriedly ran for their valises.

And many of the emigrants already seated in the cars began to wonder whether they were doing the right thing to depart beyond the boundaries.

Three more cars had to be added to the train because of lack of space. An hour late, it now started out on the journey. White handkerchiefs were waving from the station platform in farewell, and the voices of friends and relatives could be heard shouting good-byes. The train was to be accompanied by two civilians as far as the boundary line.

The train passed two stations without stopping, and then suddenly halted at a crossing in the middle of a field. As if from nowhere there arose an armed NKVD squad, which completely surrounded the train. A guard stood at the door of every car, shouting: "Examination of documents!"

The two civilians now showed their true colours. Along with two groups of armed guards they approached the end cars, commanding everybody to come out and show their documents! All the passengers were searched and their papers and valuable belongings taken away from them. Anyone trying to protest was struck on the shoulders with a rifle and brutally cursed. Every piece of baggage was taken out of the cars by the guards.

Following this "examination of documents," the people were forced back into the cars, and warned at gun-point to maintain complete silence. The doors were closed and sealed with wire, which the guards had brought along for just such an emergency. The windows also were nailed tight. All the valises in which the passengers kept their most valuable belongings were packed into the front cars.

All this activity lasted but an hour, at least presumably so, since the passengers no longer had watches. The train then moved ahead, and after a short stop at the first railhead station, it turned aside to go back to the "most democratic country on earth," under close observation of the guards.

Later on these victims found themselves in the Lukianiwska prison at Kiev. At the Lukianiwska station the men were packed into Black Crows and thus perhaps forever separated from their wives and children.

In the prison they went through the appropriate "preliminaries," and now some of them found themselves at Palkino. The men from the train were charged with espionage in favour of Germany on the flimsy evidence that they wanted to emigrate to that country. All of them were forced to sign false testimony for which they received a ten-year sentence. Some of them disappeared without trace, which meant that they had been shot in the neck at the Rosa Luxembourg Street garage, or some other torture chamber.

Nobody knew what happened to their wives and children. When they tried to find out they were either ignored, or else received the following insulting answer:

"Your wife is working in a bawdy house."

The children were taken to an institution, where they would be trained according to proper communistic precept. The mothers were deported to the Kazakstan steppes, where hundreds of thousands of female workers from the great prison of nations eked out a wretched existence at hard labour.

These new prisoners, who had been used to a normal life, exhibited a deplorable lack of initiative under the slave labour conditions. We did our best in extending a helping hand to these novices, in work and in advice, for we considered them brothers in misery, and we finally broke down the stony and cold hauteur with which we were regarded by some of the Polish officers.

The Ukrainian peasants from the West Ukraine, who comprised about a half of our new contingent, adapted themselves readily to the life of the camp; but, being people with a deeply ingrained sense of right and wrong, they found it extremely difficult to swallow Bolshevik hypocrisy, treachery and cruelty. They could not understand how a government could lie so flagrantly, twisting falsehood into seeming truth whenever it suited its purpose.

*   *   *

If this constitution were an honest document, then why were millions of the best farmers in the USSR branded with the odious name of *kulaks*, deprived of their property, the fruits of long years of unrelenting toil, and evicted from their homes with their families in the middle of winter and sent to almost certain death in Siberia?

Somewhat later, in 1943, when I was leaving the Dnieper region of the Ukraine for Volhynia and West Ukraine, I personally witnessed the havoc which the Stalin constitution had wreaked in those regions. To us, who were veterans of the Communist brutal regime, this was not altogether surprising. We had undergone even worse experiences during the long years we lived under it. One had to admire the indomitable will to live of the Ukrainian people against whom Moscow has continually been directing the full brunt of its terrorism. At this same Tarnopol I later made the acquaintance of Dr. Olynyk, whose heavily scarred neck and temple bore plain evidence of bullet wounds. I asked him how he received those marks.

He told me that they were Bolshevik mementoes, delivered while the Communists were retreating from Tarnopol in 1941.

The Communists rounded up about two hundred people and drove them ahead until they came to a ravine. Here they shot them down with machine-guns and automatics.

Dr. Olynyk fell on a pile of bodies, and lapsed into unconsciousness. When he revived he was lying on a litter of hay in a stable which served as a Ukrainian Underground hospital. A strange man was binding his head with a bandage, and a woman was aiding him. It was several months before Dr. Olynyk was able to rise.

He learned later that some Ukrainian insurgents had stumbled upon the dead bodies in the ravine, and that his groans had attracted their attention. He was the only one left alive.

At first they kept him hidden in the stable, since some of the Bolsheviks had stayed behind; and then he was taken to a hospital. The doctor informed him that he had had a miraculous escape, since the bullet had entered only a fraction of an inch from the vital spot in the temple. This was how he got his souvenirs from the "comrades."

Such slaughter was not restricted to Tarnopol. All over the Ukraine, the Bolsheviks liquidated thousands of innocent people on the flimsiest of suspicions. When the Soviet armies retreated from Lviv, before the German advance, the inhabitants found the bodies of more than nine thousand prisoners. Some had been tortured beyond recognition. Thousands more from the Kiev prisons had been taken out and shot in the Darnitsky Forest and the Misholovka Ravines.

Right in the heart of the city of Kharkov thousands were burned alive in the NKVD prison, and the same kind of evidence was found at Krenenchuk. At Nikipol eight hundred bodies were thrown into huge oil tanks, with the intention of setting them on fire. It is difficult to estimate the numbers of corpses left in the NKVD cellars, along the roads, and in the ravines at that time. Those prisoners who escaped this fate, only to eke out a precarious existence along with us in the inhospitable *taiga*, were perhaps more fortunate in that they were still alive and free to dream of liberty.

So far as I know there were only two cases of suicide among them. One man threw himself under the wheels of a lumber train; another hanged himself on a bunk when his turn came for looking after the bunkhouse in the absence of the others. Before taking his own life he had washed the floor and tidied up the bunkhouse.

There were many cases, however, of self-inflicted frostbite. Completely fagged out by the onerous work, some of the prisoners would wet their hands and hold them out in the intense cold. But it was only in cases of severe frostbite that the doctor would let them stay away from work, and the food ration still remained on the basis of work done. Resorting to this kind of subterfuge to avoid complete exhaustion was dangerous. In the first place freezing one's hands might result in amputation or rendering them useless for further work. Secondly, if it were known that the freezing was premeditated, it would mean five days in the *kartser* in semi-nakedness, almost certain death. But the administration did not care about that, since it would serve as a warning to the other prisoners. These workers must labour for the good of Moscow and help finance espionage and subversion abroad even if they were to die in the process.

Whenever anyone died in the camp, the other prisoners remarked with bitter irony that the deceased slave had failed to justify the confidence of the Soviet Government, that he had died without finishing the term assigned to him.

None of us ever attended a funeral, even when the person

being buried was one of our own relatives. But there were no real funerals. The dead person was merely dragged out by the hands and feet, and thrown into a wooden shed. After dark the bodies were hauled into the woods and hurled unceremoniously into a pit. When a fellow-prisoner died at work, he was placed on a stretcher woven from the branches of trees and carried back to camp after the day's labour was ended. Any new arrival with the slightest bit of conscience must have been shocked at the sight of these shabby, cadaverous, ragged and ghost-like creatures slowly trudging back to the camp with their dead burden.

There were a couple of dozen women in our camp, with five to ten year sentences. For the most part they were the wives and daughters of "enemies of the people." Some of them worked in the kitchen, others at the saw-mill, sorting lumber. They endured the hard labour as stoically as the men. They were segregated from the men both as regards work and living quarters. Their bunkhouse was fenced off from ours with barbed wire. There was no guard near the place, but the guards had access to it at all times. Any prisoner caught in the women's bunkhouse or found in the company of a woman was punished in the *kartser*.

Nevertheless, some of the women did become pregnant. Such women were excused from work only after eight months, when they were transferred to Camp Sama, where there was accommodation for such cases. There they did some light work until the time of delivery.

The child was left with the mother for only two months. Then she was sent to some camp to do her share of work as before, and the illegitimate offspring was taken to a children's home where children were trained as traitors like Paul Morozov, who, at the age of ten, sold his own father "down the NKVD river" and won for himself the name of an exemplary child in the USSR. There they were thoroughly indoctrinated as obedient and fanatic servants of the Soviet superstate.

· 4 ·

RICHARD WURMBRAND

A Christian in Bucharest:
The Voice of the Martyred

REVEREND RICHARD WURMBRAND inspired ten of thousands of
Christians opposed to communism for his courage in preaching
the word of God through his underground ministry that began
under the Nazi occupation of Romania and continued under the
Communist regime. His books, including *In God's Underground*
(1968), from which the following excerpt is drawn, gained an
international following.

Born a Jew, Wurmbrand had converted to Christianity shortly
after his marriage to Sabina Oster in 1936. He became a pastor of
the Norwegian Lutheran Church in Bucharest, where he and his
wife were arrested several times by the Nazi government. During
this time he began his underground ministry evangelizing Russian
prisoners of war, continuing after the Communists came to power.
Following his open opposition to the repression of Christianity,
expressed during the Communist-organized Congress of Cults in
1948, Wurmbrand was held prisoner and mentally and physically
tortured in the Central Interior Ministry prison in Bucharest. In
1950 his wife Sabina was imprisoned as well and sentenced to hard
labor on the Danube Canal project. Released in 1953, she was told
by authorities that her husband had died in prison. But in 1956, he
was released.

Wurmbrand was assigned to a pastorate in Orsova but
continued in his underground church to spread the Gospel, an
illegal activity under the regime. He was rearrested in 1959 and

sentenced to twenty-five years in prison. His case drew
international attention from Christian churches in the United
States and Western Europe. In December 1965 the Norwegian
Mission and the Hebrew Christian Alliance paid $10,000 for the
Wurmbrand family to leave Romania.

The minister came to the United States in December 1965
and testified before the U.S. Senate Internal Security
Subcommittee about his experiences as an underground Christian
in Romania. He also became a frequent speaker at anti-Communist
meetings. In 1967 he began publishing a newsletter, "The Voice of
the Martyrs" through which he organized offices in thirty countries
to protest the treatment of persecuted Christians throughout the
world. During his ministry, Wurmbrand wrote eighteen books in
English.

Wurmbrand's experiences in Romanian prisons motivated
anti-Communists in the United States to pursue their campaign.
His experiences provided a clear lesson to anti-Communists in the
West: if torture had failed to break his Christian faith, surely anti-
Communists should not bow to popular opinion that seemed less
concerned with the communist threat. The struggle against
Communism was a struggle between the forces of atheism and
belief.

In 1968, when Wurmbrand's *In God's Underground* appeared,
the United States had become mired in what appeared to be an
intractable war in Southeast Asia. For many Americans who
opposed it, this involvement in a destructive and meaningless war
in Vietnam showed how anti-Communist ideology had subverted
American ideals of self-determination and justice. Anti-Communist
ideology appeared to many Americans as an expression of
extremism and an antiquated view which failed to understand that
the United States and Communist nations could live together in
peaceful coexistence.

Although public opinion shifted against the anti-Communist
movement, activists continued their struggle in various ways. Anti-
communism continued to motivate those who opposed détente
with the Soviet Union, student anti-war protests, and the expansion
of the welfare state under Lyndon Johnson. While evangelical

Christians remained generally dormant politically, the anti-Communist message carried by Wurmbrand and others laid the foundations for the mobilization of evangelical voters in the late 1970s. That surge was sparked by other issues, such as abortion and the Equal Rights Amendment, but anti-Communist education within the churches during the 1960s and early 1970s had prepared the ground for this political involvement that would be captured by that longtime foe of communism, Ronald Reagan, in the election of 1980. When President Reagan denounced the Soviet Union as "the evil empire," his listeners knew all too well what he meant by these words. Wurmbrand had brought the same message to them a decade and a half earlier. They too had endured in their struggle against communism, and now Reagan had arrived to carry their banner in the battle for Christendom.

✠ I am a Lutheran minister who has spent more than 14 years in different prisons because of my Christian belief, but that in itself is not the reason for the existence of this book. I have always disliked the idea that a man who has been unjustly imprisoned must write or preach about his sufferings. Campanella, the great author of *City of the Sun*, was kept in prison for 27 years; but that he was tortured and lay 40 hours on a bed of iron nails we know from his medieval biographers, not from him.

The prison years did not seem too long for me, for I discovered, alone in my cell, that beyond belief and love there is a delight in God: a deep and extraordinary ecstasy of happiness that is like nothing in this world. And when I came out of jail I was like someone who comes down from a mountain top where he has seen for miles around the peace and beauty of the countryside, and now returns to the plain.

First, I should explain why, more than two years ago, I came to the West. When I was released from jail in 1964 with several thou-

From *In God's Underground* (Greenwich, Conn., 1968), pp. 5–8, 9, 26–30, 37–39, 44–45, 85–88, 155, 160–162, 253–254.

sand other political and religious prisoners, it was because the Romanian Popular Republic had adopted a more "friendly" policy to the West. I was given the smallest parish in the country. My congregation numbered 35. If 36 people entered the church, I was told, there would be trouble. But I had much to say, and there were many who wished to hear. I traveled secretly to preach in towns and villages, leaving before the police could hear that a stranger was in their district. This, too, had to stop. Pastors who helped me were dismissed by the State, and I could become the cause of new arrests and confessions obtained by torture. I was a burden to those I wished to serve, and a danger.

Friends urged me to try to leave the country so that I might speak for the underground church in the West. It was plain, from the statements of Western Church leaders, that some did not know and others did not want to know the truth about religious persecution under the Communists. Prelates from Europe and America came on friendly visits and sat down to banquets with our inquisitors and persecutors. We asked them why. "As Christians," they said, "we have to be friendly with everybody, you know, even the Communists." Why, then, were they not friendly to those who had suffered? Why did they not ask one word about the priests and pastors who had died in prison or under torture? Or leave a little money for the families that remained?

The Archbishop of Canterbury came in 1965 and attended a service. Dr. Ramsey did not know that the congregation consisted of officials and secret police agents and their wives—the same audience that turns out on every such occasion. It had listened to visiting rabbis and muftis, bishops and Baptists. After they had returned home, we read of their approving comments on freedom in Romania. A British theologian wrote a book in which he declared that Christ would have admired the Communist prison system.

Meanwhile, I lost my license to preach. I was blacklisted and constantly followed and watched. I still sometimes preached at the homes of friends who did not count the danger, so I was not surprised when, some time after secret negotiations had begun for my departure to the West, a stranger asked me to his house. He gave the address, but no name. When I called he was alone.

"I want to do you a service," he said. I recognized that he was a secret police agent. "A friend of mine says that the dollars have been received for you. Probably you'd like to leave the country at once. My friend is worried. You are a man who speaks his mind, and you are fresh from prison. They think it might be better if you were kept a while—or that a member of your family stays here to vouch for your good behavior. Of course, your release will be unconditional . . ."

I gave him no assurances. They had the dollars and that must be enough. Christian organizations in the West had paid £2,500 in ransom money for me. Selling citizens brings in foreign currency and helps the Popular Republic's budget. A Romanian joke says, "We'd sell the Prime Minister if anyone would buy him." Jews are sold to Israel at £1,000 a head, members of the German minority to West Germany, Armenians to America. Scientists, doctors and professors cost about £5,000 apiece.

Next I was summoned openly to police headquarters. An officer told me: "Your passport is ready. You can go when you like, and where you like, and preach as much as you wish. But don't speak against us. Keep to the Gospel. Otherwise you will be silenced, for good. We can hire a gangster who'll do it for $1000—or we can bring you back, as we've done with other traitors. We can destroy your reputation in the West by contriving a scandal over money or sex." He said I could go. That was my unconditional release.

I came to the West. Doctors examined me, and one said: "You're as full of holes as a sieve." He could not believe that my bones had mended and my tuberculosis healed without medical aid. "Don't ask me about treatment," he said. "Ask the One who kept you alive, and in Whom I don't believe."

My new pastorate for the underground church began. I met friends of our Scandinavian Mission in Norway, and when I preached there, a woman in the front row began to weep. Later she told me that years ago she had read of my arrest and had prayed for me ever since. "Today I came to church not knowing who would preach," she said—"As I listened I realized who was speaking, and I wept." I learned that thousands of people had been praying for me, as they still pray daily for those in Communist prisons. Children whom I had never met wrote, saying: "Please come to our town—Our prayers for you have been answered."

In churches and universities all over Europe and America I found that people—although they were deeply moved, often, by what I said—did not believe that a danger really threatened them. "Communism here would be different," they said. "Our Communists are few, and harmless." We thought the same in Romania, once, when the Party was small. The world is full of small Communist parties, waiting. When a tiger is young you may play with it: when it grows up, it will devour you.

I met Western Church leaders who advised me to preach the Gospel and avoid attacks on Communism; this advice I had also from the secret police in Bucharest. But wrong must be called by name. Jesus told the Pharisees that they were "vipers," and for this, and not the Sermon on the Mount, he suffered crucifixion.

I denounce Communism because I love the Communists. We can hate the sin, while loving the sinner. Christians have a duty to win the souls of Communists, and if we fail to do so, they will overwhelm the West and uproot Christianity among us here as well. The Red rulers are unhappy and wretched men. They can be saved, and God's way is to send a man. He did not come himself to guide the Jews from Egypt, he sent Moses. So we must win over to God Communist leaders in every field—artistic, scientific and political. By winning those who mold the minds of men behind the Iron Curtain, you win the people they lead and influence.

The conversion of Svetlana Stalin, only daughter of the greatest mass-murderer of Christians, a soul brought up in the strictest Communist discipline, proves that there is a better weapon against Communism than the nuclear bomb: it is the love of Christ.

The first half of my life ended on February 29, 1948. I was walking alone down a street in Bucharest when a black Ford car braked sharply beside me and two men jumped out. They seized my arms and thrust me into the back seat, while a third man beside the driver kept me covered with a pistol. The car sped through the thin traffic of a Sunday evening; then, in a street called Calea Rahova, we turned in through steel gates. I heard them clang behind us.

My kidnappers belonged to the Communist Secret Police.

This was their headquarters. Inside, my papers, my belongings, my tie and shoelaces, and finally my name were taken from me. "From now on," said the official on duty, "you are Vasile Georgescu."

It was a common name. The authorities did not want even the guards to know whom they were watching, in case questions should be asked abroad, where I was well known. I was to disappear, like so many others, without a trace.

Calea Rahova was a new jail and I was the first prisoner. But prison was not a new experience for me. I had been arrested during the war by the Fascists who ruled in Hitler's day, and again when the Communists took over. There was a small window high in the concrete wall of the cell, two plank beds, the usual bucket in the corner. I sat waiting for the interrogators, knowing what questions they would ask and what answers I must give.

I know what fear is well enough, but at that moment I felt none. This arrest, and all that would follow, was the answer to a prayer I had made, and I hoped that it would give new meaning to my past life. I did not know what strange and wonderful discoveries lay in store for me.

My arrest, in the widespread round-ups which were going on in this time, could have been considered an answer to my prayer, but never could I have supposed that the first man to join me in my cell would be Comrade Patrascanu himself.

When the door of my room in Calea Rahova opened, a few days after my arrival, to admit the tall Minister of Justice I supposed at first that he had come to question me in person. Why was I so honored? Then the door was locked behind him: stranger still, his shirt was open at the neck and he wore no tie. I looked down at his highly polished shoes—no laces! The second prisoner in my brand-new cell was the man who had brought Communism to power in our country.

He sat down on the other plank bed and swung his feet up; a tough-minded intellectual, he was not going to allow the transformation from Minister to jailbird to affect his poise. Wrapped in our greatcoats against the March chill, we began to talk. Although I knew Patrascanu's doctrines had shattered justice and caused so much destruction, it was possible to like him as a man and believe in his sincerity. He passed off his arrest with a shrug. It was far from being his first spell in prison. He had been arrested several times by the former rulers of Romania. It seemed that his growing popularity had banded the other Party leaders against him. At a congress a few days earlier he had been denounced as a bourgeois traitor in the class war by his colleague Teohari Georgescu, Minister of the Interior. A second charge, that Patrascanu had been "potentially helped by the imperialist Powers," was backed by Vasile Luca, the Minister of Finance, who had been in prison with him under the old regime. The accusations were driven home by Ana Pauker, another of his old friends.

They had been plotting against him for some time, Patrascanu said, but one incident in particular had told against him as a Communist. He had asked one of Georgescu's officials if there was any truth in the rumors that prisoners were being tortured. Why certainly, said the man from the Ministry; they were counter-revolutionaries who deserved no pity, especially if they held back information. Patrascanu was deeply disturbed. Was it for this, he demanded, that they had struggled all these years to bring the Party to power? His protest was reported to Georgescu, and the denunciation at the Congress followed.

"As I left the hall," he said, "I saw a new driver waiting at the car. He said, 'Your chauffeur Ionescu has been taken ill, Comrade Patrascanu.' I stepped in, two secret policemen got in after me— and here I am."

He was sure that he would soon be reinstated, and when supper came I began to think he might. Instead of boiled barley, he was given chicken, cheese, fruit and a bottle of hock. Patrascanu took a glass of wine and pushed the tray over, saying he had no appetite.

While I tried not to eat too ravenously, he told amusing stories. One was about the Swiss senator who wanted to be Navy Minister. "But we have no navy!" said the Prime Minister. "What does that matter?" the senator asked. "If Romania can have a Minister of Justice, why shouldn't Switzerland have a Minister of the Navy?" Patrascanu laughed heartily at this anecdote, although it ridiculed the "justice" he had created, and of which he himself was now victim. Next morning Patrascanu was escorted from the cell, I supposed for interrogation. He returned bad-temperedly in the evening to say he had not been answering questions but giving a lecture at the university, where he taught law. The Party wanted his arrest kept secret for the time being, and he, with thirty years of Communist discipline behind him, had to fall in with their wishes. He talked to me because he could talk, even outside prison, with nobody else. To reveal, even to his wife, that he was "under examination," or to ask anyone's advice, would be a capital offense. This isolation preyed on his nerves, as it was intended to. He could be himself only with me, because he had no reason to believe that I would ever see the outer world again.

As Patrascanu told me something about his early life, I was interested to see that he had become a Communist not through any objective judgment, but in revolt against early troubles. His father, a well-to-do man, supported the Germans so enthusiastically in World War I that, after the victory of the Allies, the whole family was ostracized. Young Patrascanu had to go to Germany for a university education, and on his return joined the only political party which offered him a welcome. His first wife, a Communist, died in the Stalinist purges, and when he remarried it was to another Party member, who happened to be a school friend of my wife.

I tried to show Patrascanu the source of his convictions. "You are like Marx and Lenin," I said, "whose ideas and actions were also the outcome of early suffering. Marx felt genius within him, but as a Jew in Germany when anti-Semitism was rampant, he could find no outlet for it except as a revolutionary. Lenin's brother was hanged for an attempt on the emperor's life—rage and frustration made him want to overturn the world. It has been much the same with you."

Patrascanu dismissed the idea. His nerves found an outlet in tirades against the wickedness of the Church. The evil days of the Borgia Popes, the Spanish Inquisition, the savagery of the Crusades, Galileo's persecution, were all surveyed.

"But it's the crimes and errors of the Church which give us so much more to admire in it," I said.

Patrascanu was startled. "What do you mean?"

I said, "A hospital may stink of pus and blood; in that lies its beauty, for it receives the sick with their disgusting sores and horrible diseases. The Church is Christ's own hospital. Millions of patients are treated in it, with love. The Church accepts sinners — they continue to sin, and for their transgressions the Church is blamed. To me, on the other hand, the Church is like a mother who stands by her children even when they commit crimes. The politics and prejudices of its servants are distortions of what comes from God — that is, the Bible and its teachings, worship and the sacraments. Whatever its faults, the Church has much that is sublime in it. The sea drowns thousands of people every year, but no one contests its beauty."

Patrascanu smiled. "I could make much the same claim for Communism. Its practitioners are not perfect — there are scoundrels among them — but that doesn't mean there's anything wrong with our theories."

"Then judge by results," I said, "as Jesus advised. Sad deeds have stained the history of the Church, but it has lavished love and care on people all over the world. It has produced a multitude of saints, and it has Christ, the holiest of all, at its head. Who are your idols? Men like Marx who was described as a drunkard by his biographer Riazanov, director of the Marx Institute in Moscow. Or Lenin, whose wife tells us he was a reckless gambler, and whose writings drip with venom. 'By their fruits ye shall know them.' Communism has wiped out millions of innocent victims, bankrupted countries, filled the air with lies and fear. Where is its good side?"

Patrascanu defended "the logic of Party doctrine."

I said doctrines as such meant nothing. "You can do atrocious acts under polite names. Hitler talked about a struggle for *Lebensraum* (vital space) and murdered whole populations. Stalin said 'We must care for men like flowers,' and he killed his wife and yours."

Patrascanu looked uncomfortable; but he was frank. "Our long-range purpose is to communize the world. There are few who want to go all the way with us, but we always find some who are willing for their own reasons to go with us for a time. First we had the Romanian ruling classes and the king, who backed the Allies against the Nazis. When they had served our purpose, we destroyed them. We won over the Orthodox Church with promises, then used the smaller sects to undermine it. We used the farmers against the landlords and later the poor peasants against the rich farmers—and now all of them will be collectivized together. These are Lenin's tactical ideas, and they work!"

I said, "Everyone knows that all your fellow-travelers have been jailed, executed or somehow destroyed in the past. How can you hope to go on using people and throwing them away?"

Patrascanu laughed. "Because they are stupid. Here's an example. Ten years after World War I, the great Bolshevist thinker Bukharin opposed Trotsky's plans for making world revolution by force of arms. He argued that it was better to wait until the capitalist countries came to blows among themselves; Russia could then join the winning side and take the lion's share of conquered countries. A remarkable prophecy—but no one took it seriously. If the West had known that half of Europe and two-thirds of Asia would become Communist as a result, the last war would never have taken place. Fortunately our enemies don't listen to our argument or read our books, so we can speak openly."

I pointed out a flaw in his argument. "Don't you see, Mr. Patrascanu, that as you used people and then cast them aside, so your comrades have used you and thrown you away? Haven't you blinded yourself to the evil logic of Lenin's doctrine?"

For once Patrascanu's bitterness was unconcealed. He said: "When Danton was driven to the guillotine and saw Robespierre watching from a balcony, he called out, 'You will follow me!' And I assure you now that they will follow me—Ana Pauker, Georgescu and Luca, too."

So they did, within three years.

The Secret Police had been patient, I was told, but now it was time for some results. Colonel Dulgheru, their grand inquisitor, never failed to get them. He sat at his desk, still and menacing, with delicate hands outspread before him. "You've been playing with us," he said.

Dulgheru had worked before the war at the Soviet Embassy. Then, under the Fascists, he was interned and thus fraternized with

Gheorghiu-Dej and other imprisoned Communists. They noted his tough qualities, intelligence and ruthlessness. So here he was, with delegated powers of life and death.

At once, Dulgheru began to question me about a Red Army man who had been caught smuggling Bibles into Russia. Until now the interrogators seemed to know nothing about my work among the Russians, but although the arrested soldier had not given me away, it was discovered that we had met. Now, more than ever, I had to weigh every word, for in fact I had baptized the man in Bucharest and so enlisted him in our campaign.

Dulgheru's questions were persistent. He thought he had scented something important. In the weeks that followed, I was worn down by a variety of means. The beds were removed from the cell and I had barely an hour's sleep a night, balanced on a chair. Twice every minute the spy-hole in the door gave a metallic click, and the eye of a guard appeared. Often when I dozed he came in and kicked me awake. In the end I lost all sense of time. Once I awoke to see the cell door ajar. Soft music sounded in the corridor: or was it an illusion? Then the sound became distorted and a woman's voice was sobbing. She began to scream. It was my wife!

"No, no! Please don't beat me. Not again! I can't bear it!"

There was the sound of a whip hitting flesh. The screams rose to an appalling pitch. Every muscle in my body was strained in a rictus of horror. Slowly the voice began to die away, moaning; but now it was the voice of a stranger. It faded into silence. I was left drained of feeling, trembling and drenched with sweat. Later I learnt that it was a tape-recording, but every prisoner who heard it thought that the victim was his wife or sweetheart.

Dulgheru was a refined barbarian, patterned on the Soviet diplomats with whom he had mixed. "I order torture with regret," he told me. Being all-powerful in the prisons, he could dispense with notes and witnesses, and often came alone to my cell at night to continue interrogation. One critical session dragged on for hours. He asked about my contact with the Church of England Mission. What had I done there? I said that I'd visited Westminster Abbey. He became more and more incensed.

"Do you know," he said with venom, "that I can order your execution now, tonight, as a counter-revolutionary?"

I said, "Colonel, here you have the opportunity for an experiment. You say you can have me shot. I know you can. So put your hand here on my heart. If it beats rapidly, showing that I am afraid, then know there is no God and no eternal life. But if it beats calmly, as if to say, 'I go to the One I love,' then you must think again. There *is* a God, and an eternal life!"

Dulgheru struck me across the face, and immediately regretted his loss of self-control.

"You fool, Georgescu!" he said. "Can't you see that you're completely at my mercy and that your Savior, or whatever you call him, isn't going to open any prison doors? You'll never see Westminster Abbey."

I said, "His name is Jesus Christ, and if He wishes He can release me, and I shall see Westminster Abbey, too."

Dulgheru glared at me as if struggling for breath. Then he shouted, "All right. Tomorrow you'll meet Comrade Brinzaru."

I had been expecting this. Major Brinzaru, the colonel's aide, presided over a room where clubs, truncheons and whips were kept. He had hairy arms like a gorilla. Other interrogators used his name as a threat. The contemporary Russian poet Voznesensky writes, "In these days of untold suffering, one is lucky indeed to have no heart," and Brinzaru was lucky in this way. He introduced me to his range of weapons. "Is there any you fancy?" he asked. "We like to be democratic here."

He displayed his own favorite, a long, black rubber truncheon. "Read the label." It was inscribed, "MADE IN U.S.A."

"We do the beating," said Brinzaru with a show of yellow teeth, "but your American friends give us the tools." Then he sent me back to my cell to think about it.

The guard told me that Brinzaru had worked before the war for a prominent politician and been treated as one of the family. After the Communist take-over which hoisted him up the ranks of the Secret Police, a young prisoner was brought to him for questioning. It was the politician's son, who had tried to start a patriotic movement. Brinzaru told him, "I used to hold you on my knee when you were a baby!" Then he tortured the lad and executed him with his own hands.

Curiously, Brinzaru did not give me the threatened beating: On his nightly round of inspection, he flicked the spyhole cover back to watch me for a moment. "Still there, Georgescu? What's Jesus doing tonight?"

I said, "He's praying for you." He walked away without replying.

Next day he was back again. Under his supervision, I was made to stand facing a wall with my hands raised above my head so that my finger tips just touched it. "Just keep him there," Brinzaru told the guard before leaving.

At last, the torture began. I do not want to make much of it, but it must be told because these things were common to all Secret Police prisons. First I stood for hours, long after my arms had lost all feeling, and my legs began to tremble and then swell. When I collapsed on the floor, I was given a crust and a sip of water and made to stand again. One guard relieved another. Some of them would force you to adopt ridiculous or obscene postures, and this went on, with short breaks, for days and nights. There was the wall to look at.

I thought of the walls referred to in the Bible, recalling a verse from Isaiah which saddened me: God says that Israel's wrongdoings put a wall between Him and the people. The failures of Christianity had allowed a Communist triumph, and that was why I had a wall before me now. Then I remembered a phrase, "With my Lord, I jump over the wall." I, too, might jump this wall into the spiritual world of fellowship with God. I thought of the Jewish spies who returned from Canaan to report that the cities were great and walled—but as the walls of Jericho came down, so the wall before me must also fall at the will of God. When pain was overwhelming me, I said to myself a phrase from the Song of Songs: "My beloved is like a roe or a young hart; behold, he standeth behind our wall." I imagined that Jesus stood behind my wall, giving me strength. I remembered that, as long as Moses held up his hands on the mountain, the chosen people went forward to victory; perhaps our sufferings were helping the people of God to win their battle, too.

From time to time, Major Brinzaru looked in to ask whether I was willing to co-operate. Once, when I was on the floor, he said, "Get up! We've decided to let you see Westminster Abbey, after all. You start now."

"Walk!" ordered the guard. I tried to pull my shoes on, but my feet were too swollen. "Come on! Hurry! Keep going round! I'll be watching from outside."

The cell was twelve paces round: four steps, one wall; two steps, the next; then four; then two. I shuffled around it in torn socks. The spy-hole clicked. "Faster!" shouted the guard. My head began to spin. "Faster—or do you want a beating?" I bumped painfully into a wall. My eyes stung with sweat. Round and round, round and round. Click! "Halt, turn about! Walk!" Round, round in the opposite direction. "Faster!" I stumbled, and picked myself up. "Keep moving!" When I fell the guard charged in and cracked me across the elbow with a club as I struggled up. The pain was so agonizing that I fell again. "Get up! Get moving! This is the *ma-nege!*"

Nearly everyone had to go through the *manege*, or training ring as it was known. Hours went by before you got a cup of water or anything to eat. The thirst drove out hunger. It was even fiercer than the stabbing of hot knives that ran up your legs. Worst of all was having to start walking again after being allowed a few minutes rest, or a few hours at night in a stupor on the floor. Stiff joints, cracked muscles, lacerated feet would not support the body's weight. You clung to the walls, while guards screamed orders. When you could no longer stand, you went on all fours.

I do not know how many days and nights I spent in the *ma-nege*. I began to pray for the guards as I moved. I thought of the Song of Songs, in which we are told of the holy dance of the Bride of Christ in honor of her bridegroom. I said to myself, "I will move with as much grace as if this were a dance of divine love, for Jesus." For a while it seemed to me that I did. If a man wills to do every-thing that he has to do, then he does only the things which he wills—and the hardest trials, being voluntary, become easier. And as I went round and about, it seemed as if everything was revolving around me. I could no longer distinguish one wall from another, or a wall from the door, just as in divine love one does not distinguish between good and evil men and can embrace everyone.

*   *   *

I had been seven months in Calea Rahova prison. It was October and the winter was already on us. We suffered much from cold now, as well as hunger and ill-treatment, and months of winter lay ahead. Gazing from my window at the sleet falling on the prison yard, I shivered, yet my spirits were not low. Whatever I could do for God by patient love in jail would be small, I thought, but the good in life always looks small in comparison with the amount of bad. While evil in the New Testament is depicted as a huge beast with seven horns, the Holy Spirit descended as a little dove. It is the dove which will defeat the beast!

One evening, a plate of savory goulash appeared, with four whole slices of bread. Before I could eat it, the guard returned and made me gather up my things and follow him to a place where other prisoners were lined up. Thinking of my lost goulash I went by truck to the Ministry of the Interior. This splendid building is much admired by tourists, who do not know that it is built over an extensive prison with a labyrinth of corridors and hundreds of help-less inmates.

My cell was deep underground. A light bulb shone from the ceiling on bare walls, an iron bedstead with three planks and a straw pallet. Air entered through a pipe high in the wall. I saw there was no bucket and I would have to wait always for the guard to take me to the latrine. This was the worst imposition for every prisoner. Sometimes they made you wait for hours, laughing at your plead-ings. Men, and women, too, went without food and drink for fear of increasing their agony. I myself have eaten from the dish in which I fulfilled my needs without washing it, because I had no water.

The silence here was practically complete—deliberately so. Our guards wore felt-soled shoes and you could hear their hands on the door before key found lock. Now and again there was the far-off sound of a prisoner hammering steadily on his door or screaming. The cell allowed only three paces in each direction, so I lay down and stared at the bulb. It burnt all night. Since I could not sleep, I prayed. The outside world had ceased to exist. All the noises I was used to, the wind and rain in the yard, steel boot studs on stone floors, the buzz of a fly, a human voice, were gone. My heart seemed to shrink, as if it, too, would stop in this lifeless silence.

*   *   *

For some time there had been frightened talk of a system of "re-educating" prisoners, which was practiced at Suceava and Piteshi jails. It was carried out not with books, but by beating. The tutors were usually turncoat Iron Guards, who had been formed into an "organization of prisoners with Communist convictions" (PCC).* We heard the names of Turcanu, Levitkii and Formagiu as the organizers of these groups. They seemed to be behaving like savages.

We feared that the process would be introduced among us; but Boris** scoffed. He could not believe that his former associates of the Left would allow atrocities.

He said, "They know that 'terror can never uproot ideas.' That's what Karl Kautsky, the Social Democrat thinker, wrote at the start of the Russian revolution."

I said, "Yes. I remember what Trotsky, who was War Minister, replied: 'Mr. Kautsky, you do not know what terror we will apply.' It's ironic that Trotsky's own ideas have been as effectively uprooted by terrorism in Russia as has Capitalism."

The Abbot [a jailed Roman Catholic priest] said, "I fear that terror and torture, applied ruthlessly and long, may crush any man's resistance, without a miracle of God."

"I don't believe in miracles," said Boris. "I'll get along without them. Nothing has touched my convictions yet."

The prison's atmosphere grew worse after a brief visit by the

---

*Iron Guards were a nationalist, anti-communist, and pro-fascist organization that emerged in the 1930s in Romania.

**Boris Matei, a worker and communist, was jailed for writing an anonymous letter to a party boss complaining about work conditions in his factory. The secret police tracked down his name by examining 10,000 handwriting samples of workers in the plant.

"re-education" leader Formagiu, from Piteshi, with instructions to inaugurate the system. Up to now, although you were tormented for most of the day, you knew that sooner or later the guards would go to eat or sleep. Now the "prisoners with Communist convictions" moved in with us.

They had the power to beat and bully at will, and had rubber truncheons for their work. They had been handpicked by the authorities from the worst and most violent prisoners, and there was no escape from them: to every fifty prisoners there was a group of ten or twenty "PCC" men, and the number grew steadily. Those who declared themselves ready to become Communists had to prove their conversion by "converting" others in the same way.

Crude violence was punctuated by sessions of more refined cruelty, under medical supervision to ensure that prisoners did not die. Doctors were often PCCs themselves. I knew a Dr. Turcu who, after examining a cellmate, would advise a pause, give the man an injection to increase his resistance and tell the re-educators when to start again. It was Turcu who decided when the man had reached his limit and might be thrown back into his cell until next day.

A wave of madness swept the prison. Tuberculosis patients were stripped, laid on the stone floors and drenched with buckets of freezing water. Pig swill was thrown on the ground before men who had been starved for days; with hands tied behind their backs they were forced to lick it up. No humiliation, however vile, was spared. In many prisons men were made by the PCC bullies to swallow excrement and drink urine. Some wept and begged at least to be given their own, not that of others. Some went crazy and began to scream for more. Convicts were also made to perform sexual perversions publicly. I had not thought that such mockeries of body and soul were possible.

Those who clung to their faith were the worst treated. Christians were tied for four days to crosses, and daily the crosses were placed on the floor. Then the other prisoners were ordered to defecate on their faces and bodies. After this, the crosses were put up again.

A Catholic priest brought into Room Four told us that in Piteshi jail, on a Sunday, he had been pushed into the latrine cesspit and ordered to say Mass over excrement and give men Communion.

"Did you obey?" I asked.

He buried his face in his hands and wept. "I've suffered more than Christ," he said.

These things were done with the encouragement of the prison administration, on orders from Bucharest. Turcanu, Formagiu and the other specialists were taken from jail to jail, recruiting PCCs and seeing that the campaign did not flag. Party leaders, even men from the Central Committee, like Constantin Doncea and the Undersecretary of the Interior Ministry, Marin Jianu, came to watch the sport. Boris, who had worked with Jianu, broke through the guards to protest, but if Jianu recognized his former colleague he did not admit it. "We don't interfere when one swine beats another!" he said; in other words, the Party dissociated itself from the torturers, but allowed them to torture. "Take him away," said Jianu. Boris was beaten until he screamed for mercy.

The old union fighter broke down completely. Exposed to humiliation and torture day and night, something had burned out in him. He crawled to kiss the hands of the men who beat him.

"Thank you, comrade," he said. "You have brought me to the light." Then he began to prate about the joys of Communism, and how criminal he had been to persist in error. After such a collapse his self-respect demanded a total shift of loyalty; otherwise he would have appeared ridiculous in his own eyes. Boris joined the PCC group. One of the first he used his truncheon on was Dr. Aldea.

The re-education system—imported from Russia—brought incredible results. Victims blurted secrets they had kept back under months of interrogation. They denounced friends, wives, parents. So thousands more arrests were made.

*   *   *

A desire to show Communism in a better light before the summit meeting diminished some of the worst excesses in the prison system. At Salcia, where punishments had included hanging prisoners by the heels and plunging women in icy water for hours, the whole staff was arrested. Official evidence said fifty-eight people had died in the competitions between "brigade leaders" to see who could work to death the most prisoners—in fact, Salcia survivors who came to Craiova said there had been at least 800 deaths.

With a show of judicial indignation, the Salcia staff were given long sentences, and the purge had a chastening effect in other jails. Beatings stopped. Guards became carefully polite. When the Jilava commandant, Colonel Gheorghiu, asked for complaints, and had a plate of barley thrown at him, the culprit suffered nothing worse than a day in solitary confinement.

The reforms were short-lived. Soon beatings and insults became routine once more; and a year or so later, when the trials had been forgotten abroad, the mass-murderers of Salcia were reinstated, with promotion. Only the common law prisoners, who had acted as their tools in torturing others, stayed in prison.

During this shake-up in the jails, I was moved several times. These nightmare journeys have merged into one in my mind. I close my eyes and see a frieze of stubble-chinned, shaven-headed convicts, jogging gently with the movement of the train. Always we wore fifty-pound chains, which chafed us through our clothes and made sores that took months to heal in our undernourished state.

On one journey we came to a halt during the night, and the silence was broken by a wail of anguish: "I've been robbed!"

I sat up to find little Dan, a petty crook from Bucharest, moving from one prone figure to the next, shaking everyone awake. Dan was cursed and cuffed, but he went on howling, "I had five hundred lei hidden away and it's gone! It's all I had in the world!"

In the hope of quieting him, I said, "My friend, I hope you don't suspect a pastor of stealing, but if you do you may search me to the skin."

The others also allowed Dan to search them for the sake of peace, but nothing was found. The train moved off at last and, one by one, we fell asleep. I was awakened at dawn by a new and worse uproar. All the other eighteen prisoners had been robbed as well.

"I knew we had a thief among us!"

Dan cried. Days later, at Poarta-Alba, our next stop, I told the story to a man serving a year for theft. Bursting with laughter, he said, "I've known Dan for years. He simply wanted to find out where each of you kept anything worth lifting!"

*   *   *

I was moved back to Vacaresti, the prison-hospital where I had spent a month after my solitary confinement in the cells beneath the Ministry of the Interior. The place was more crowded than ever. Tubercular patients had to share rooms and exchange infections with sufferers from other diseases.

Two Secret Police officers who came to interrogate me asked quizzically what I thought of Communism now. "How am I to say?" I replied. "I know it only from the inside of its prisons."

They grinned, and one said, "Now you can learn about it from a VIP; Vasile Luca—the old Minister of Finance—is in your cell."

Luca's dismissal for currency scandals in March 1953 had helped to bring down the Ana Pauker clique. With Theohari Georgescu, Minister of the Interior, he had been expelled from the Party, and now all three were in various prisons with the victims of their five-year reign. In his days of power, Luca was much flattered, but little loved. Now guards and prisoners took the chance to show their contempt. Luca sat alone, in a corner of our cell, biting his knuckles and muttering to himself; old, ill, and unrecognizable as the man whose photograph had appeared so regularly in the newspapers.

Luca could find no relief from his sufferings. A Christian, whatever his troubles, knew that for his faith he was treading the road that Christ had trod, but Luca, who had worked all his life for Communism, had neither hope nor belief left. If the Nationalists came to power, or the Americans arrived, Luca and his comrades would be the first to hang. In the meantime, they were punished by their former Party friends. Luca was close to the breaking point when we met.

After his political disgrace, he told me, he was forced to confess under torture to absurd charges. A military court condemned him to death, but the sentence was commuted to life imprisonment.

"They knew I wouldn't last for long," he said, coughing. He was given to outbursts of rage against his Party enemies. One day, when he could not eat the food pushed into our cell, I offered him my bread. He took it hungrily.

"Why did you do that?" he growled.

"I've learned the value of fasting in prison."

"And what might that be?"

I said, "Firstly, it shows that the spirit is master of the body. Secondly, it saves me from the quarrels and hard feelings over food which are so common. Thirdly—well, if a Christian does not fast in jails, what means has he of helping others?"

Luca admitted that the only help he had been given since his arrest had come from Christians. Then his bile rose again.

"But I know far more clergymen who are first-rate scoundrels. As one of the Party's Central Committee I kept a firm hand on sects and religions. My department had a file on every priest in the country—including you. I began to wonder if there was a priest in Romania who wouldn't soon be knocking at my back door after dark. What a band of brothers!"

I said that man might degrade religion, but religion ennobled man much more. This was shown by the host of saints: not only those of old, but the many great saints who could be met today.

Luca grew angry. His spite against the world would not allow him to admit goodness in anyone. He recited familiar atheist arguments about the Church's persecution of science. I reminded him of the great scientists who have been Christians—from Newton and Kepler to Pavlov, to the discoverer of anaesthetics, Sir James Simpson.

Luca said, "They conformed to the conventions of the time."

I said. "Do you know the declaration of Louis Pasteur, who discovered microbes and vaccination? *Je crois comme une charbonniere le plus que je progresse en science.* He believed like a coalminer, like a woman coal-miner of the last century. This man who spent most of his life at the head of a body of scientific studies had faith of the simplest human creature."

Luca said indignantly, "What of all the scientists the Church has persecuted?"

I asked if he could name them.

"Galileo, of course, who went to prison. Giordano Bruno, whom they burned . . ." He stopped.

I said, "So you can only find two cases in two thousand years! That's a triumph for the Church by any human standards. Compare the Party record in the last ten years, here in Romania alone. Many thousands of innocent people shot, tortured and imprisoned; you yourself sentenced on the strength of perjured evidence obtained by threats and bribes! How many miscarriages of justice do you think there have been in all the countries under Communist rule?"

One evening I spoke of the Last Supper, and Jesus's words to Judas, "What you have to do, do quickly."

Luca said, "Nothing will make me believe in God, but if I did, the one prayer I'd make to Him would be, 'What you have to do, do quickly.'"

His condition worsened. He spat blood, and in his fever a cold sweat broke out on his forehead.

At this time I was moved to another prison. Before I left, he promised to give thought to his soul. I have no way of knowing what happened, but when a man starts to argue with himself, the chances of finding the truth are small. Conversions are usually instantaneous. The message pierces the heart, and from its depths something new and healing breaks out at once.

I met many like Luca at that time, and often discussed with friends how Communist leaders and their collaborators should be dealt with when Communism fell. Christians opposed revenge but were divided among themselves: some who thought that forgiveness should be complete, and those who said that Jesus—in telling Peter to forgive men who had wronged him "Not seven times, but seventy times seven"—had fixed a limit which the Communists had long overstepped.

My view is that, having judged each man singly, with understanding of the evil forces that made him, we have only the right, without being vindictive, to put the wrongdoer into a position where he can do no further harm. Communists already spend much time and effort in punishing each other. Stalin poisoned

Lenin, it is said. He had Trotsky murdered with an ice-pick. Khrushchev so hated his "comrade" that he destroyed his reputation and despoiled his tomb. Luca, Theohari Georgescu, Ana Pauker and so many more were victims of their own cruel system.

· 5 ·

BELA SZASZ

The Purge: The Tale of a Hungarian Communist

BELA SZASZ'S *Volunteers for the Gallows*, first published in
Brussels in 1963, became a modern classic among prison memoirs.
In its first year the book was translated into French and German,
and finally into English in 1971. Szasz took six years to write the
book after he emigrated from Hungary following the 1957 uprising
against the Soviets. He brought a certain detached quality to the
book as he described his arrest and torture by the secret police
during a purge of the Hungarian Communist party in 1949, in
response to Tito's Yugoslavian government's break with the Soviet
Union. Fearing "liberalization" in the Hungarian party, the Soviets
initiated a campaign against the Laszlo Rajk faction.

The purge against Titoists in "people's democracies" began in
late 1948 when the Cominform, established by the Soviets in 1947
to include all international Communist parties then in power,
condemned "deviationism" in Tito's regime in Yugoslavia. The
repression against Titoists took the form of show trials designed to
confirm Moscow's suspicions of espionage. The first major trial
opened in Romania in 1948. By the next year, purges of
Communist parties in countries bordering Yugoslavia spread, first
to Albania, where the party had close ties to Yugoslav Communists,
then to Hungary. The focus of the Hungarian purge was Lászlō
Rajk, a veteran of the Spanish Civil War and a resistance fighter
during the German occupation of Hungary in World War II.
When the Communist regime came to power in Hungary, Rajk
was made minister of internal affairs. In this position he headed a

brutal campaign against non-Communist democrats before he became minister of foreign affairs. With his arrest, the "chickens had come home to roost." As Karel Bartošek describes in his essay on central and southeastern Europe in *The Black Book on Communism: Crimes, Terror Repression* (1999), Rajk was tortured and blackmailed until he confessed in court to cooperation with "enemies of people's democracy." He was executed on October 16, 1949.

Following the Rajk trials, ninety-four people in Hungary were arrested and sentenced to prison terms. Of these, fifteen were executed while eleven others died in prison. The total number of dead were about sixty, including suicides among prisoners, relatives, and others involved in this affair. The trials were designed to prove the existence of a huge international anti-Soviet conspiracy.

Szasz was one of the victims of this purge. He had returned to Hungary after the war, anxious to support the new regime. He entered the ministry of foreign affairs and then was appointed head of the press department at the ministry of agriculture. Szasz brought to his press duties an international background. Born to a family of Hungarian gentry, he studied at the University of Economics before transferring to Peter Pzmny University to study French and Hungarian. While studying at the Sorbonne in Paris he became a Communist, and when he returned to Hungary he was arrested in 1932 and spent three months in prison. In 1937 he studied film in Paris and then traveled to South America where he worked for the Gaumont Studies. He was also involved in a number of popular-front anti-Nazi groups in South America.

He was arrested in May 1949, charged with being part of the Rajk conspiracy. Endlessly tortured and deprived of sleep by the Hungarian secret police and KGB officers, he nonetheless refused to confess and was sentenced to ten years' imprisonment. Only after Stalin's death in 1953 was Szasz released from prison as a rehabilitated victim of Stalinism. In October 1956 the remains of Rajk and his comrades were reburied in Budapest, where Szasz spoke at the funeral. Soon after, the Hungarian revolution broke out and was suppressed by Soviet tanks. Szasz was offered a position in the new government but instead asked for a passport, which was granted in March 1957. He died in exile in England in 1988, after publishing a number of books and translations.

Throughout the cold war, Hungary held a particular importance for anti-Communists. As a Roman Catholic country, it suffered a Communist oppression equal to that of Poland. In Hungary, József Cardinal Mindszenty suffered twenty-three years of Communist torture and imprisonment for his unflinching opposition to totalitarianism, becoming a living martyr for Catholics throughout the world. Only a year after the publication of Szasz's book in English, Cardinal Mindszenty, forced to leave Hungary, took up residence in Vienna, Austria. When Hungarian freedom fighters rose up against their Communist oppressors, only to be crushed by the Soviets as the United States stood by watching, anti-Communists perceived U.S. inaction—however unrealistic intervention might have been—as a lack of courage among American policymakers. Memoirs such as Szasz's showed, however, that the people behind the Iron Curtain did not lack for courage, and if given proper support and encouragement would overthrow the yoke of communism. This faith that one day the people of Eastern Europe would rebel against their Russian oppressors continued to sustain anti-Communists in the United States well into the 1990s, when the Soviet Union finally collapsed.

🆄🆁 "Which espionage organization have you been working for?"

"Now really . . ." I replied breaking into laughter, partly because these dignitaries enthroned behind the T-shaped table looked ludicrous enough, partly because it didn't even occur to me to take Péter's [Gàbor Péter, head of the Hungarian Secret Police] question seriously and, therefore, I drew the only possible conclusion, namely that I was the victim of some childish prank, that they were playing a game, making a fool of me. I was not concerned that Péter had

From *Volunteers For the Gallows*, (New York, 1971), pp. 8–13, 120–124, 136–146, 150–153, 156, 175–179.

dropped the familiar second person singular and addressed me as
though I were a stranger: perhaps that was part of the joke too.
When I replied, I addressed him by his first name.

"Don't make me laugh, Gàbor . . ."

"We'll see who has the last laugh," Gàbor Péter shouted jumping up from his chair, "when we come to your contemptible doings
in South America." Then he sat down again, glaring at me.

"Who is Wagner?" he asked, smiling ironically with the air of
one dealing a deathblow to his enemy.

"Wagner?" I mused, recalling first the music teacher of my
school days, then an old acquaintance, an historian, deported by
the Nazis. Neither could be the Wagner in whom superficially . . .

Péter seemed interested. Then suddenly it came to me:

"Do you mean the Hungarian consul in Bratislava?" I asked. "I
know him only superficially."

Péter waved his hand and, as if this had been a cue, the others
sitting at the head of the table broke into a chorus of synthetic
police-laughter.

"No, that isn't the Wagner I am thinking of," Péter said with a
drawl. "I am thinking of the Wagner from whom you brought
Szönyi an illegal message with a password!"

"Tibor Szönyi!" I exclaimed, surprised because, as far as I
knew, Szönyi was still head of the Communist Party's cadres department, a post carrying at least ministerial rank in the state administration, as it was the cadres department that suggested, or even
decided on its own authority, to what posts Communist Party members should be appointed in the state administration, the Party, the
army, or the so-called mass organizations. When I was transferred
from the Foreign Ministry to the Ministry of Agriculture, it had
been Tibor Szönyi and his assistant, András Szalai, who informed
me of the decision and discussed it with me. Szönyi had explained
to me, in a dull party jargon hardly in keeping with his erudition
and intellect, why, though I knew next to nothing about agrarian
problems, it was important that I should assume the direction of the
press department of the Ministry of Agriculture instead of remaining at the Foreign Ministry. Had someone really brought this cold,
rigid party functionary an "illegal" message? Even supposing this

someone was I, why should we have used a password as we did in the underground Communist movement, when contact had to be established between two party members or fellow travelers who did not know each other? I repeated my train of thought aloud, but Péter interrupted impatiently:

"You'd better tell us the password."

"I know of no password."

"Then let me tell you what it was. It was 'Wagner notifies Péter.' And what was the message?"

"I don't know anything about a password or a message."

"Fetch Szönyi," Gàbor Péter ordered.

Any development of this farce would have surprised me less than Szönyi's appearance. Yet he appeared. Seconds later, there stood on my right, also at the foot of the T, the head of the Communist Party's cadres department, in a somewhat crumpled grey suit and a blue jersey sports shirt without a tie.

"Did this man bring you a message?"

"Yes, he did," Szönyi nodded, taking care not to look at me.

"One with a password?"

"Yes. One with a password."

"What was the password? Tell him to his face!"

Szönyi, though he turned his face towards me, avoided my eyes. "Wagner notifies Péter," he said—

"And when did I give you that message?"

Szönyi looked up in perplexity, his gaze crept up from my shoes to my face, then slid away above my head. He stared into the air as if he were thinking, then said slowly, in a low voice:

"Last year, on the 4th of May."

"And where did I give it to you?"

"In my office," Szönyi replied, this time without hesitation.

"Well," I said, relieved, "this makes matters infinitely more simple. I went to see Szönyi quite a few times, so I know that his office keeps a record of every incoming telephone call, whether Szönyi takes it or not, and of every visitor, whether he is received by Szönyi or passed on to one of his subordinates. This record will show whether or not I saw Szönyi on the 4th of May last year. And there is something else too! As I had no permanent pass, I would have had to ask for an entrance slip at the gate. If I entered Party Headquarters at that period there must be a record of it. Unless I had business there, I didn't go to Party Headquarters for months at a time, so it should take you only a few minutes to find out that Szönyi is not telling the truth."

"Do you maintain your statement?" Péter turned to Szönyi. "I do."

"And you too?" he asked me. "Naturally."

"In that case," Gàbor Péter shrugged impatiently, "give them both a soling."

Soling, an expression borrowed from the shoemaking industry, was already used in the vocabulary of the pre-war Hungarian police to describe an ancient but piously preserved mode of interrogation. The bare soles of the suspected person were beaten, first with a cane, later with a rubber truncheon, until he declared himself ready to confess. Szönyi presumably knew from experience what *soling* meant, for at Gàbor Péter's words his features twisted into a plaintive begging expression, he raised his shoulders and held out his hands, palms upward, towards Péter in a gesture of helplessness, but a guard grasped his arm and led him out. This was my last meeting with the former head of the cadres department. Later, in one of the cells of the Marko Street prison, I discovered traces of his presence. He had scratched his name into the ancient layer of whitewash, connecting it skillfully, in a wreath of vines, with the words, "Little Flower"; next to it he had kept a diary which showed that his arrest had taken place one week before mine. By the time I came across Szönyi's handwriting, my own bouquet of recollections and the words "Little Flower" had reconciled me to him; but for the present I was still resentful, I was still angry with him, rather than the secret police, because I felt he was deliberately fooling Gàbor Péter and his men and was accusing me falsely, perhaps to protect someone else.

I was still convinced of this when I entered the small room where a powerfully built man was waiting for me. Later I had occasion to see him repeatedly and from information gathered and remarks dropped, I discovered that his name was Detective Inspector Gyula Prinz, that once upon a time he had been a detective in Horthy's criminal police, but having supported the rather weak Hungarian resistance movement he was, after 1945, rewarded by being promoted detective-inspector in the ÁVH. Prinz, with the rubber truncheon swinging from his wrist, pointed almost apologetically, almost mildly, to the floor:

"Take off your shoes, please, and lie down on your stomach."

We were alone in the room. Prinz muttered something and shrugged his shoulders with embarrassment. Perhaps it was his irresoluteness that disarmed me. After all, I thought, he's only obeying an order and I complied readily. Prinz hit the soles of my feet ten blows each with his truncheon. I took hold of myself so as not to groan but I think that if I bore this first *soling* more easily than the subsequent ones it was not merely because the truncheon came down on healthy, still unbroken skin, still uninjured tissues, but also because Prinz swung the truncheon from at most shoulder height, not in a three-quarter arc, like the experts I encountered later.

I was led back into the big room and again made to stand at the foot of the table.

"Well, do you admit it now?" Péter asked sneeringly.

"Szönyi is lying," I replied, "and you can prove it in half an hour if you examine the entrance slips at Party Headquarters and the diary of Szönyi's secretary . . ."

"I didn't ask you for advice. You had better realize that you can count on nobody's support, nobody's protection here. You understand? The Party has delivered you into our hands. Will you admit that you brought Szönyi an illegal message?"

"How can I admit it."

"Give him some more of the same," Péter shouted, pointing at the door.

This time I was taken to another room where I found myself surrounded by five or six men. I believe I never told anyone during my long imprisonment something that, at the time, seemed absolutely natural to me, namely, that when one of the detectives hit me in the face, I returned the blow with equal force. A couple of years later my action appeared improbable to me: more than that, as if invented by myself.

I was obeying some ancient impulse, maybe the bidding of my

upbringing, or perhaps I was living up to the code of honour preva-
lent in the provincial environment of my youth, though intellectu-
ally I regarded these interpretations of honour as comically obsolete
and unrealistic. According to the standards of that code my first experience of the bastinado almost amounted to a voluntarily undergone test, but the first blow in the face was so obvious a humiliation
that retaliation was instinctive, regardless of the consequences.

It did not take the five or six men long to overpower me with
their fists, kicks and blows with truncheon and gun-butt. Then they
stamped on me, sat astride my back, bent back my legs and held
them while one of their colleagues beat my soles, swinging his truncheon through three-quarters of a circle. When I was led back to
the big room I was unable to open my right eye and my face as well
as my clothes bore witness to what had happened in the next room.

"What did you do to him?" Péter asked his men.

"He fell," a rough voice behind me replied, drawing out and
deepening the vowels so as to lend the answer, with its suburban
overtones, a shade of vacuity.

The upper group at the T-shaped table rewarded this wit with
hooting laughter, then Péter looked at me mockingly:

"Will you admit it now?"

"Not even if you put me through this treatment a hundred
times. Szönyi is lying and you can easily prove it."

"Take him away," the head of the secret police commanded
and my guards led me back, pushing and pulling me down the
darkened staircase to the cellar, where they flung me into the cell.

While I was pacing to and fro in the little cell, or trying to
squat on the bunk with my head between my shoulders, then lie on
it with knees bent, two ÁVH squad-cars stopped in front of No. II,
Üllöi Street, the large block of flats where I lived. At a barked command, troops armed with rifles and tommy guns jumped out. One
group, so the inhabitants of the flats told me later, spread out in
open formation, then cautiously, hugging the wall, worked their
way up to my flat on the fifth floor. Armed troops occupied the
landings, the backstairs and, with an encircling maneuver, blocked
the exits. Plain clothes security men, accompanied by uniformed
police with tommy guns, opened my flat, and the search began.

What was the purpose of all this? When the squad-cars arrived I had been in the hands of the ÁVH for two solid hours. I think the principal aim was not to intimidate the civilian population, but to create tension in the ÁVH organization and fill both officers and men with the sense of an immediate threat to their safety, if not their lives.

*   *   *

The investigators proved to be conservative. They remained true to their truncheons all through the second day. If this time they concentrated on my kidneys, they did not neglect the soles of my feet, for which purpose they repeatedly resorted to the carpet-rolling process. There were six or seven of them taking turns in such a way that there were always four in the room with me.

They must have realized that my purple-blue, swollen soles, as well as the other parts of my body that had been belabored with the truncheons were, in their maimed condition, incomparably more sensitive than on the first day. One even hinted at this by declaring that increased exertion was superfluous as the truncheon was becoming more and more effective and the pain I suffered more and more unbearable, so that it could be only a question of time, a short time at that, before I would give in and confess to anything including multiple homicide.

I took these allusions to be simply rhetoric; it seemed to me that Szönyi's accusations must really have convinced the investigators that they had caught a spy. However, it seemed somewhat suspicious, even bewildering, that they made no attempt to check even the most easily ascertainable evidence in Szönyi's accusation, that they took no steps to find out whether I had indeed been to see Szönyi or entered Party Headquarters at all at the time in question.

I believed, like hundreds of others, that I was the victim of a "fatal" error and it never entered my head to admit even part of the false accusation in order to gain temporary, or perhaps even permanent respite from physical torment.

*   *   *

[After prolonged interrogation, Szasz was sent to the Marko Street prison but then transported back to the secret police headquarters to undergo further questioning. — ED.]

Though the Andrássy Street Headquarters of the ÁVH had not changed outwardly, inside it was still being reconstructed over and over again, then, like a toy children have grown tired of, it would be demolished anew and restored to its original shape. Cars no longer stopped before the main entrance or the side-entrance in Csengery Street, but drove from Csengery Street into the courtyard, one corner of which had been surrounded by a wall some twenty feet high. Opposite the gate they had erected a great wooden tower, from the top of which a fierce-eyed tommy-gunner watched the prisoners alighting from the cars. I could no longer have run into Gàbor Péter at a turning in the stairs, since the prisoners were being taken up by obviously temporary but very ingenious secret routes. The changes were most noticeable and significant on the ground floor, for this is where the MVD had set up its headquarters.

The corridor leading towards the right from the Andrássy Street main entrance had been walled up, just enough room being left for a narrow iron door. The Soviet section had been newly painted, the worn furniture replaced by brand new furnishings, and the corridors were thickly carpeted. Even for ÁVH members, access to the sacred abode of the MVD was solely through the iron door. My guard knocked on this door when he led me upstairs.

Someone peeped out through the spy hole in the narrow door. My guard must have whispered a code word into the hole, for the door was opened to admit us. After a few steps the corridor broadened into a small lobby. Here I was made to wait. While I waited, the Russian Colonel who looked like a sergeant and the bald MVD officer with the intellectual face crossed the lobby. From one of the rooms I saw Vajda emerging, the brutal-faced young detective who had arrested me at the Ministry of Agriculture.

"This character has given me a lot of trouble," Vajda remarked to one of his colleagues idling in the corridor. Then he turned to me: "Are you still so stubborn?"

At that moment, Ernö Szücs, Gàbor Péter's deputy entered the lobby. He motioned to me to follow him.

Szücs led me into a small room. He spoke shortly, hurriedly, about the trial in preparation. He used Károlyi's expression which I was to hear frequently thereafter, like a "leitmotiv" in background music: "We want to deal the Imperialists a heavy blow." And I— Szücs added—unless I sided with the enemy, must put myself at the disposal of the Communist Party, the Soviet comrades, the ÁVH. Rajk* had come to his senses, he now saw the situation quite clearly. I could convince myself of this personally, not merely on the basis of written statements. For they would again confront me with Rajk.

We proceeded into a larger room. Rajk was sitting by the opposite wall with his legs crossed. He was no longer wearing his grey summer suit, as at our first confrontation, but a brown suit, sandals and thick woollen socks. This was indeed a privilege, for the rest of us were without socks, our shoes had no laces and we were wearing the same suits in which we had been arrested. Rajk was thinner, paler than when I last saw him, but the ghastly network of wrinkles, had disappeared from his face. He gave me a friendly, though somewhat embarrassed and melancholy smile. Szücs sat down at the long side of the oblong table and made me sit at the short end, then, from the papers lying before him, he read, to my surprise, a formal text of our confrontation even before it had taken place. In the text, the two persons confronted declared by way of introduction, that they were neither related to each other nor on bad terms. When the Colonel reached the end of this paragraph he looked up from the paper:

"Well, László Rajk?" he asked.

Rajk did not look at Szücs, his eyes sought mine and his hand rose in a restrained but hopeless gesture. He tried to smile, then said in a loud voice:

"*I* feel no hostility." He pronounced this *I* emphatically, as if

---

*László Rajk was appointed Minister of Foreign Affairs in 1948. Three years earlier Rajk had been appointed to serve as head of the Ministry of Interior. He was looked upon as the top man among communist leaders, neither trained in Russia nor sent home by Moscow. He had served in the Hungarian Brigade during the Spanish civil war and had been active in the Hungarian Resistance movement during the German occupation.

he wanted to stress that he had no cause to take anything amiss but would not be surprised if I were resentful.

My expression as I entered the room with the memory of the electric shocks in my muscles must have been rather gloomy. My depressing appearance was scarcely enhanced by the circumstance that I had washed my shirt at the Marko Street prison but could not put it on because it was still wet when they came to fetch me; now, in the absence of a shirt, it was my skin that peeped through the holes of my torn pullover.

I returned Rajk's look and suddenly recalled the scene in the corridor of the University when he had told me perhaps rhetorically, but without bombast, "It's no use, there is but one solution: Lenin." It was with these words that the young historian had set out on the road of a professional revolutionary. Now, looking into his sunken but flushed face, into his tired eyes that looked into mine, I knew beyond all doubt that Rajk had no illusions left, that he realized he had come to the end of the road.

Szücs's pencil was tapping impatiently on the table:

"And you?" he asked, "And you?" He looked at me insistently and his shoe beat rhythmically on the floor. "Come on, answer. Are you on bad terms with László Rajk?"

"I don't bear him any grudge," I replied looking at Rajk, not at the Colonel.

Like Rajk's answer a few seconds before, mine did not refer to Szücs's formal question and it must have been obvious to him that we were both thinking of the statement my former fellow-student had made against me. But the Colonel took no notice of our dialogue, for our quarrel or reconciliation had no longer any influence on the set course of events.

Without further remark, Szücs began to read a previously prepared deposition. In this, Rajk mentioned briefly our university years, our subsequent meetings, but gave a more detailed account of our meetings after my return home, describing when, where and how often we had met. He declared that he had proposed my appointment to the Ministry of Foreign Affairs in the Party's organizational committee because, on the one hand, he had come to know my Trotskyite attitude from our conversations, on the other, because according to reliable information I had been recruited by the British Intelligence Service in South America. As I had returned to Hungary as an agent of the Imperialists, he—as a fellow-agent—wanted to help me carry on my espionage activity with the greatest possible success.

At the trial, this statement was referred to by the Public Prosecutor, Gyula Alapi. Rajk, he said, had created a wide espionage network:

> Wherever possible he appointed the agents of the Imperialists, especially former Trotskyists, agent provocateurs and spies to high position. It was thus that important offices in the Ministry of Foreign Affairs fell to Béla Szász, an agent of British intelligence. (Ibid., p. II)

In Szücs's papers, Rajk's confession was followed by mine. As far as I remember, apart from the customary biographical details which, by the way, were accurate, the text was but a summary, prepared from the notes of the Russian Lieutenant-Colonel, of my meetings at the house of my Danish friend, with the Englishman and my conversations with him concerning my return to Hungary. As this dialogue, condensed into *oratio obliqua*, contained no evidence to prove either my recruitment or that I had been sent home by the British Secret Service, in a negative way it actually contradicted Rajk's statements. All the more so as the report did not even accuse me of attempted espionage, let alone espionage itself.

I had a side look at Szücs. He had put on weight since I last saw him. His uniform was buttoned over his quivering stomach and broad rings of fat stood out like pumped-up tires.

As the Colonel articulated each word clearly, almost joyfully, it occurred to me as I watched his apparently unjustified self-satisfaction, that they were probably putting together these two contradictory statements to prevent me from referring to this contradiction later, or even from behaving like Hans Andersen's courtiers lost in admiration at the Emperor's new clothes. Still, I reflected, only for its internal use could even voluntaristic Soviet police-logic consider these two conflicting reports as being in agreement. If they intended to put me, too, on public trial, they could not rest content with this. The MVD could "deal the Imperialists a blow" with the aid of my confession only if I admitted not merely that in South America I had talked about my return home with an Englishman whose name I could not even remember, but if I also confessed what espionage reports I had passed on, when, and to whom.

In that case, this confrontation with Rajk would not be an end but a beginning. Here, the Governor's men could only pause, they could not stop. They might return to Szönyi's statement concerning the mysterious Wagner, come back to Péter Hain, to Colonel Káratson. They might fling me back into the nights and dawns of the first month to mould me into a well-mannered, zealous spy. Although I foresaw with misgiving that my physical strength and my moral resistance would give out in a single day if I had to go through the same experience a second time, I was still filled with an indifferent, light-minded calm, and amused myself by maliciously calculating the weight of Szücs's quivering tires of fat.

When at last the Colonel finished reading, he looked at us and said nonchalantly:

"Well, sign!"

Rajk walked over to the table and signed his name with a flourish on each page of the report, even those that should have been signed by me, since they contained the text put into my mouth. Szücs noticed this only when he pushed the file over to me. He glanced at Rajk reproachfully.

"Now really," he said, "you should know the rules better by now . . ."

Perhaps Rajk did. Perhaps he indicated with this indifferent handout of his signature that he was beyond caring, that he would sign anything; or that I should accuse him without compunction, if by doing so I could improve my own position. Perhaps he had acted without thinking. Because he no longer cared about anything, or paid any attention to what was going on around him. . . .

In more than one case the various methods of awakening a sense of guilt contributed, particularly among arrested communists, to the admission of espionage and conspiracy. Some of them insisted for years afterwards that they had truly committed the fictitious crimes with which they were charged, even when they mixed

with other prisoners in gaol and it could have become clear to them
from daily conversation that not only they, not only certain other
persons, but, at a conservative estimate, over ninety-five per cent of
the political prisoners had been sentenced on the basis of purely invented charges.

At times, dissecting year by year the life of the man entrusted
to their care, the interrogators would try to instill into him a sense of
guilt not with reference to the party, but by laying great emphasis
on some personal matter in his past. One of my cell-mates, for instance—the son of a protestant theologian turned freethinker and
then communist—tried to convince me amidst innumerable *mea
culpas*, that fundamentally he had deserved his punishment, not, of
course, because of any espionage activity as alleged in the indictment but because of having been twice unfaithful to his wife many
years before his arrest.

*   *   *

[Szasz remained in prison while the purge of the party continued.
Rajk was placed on trial, during which Szasz was accused of being
both a British and an American spy. While in prison he was given a
transcript of the trial.—ED.]

When, in the last year of our imprisonment, we were given
books to read, we obtained from the prison library the *Blue Book* of
the Rajk trial. In this it was Szönyi's [former head of the Hungarian
Communist party's cadre department] questioning that threw the
clearest light on what was not exactly a side-issue in the trial: the
Party purge, and particularly a certain trend within it. The produc-
ers of the trial put Szönyi in the spot-light as the symbol of a category, for his confession was made up in such a way as to throw
suspicion not only on himself, not only on those in the dock with
him, but on all those who had returned home from the West, especially the intellectuals.

Szönyi's confession insinuated that all those who had lived in
the West, or shown an interest in Western culture, were the agents,
or at least the potential agents, of one or another of the Imperialist
powers.

From Szönyi I at last obtained a reply to the question that had
for long preoccupied me, although it had no bearing on the identity
of Noel Field or of Wagner, about whom Gàbor Péter had questioned me during that first hour of my arrest and his men for weeks
following, in a rather unfriendly manner.
All this emerged clearly from Szönyi's account of the preliminaries of his return home:

> In the summer of 1944, towards the end of the war, in its last year,
> it had become obvious that a part of the East European and Cen-
> tral European countries would be liberated by the Soviet troops.
> At that time the American intelligence service, under the leader-
> ship of Allan [sic] Dulles, began to concentrate on the task of
> bringing into its organization spies from the political émigrés
> there, especially from the left-wing communist groups. The pur-
> pose of this was to infiltrate these people into the territories liber-
> ated by the Soviet troops, to carry out underground activity
> against the Communist Parties there. It was in the course of this
> activity that I came into contact with the American spy organiza-
> tion. The chief helpmate and closest collaborator of Allan Dulles
> in his work of organizing spies from among the political émigrés
> was Noel H. Field, who was officially the head of the Unitarian
> relief organization called the Unitarian Service Committee. In re-
> ality he was a direct collaborator of Dulles in the spy organization.
> (Ibid., p. 146–147)

After that there is a lot about Allen Dulles (the *Blue Book*
spelled his name everywhere as "Allan"), and there is a great deal
about the Yugoslav, Czech, Polish political refugees who had also
been recruited by the American secret service. Szönyi continues:

> I met Dulles regularly until my return home in January, 1945. My
> formal enrollment into the American spy organization took place
> at the end of November, 1944, in Berne. At this meeting Dulles
> explained to me at length his political conception for the period
> after the war and told me that the Communist Parties would obvi-
> ously become government parties in a whole series of Eastern Eu-
> ropean countries which would be liberated by Soviet troops. So

support for an American orientation and the American collaboration policy should be carried on first of all within the Communist Party. (Ibid., p. 148)

Finally, Szönyi concludes this part of his confession as follows: "Later I met Dulles more than once. I agreed with him that after our return home we would remain in contact with each other, and I would use in this contact the cover-name 'Péter' and he the cover-name 'Wagner.' " (Ibid., p. 148)

More than four years later, turning the pages of the *Blue Book* in my prison cell, I at last understood the question Gàbor Péter had asked me at the T-shaped table, I understood what that alleged password: "Wagner's message to Péter . . ." meant. But my conscience did not bother me, not even when I remembered Szücs's wasted efforts, for after all, I had put no spoke in their wheel; they had found understudies to play my role, a prisoner in the Andrássy Street cellars and someone living beyond their reach abroad. But the most important role, the one written for László Rajk, could be played by no one but László Rajk himself.

*   *   *

Communist ideology had, for decades, proclaimed the irreconcilable conflict between socialism and capitalism. Although during the war there had been a *treuga dei* [new party line] on the open propaganda front, speakers at secret or private communist meetings, such at least was my experience in South America, depicted the Western allies as enemies capable of any trickery at any time, and stressed that it was the task of the communists during the ideological armistice to secure the greatest possible number of strategic positions within the fortresses of the allied capitalist front, since the final showdown, the ultimate settlement was unavoidable.

The public prosecutor ascribes the same train of thought and action to the other side when he declares:

For it becomes evident from the material of the trial that the American intelligence services were already getting ready during the war against Hitler for the fight against the forces of socialism and democracy. They did this not only by diplomatic and political methods but with the base means of internally disorganizing the democratic forces and revolutionary workers' parties. Behind Rankovich there are the shadows of Mr. Field and Mr. Dulles. (Ibid., p. 269)

Belkin did not turn the point of the confessions directly against the West, and even the shadow of Allen Dulles conjured up by them must be considered as nothing but an instrument to blacken the Yugoslavs. This is how the public prosecutor proclaimed the primary and true aim of the trial, its "international significance" as he put it:

> It is true and right that the Hungarian People's Court, passing sentence on László Rajk and his gang of conspirators, should also pass sentence, in a political and moral sense, on the traitors of Yugoslavia, the criminal gang of Tito, Rankovich, Kardelj and Djilas. The international significance of this trial lies particularly in the fact that we are passing sentence on the Yugoslav deserters and traitors to democracy and socialism. (Ibid., p. 264–265)

According to the editors of the text these traitors and deserters had never even intended to bring about any form of socialism. For this is what, according to Rajk's confession, Rankovich had said:

> . . . that neither Tito nor the rest of the members of the Yugoslav government wanted a people's democratic regime even after the Liberation, and through it the building of socialism in Yugoslavia. If they as a government were still compelled to take such revolutionary measures which in essence and de facto began to lead towards the liquidation of capitalism, this was not because they wanted to carry out this programme in earnest, but because they were compelled to do so under pressure from the Yugoslav working masses. (Ibid., p. 62)

In order to heap even more coals on the heads of the Yugoslavs, Governor Belkin did not shrink from the logically as well as technically impossible accusation that the Western Powers had handed their espionage organizations over to Tito, so much did they trust him, so closely did they co-operate with him. Rajk is made to say:

> At the same time Martin Himmler told me that in all probability this would be my last talk with him and with the representatives of the American intelligence agencies in general, for they would hand over their whole network to the Yugoslavs, and in the future I would get instructions for further work through Yugoslav channels. (Ibid., p. 48)

These tasks incumbent no longer upon the Western Imperialists but upon Tito, were the following. First, Rajk said:

> they wanted to ensure their full right to command armed forces, that is, the army and the police . . . Keeping in view, of course, the final aim of shaping a bloc of states, Tito demanded such a foreign policy, and its guarantees from Hungary, as would always be in harmony with the foreign policy of Yugoslavia, that is, that her foreign relations, too, should be subordinated to the Yugoslav government. (Ibid., p. 74–75)

By the end of September, 1949, when this indictment was heard, the plans ascribed to the Yugoslavs in Hungary had long since been carried out by the Soviet Union, naturally to her own benefit. Hence the Philippic oration of the Public Prosecutor was not intended merely to win the laurels so easy to gain and so easy to lose in the people's democracies, but also to serve as a thinly-veiled threat. A threat to all those who observed that the Prosecutor's statements applied not to Yugoslavia but to the Soviet Union, not to Rajk and his colleagues, but to the party functionaries sent back from Moscow to Hungary; for this is what Alapi said:

> It is also obvious, honored People's Court, that the conspiracy of Rajk and his company was aimed to sell Hungarian independence and to liquidate national sovereignty. This gang was formed to put Hungary under a foreign yoke, to make our fatherland a foreign colony, to form its government from foreign spies and agents and to create in the place of an autonomous and independent Hungary a system which would have carried out the or-

ders of agents, dancing to the tune played abroad, and which would betray Hungarian national interests. (Ibid., p. 262)

The party leaders sent home from the Soviet Union were, naturally, champions of Hungarian independence, they represented national interests and did not dance to "the tune played abroad," and that was why the Yugoslavs told Rajk:

> . . . that Tito was absolutely determined that at the time of the coup d'etat, at the same time as the coup d'etat, the Hungarian government would have to be arrested and three of its members, Rákosi, Gerö and Farkas, would immediately have to be killed during the first action. (Ibid., p. 73)

In fact, Rákosi, Gerö and Farkas all returned to Hungary in the wake of the Soviet army. And the collaboration or working relationship of two of them—Gerö and Farkas—with the Russian secret police, was so close and of such long standing that even the least well-informed were aware of it, from Spain to Hungary. In addition, most communists who returned from the Soviet Union, such as Rákosi, Gerö and Farkas, kept two passports in their desks, one Russian and one Hungarian. This was proved in 1956, when numerous Muscovites fled the country with Soviet passports in their pockets. By choosing these men as the selected victims of assassination, the editorial board working on the text of the confessions intended not only to surround them with a somewhat ambiguous halo; they also wanted to make it quite clear in Soviet liturgical jargon that Rákosi, Gerö, Farkas and others of their kind represented the true faith in contrast to the heretics. The trial was to be the party's crusade against the heretics.

The social-democratic parties were let off lightly for the present. Indeed, one of the secondary aims was to ascribe the failures of the people's democratic system in Hungary to the subversive activities of the accused. Foreshadowing new trials and a large-scale mustering of forces and likely maneuvers in the crusade were also those parts of the confessions which, according to Alapi, showed that:

> . . . the destructive work of the traitors and spies [was] conducted not only in our country, but in all the countries of the people's

democracy ... from Albania to Poland and from Rumania to Czechoslovakia (Ibid., p. 269). What is more: Tito and his clique, hand in hand with the imperialist intelligence services, carried on their work of dissolution not only in every people's democratic country but also in those capitalist countries which have strong labor movements, communist parties with a strong influence on the broad masses. (Ibid., p. 256)

In other words, Tito's heresy was threatening the harmony of Moscow's magnetic circles over the entire range of their power fields, that is, over the whole world. And this not merely by giving fresh impetus to the centrifugal forces in the fluctuating play of centrifugal and centripetal forces, but also by the threat that Belgrade might become a new core, that new magnetic circles might develop around it, which would cut across, perhaps even disrupt, the concentric Muscovite power fields.

This was such an important stake that the leaders of the Soviet Union felt compelled to take the risk inherent in the improbability of the accusations and confessions that followed each other in the Rajk trial and its successors, both in Hungary and in other countries in the Soviet orbit.

*   *   *

In our cells, as in the Andrassy Street cellar, the light was left on all night and as we were never allowed into the yard, only two events broke the week's monotony: the appearance of the ÁVH barber and when, late on Friday evenings, we were led singly and almost surreptitiously to the shower-room. Comparable to these pleasures was the gleaning of information by spying. In the corners of our feeding hatches, decades of continuous use had worn holes into the thick iron doors. Although the angle was difficult, we were able to peer out at the opposite gallery and see the door of one, or perhaps two cells. Our guards would, from time to time, fill up these crevices from the outside, but by using a bristle torn from a broom head I could, with a few hours' cautious labour remove or pierce the filling, and watch, for instance, when they took away for his trial Arpad

Szakasits—former Secretary General of the Hungarian Social Democratic Party, dressed in a dark suit and an open collar. At the moment of my arrest he was still president of the Republic.

Every time I was transported back to the Andrassy Street cellar,
the change interrupted the often unreal, apparently peaceful
rhythm of life to which I grew accustomed in the Marko Street
prison, but it also shook my peace of mind which I hoped had been
stabilized. They would keep me there for days, sometimes for
weeks, questioning me about myself and others. In the spring of
1950, I was again charged with having been a police informer and
interrogated about Peter Rain, and, particularly, about the military
attaché in Paris, Colonel Karátson.

Though my interrogator did not use a rubber truncheon, he
would, just as Farkas used to in the old days, tear up my notes in
which I described how I met Karátson and what we had talked
about, and threaten me with extremely unfriendly methods if I
didn't write the truth on the fresh sheet of paper put down before
me. After I had scribbled in this way eight identical depositions, my
interrogator declared that his patience was exhausted, that I would
now be locked in a cell from which few people had emerged alive
and there I would stay until I was ready to confess, or until my confession was no longer needed, because from the cell they could
send me straight down for cremation.

The cell was indeed rather oppressive. Subsoil water had
seeped through its floor forming small lakes varying from one to
three inches deep. Only at the threshold and under the bunk did
two muddy little concrete islands emerge from the water. In a few
hours my clothes were saturated with damp and I was shivering
from head to foot. I stamped my feet on the concrete islands or
squatted on the bunk with my legs drawn up. In this way I cele-
brated the first anniversary of my arrest. But I did not take the
threats of the ÁVH officer too seriously and I had no intention of
making a confession. I was not mistaken: after having shivered, sat
petrified and gasped for air in the icy mist for over three weeks, I
was returned, without a word of explanation, to the steam-heated
cell of the Marko Street prison.

My first concern was to find out who inhabited the cells next to mine. I received no reply from the cell on my right, but from the left someone answered my knocking and introduced himself as Miklós Szücs. I was flabbergasted, because Miklós Szücs was the brother of the deputy head of the ÁVH. But in the war, while Ernö Szücs had fled to the Soviet Union, Miklós had spent the war years in England, to become after the war London correspondent of the official Hungarian Party organ, *Szabad Nép*, and later head of the Foreign Ministry's London Information Bureau. In 1949, he was re-called, then arrested and accused of having been a British spy. In his case, no physical methods of persuasion had been applied. Per-haps it was this circumstance that still made him hope for an objec-tive investigation, or perhaps he counted on his brother's prestige when, through the wall, he spoke of himself as a faithful commu-nist. He declared he had full confidence in the party and that he had no doubt his innocence would soon be proved and he would be released.

Any argument, any contradiction seemed senseless, and what is more, cruel, so this conversation was not continued, but every sin-gle day we played a game of chess. The guards did not prevent us from moulding chess figures from bread; I sat next to the wall, Szücs lay down on his bed on the other side and we would convey our moves to each other by means of low knocks. The guards sus-pected us but never caught us in the act and so, like two old-age pensioners confirmed in their habits, every morning at nine-thirty, we would sit down to our chessboard. We went on playing chess through the spring, through the summer, until, sometime in Au-gust, Szücs was removed.

Strangely enough he was partly right, because they released him in the autumn. But he had but a few days in which to celebrate the triumph of his faith in the party, for he was shortly rearrested. And this time there was no mercy. When an acquaintance saw him in the ÁVH cellars, he was being dragged along by two investigators because he could no longer walk. Half-conscious, he kept repeat-ing, "Don't touch me, don't touch me, I'll sign anything." He could no longer count on his brother for it was precisely against the Colonel that they were trying to obtain damning evidence from Miklós Szücs. His release had been nothing but a trap set for his brother which enabled the ÁVH to ask Ernö Szücs why Miklós had made no admission during the months of his first arrest? And why, when he was rearrested, he admitted his crimes within a few days when the investigation was not in the hands of the Colonel? The reason was clear. Obviously they were birds of the same feather, both agents of foreign Imperialist powers.

Not even in 1956 did it become clear why the deputy head of the ÁVH had lost the confidence of his Russian and Hungarian superiors. But, side by side with a number of fanciful stories, there circulated two plausible accounts concerning the closing scenes of Colonel Szücs's career. According to one of these the Colonel committed suicide when he learned of his impending arrest; according to the other he had been beaten to death by ÁVH investigators. What is certain is that no prisoner came across the Szücs brothers in prison, and neither of them emerged in 1956 when all prison doors, even the secret ones, were thrown open. Thus, it is more than probable that neither survived the Colonel's fall from favor and that both the London and the Moscow Szücs met the same fate.

*   *   *

After a second X-ray examination, my diagnosis was modified: the X-ray picture of my back showed tuberculosis of the ribs only, not of the spine. Cavities of half an inch and one inch were measured on three of my ribs. I listened to the advice of my neighbour, the professor of medicine, rather than to that of the dentist. Following the Professor's instructions, I ate everything they put before me, whether I felt like it or not, and as soon as the weather turned milder, opened the window and exposed my back to the sun. By late spring I had put on a few pounds, found it a little easier to move and the thermometer, although it still indicated a slight fever, did not jump over 100° in the evenings.

Once or twice a month we would straighten out the legs of a couple of our fellow-prisoners—they were not always the aged—and tie up their chins, then the orderlies would grab the corners of the dead prisoner's last sheet and carry him in it down to the dissecting theatre. Meanwhile the others, whether they were able to use their limbs or not, were busy scribbling or dictating to their companions pleas for clemency or for a re-trial. But it was not on these memoranda, whether elegantly or primitively worded, that our fate depended, but solely on the outcome of the battle raging between Mátyás Rákosi and Imre Nagy [two factional leaders in the Hungarian Communist Party].

About this time the conflict was nearing its turning point. The Communist Party had formed a committee of three, designating Imre Nagy, Ernö Gerö and Mátyás Rákosi as its members. The task of this committee was to consider the case of the political prisoners and decide whether the re-trials should also be extended to those sentenced in the Rajk Affair. Rákosi fought tooth and nail against this extension, for in 1949 he had taken all the credit for the unmasking of Trotskyite traitors and spies. But he was defeated. Ernö Gerö sided with Imre Nagy in favor of the re-trials. It may well be that he did so only in the hope that Rákosi might fall and he would take his place, but he may have received direct orders from his Moscow superiors to side with Nagy. In those days, the directives handed down by the Kremlin to the Hungarian Party leaders were not synchronized; most of the Hungarian leaders were bound by political and personal ties of dependency to a variety of Soviet statesmen or Party factions. Thus, splits in the inner Soviet circles inspired secret intrigue and raised open conflict in the Hungarian Communist Party, too. Whatever the reason, Imre Nagy with Ernö Gerö's help won this round and the re-trials were extended to the Rajk affair. But Rákosi was still on the warpath; whenever and wherever he had found an opportunity to do so, he obstructed and delayed the processes of revision.

"Indeed, it wasn't easy," Imre Nagy said musingly when, early in 1956, we stood talking while his grandchildren and my son were tobogganing down the slopes of Pasarét.

At the time Nagy said this, Rákosi was again in the saddle; Imre Nagy had not only been forced to resign his Premiership, but had been condemned by the Central Committee of the Communist Party for "rightist deviation" and Rákosi had succeeded in having him expelled, not merely from the Political Committee but also

from the Party. Had all this happened a year and a half earlier, we prisoners would certainly not have been transferred in May, 1954, to the new Fö Street headquarters of the ÁVH. Because it was in May that our guard entered the ward and spelled my number out from a sheet of paper. "474-D-893," he said.

We traveled in the coffin. This was the prison nickname for the prison van, the inside of which had been divided into small cubicles that could be locked one by one. In the cubicles we could not stand upright and breathing was difficult. At ÁVH headquarters we were put into dark, but clean, well-ventilated cells, furnished with bed, table and chair, not in the cellar, but on one of the upper floors. Soon I was led before a young ÁVH officer. He introduced himself as Lieutenant Kása, for, miraculously, this time, an ÁVH officer actually introduced himself. He produced my deposition and went through it point by point, asking me what was true and what was not. Later he had me transferred from my cell to a bright room and gave orders that I should receive butter and cheese, in addition to the already by no means stingy diet; within a few days, he produced a new deposition for me. . . .

In the prison infirmary I was isolated from the others and not allowed to see any of my companions. Weeks went by, then months; not until the end of August did Lieutenant Kása reappear. He placed a gigantic sheaf of documents before me; I was to read them and if I agreed with the contents, put my name to them. The thick wad of typed pages refuted not only the deposition prepared in the trial and which contained hardly any damning evidence, but also the statements in the *Blue Book* that referred to me. The Lieutenant informed me amicably that in two or three weeks they would hear my case anew, and I could have every confidence in the outcome.

Experience had taught me to expect a wait of several months rather than several weeks, but this time I was mistaken. Although I was not yet brought before the court, a few days after the Lieutenant's visit, several of us were transported to the Fö Street headquarters of the ÁVH. No sooner did we reach the building than they led us into a large room containing a display of new shirts and underwear, suits and shoes. Obeying instructions, we discarded our prison uniform and, wasting little time on selection, dressed quickly from top to toe. . . .

During those few weeks when the possibility of release was no longer the creation of an overheated brain, I had begun to fear that when, at last, I walked out of prison, I would lose my self-control and be carried away by ridiculous, tearful emotions. I was wrong. All three of us prisoners walked out into the street with almost wooden faces, as if we had just left our club; we exchanged a few commonplace observations and looked around for a taxi. We had to walk quite a distance before we found a cab. Here we took leave of one another. Each of us carried a bundle under one arm, a small bag of granulated sugar, our collection of bits of string and rags, and a few cigarettes.

My bundle, my pallor and ill-fitting clothing immediately made clear to the taxi-driver where I had come from. He asked no questions—I was not the first of the kind he had come across—but started a quiet, friendly conversation. I went to endless trouble before I could get him to accept the fare, one fifth of the wages I had earned during five years of captivity. After taking leave of the friendly taxi-driver, I was held up by an unfriendly, locked door on the fifth floor of the Üllöi Street block of flats. My mother, who had daily awaited my return for five years, had gone to see my brother in the provincial town where he worked.

I stood bewildered in the corridor beside the empty dustbin. And here I was discovered by the tenants. A neighbor ran down to the janitor for a master-key, opened the front door, and I stepped into my mother's room. I politely put my dirty bundle on the floor and sat down in the ancient armchair inherited from my great-grandparents.

Soon the doorbell rang and at short intervals the neighbors marched in. In antique silver jugs or plain earthenware coffeepots, they brought for the prisoner they had hardly known, his first snack. For I had arrived home just at coffee-time. In a moment five cups of coffee steamed on the table and the heavenly fragrance of coffee, bread and butter and pastry hovered above the old furniture transforming the room into an oriental paradise.

One of my companions who had walked out of the prison gate

with me was luckier than I, for arriving home he was met by his entire family. The other found his wife, and they set out immediately towards the school, to pick up their little girl. As the children streamed out of the building and dispersed noisily, the returned prisoner felt suddenly confused. Zsuzsi had been a little over two years old when her father had been taken away. More than five years had gone by since he had last seen her. The released prisoner glanced irresolutely at the crowd of children, then turned to his wife:

"Which is mine?"

· 6 ·

ROBERT LOH

Nightmare from the Red Chamber: A Tale from Communist China

WHEN Robert Loh's *Escape from Red China* appeared in 1961, most Americans still knew little about Communist China. China's intervention in the Korean War (1950–1953) on October 27, 1950, made her an enemy of the United States, but in the intervening years news from China had been effectively cut off from the West. China "watchers" carefully scoured official publications from China, refugee reports, and information gathered by embassy officials stationed in Beijing, in order to piece together a picture of what was happening there. Loh's book provided a wealth of detailed information about life and politics in the early years of the Communist regime under Mao Zedong, who had come to power in 1949, ousting the nationalist government of Chiang Kai-shek.

The Chinese Communist revolution—the "loss of China," as President Truman's critics called it—created deep fear among anti-Communists in the United States. Communists had seized power in the most populated nation in the world, which was perceived by anti-Communists as another step in the Communist quest for world domination. Conservatives within the Republican party were quick to blame the Truman administration for the "loss" of China, charging that Truman had failed to provide sufficient military support to the Nationalists. Further accusations were made that General George C. Marshall's mission to China in 1946, and Marshall's subsequent attempt to arrange a political settlement between the Nationalists and the Communists, had played into the hands of the Red Chinese insurgents. Some anti-Communist circles believed that naive liberals or perhaps Communist agents in the federal government had persuaded Truman that Mao was simply an agrarian reformer. Once again, anti-Communists argued, liberals had been taken in by Communist propaganda. They pointed to innocents such as former Republican presidential candidate Wendell Willkie, who after meeting Chou En-lai, the Chinese Communist leader in Chungking at the height of World War II wrote, "If all Chinese communists are like himself, their movement is more a national and agrarian uprising that an international or proletarian conspiracy." For anti-Communists, Mao's rise to power proved all too well the liberal unwillingness or inability to grasp the insidious nature and extent of the "Communist conspiracy."

Loh's book was read by anti-Communists as a story of betrayal characteristic of the Communists. And, his description of Chinese Communist techniques of indoctrination through "mass criticism," intimidation, and repression provided a fresh insight into totalitarianism. Loh's story, unlike other literature coming from the "gulag," was not about imprisonment but about how the threat of imprisonment and death was employed by the new rulers of China to root out dissent and "brainwash" an entire people.

Like many young Chinese who had been educated abroad, Loh welcomed the overthrow of the corrupt Nationalist government and the victory of the Communists who promised agrarian reform, economic development, and better government. Since the mid-nineteenth century, when European and Japanese imperial powers had humiliated China through their imposition of "spheres of influence," young Chinese students had yearned for their country to overcome its backwardness and take its place as an equal among nations.

Born in Shanghai in 1924, Loh had studied at the University of Shanghai and in 1949 had earned a master's degree at the University of Wisconsin. Against the advice of his father, who fled China when the Communists came to power, Loh decided to remain in China to contribute to the revolution. His idealism was shared by other young people, many of whom returned from living abroad to join in making a better society in China.

In the first years of the revolution, the Chinese government promised not to purge non-Communists from the civil service, nor to eliminate private enterprise. Capital development was welcomed, provided the "bourgeois" business class accepted the socialist revolution. Loh put his educational training to work by becoming a manager for the Foo Sing Flour Mill in Shanghai, where he worked from 1952 to 1957. His faith in the revolution was quickly lost as Mao's government launched a series of mass campaigns, first against civil servants and intellectuals, then against businessmen. The attack on the national bourgeoisie began in June 1952 when Mao declared that "the contradiction between the working class and the national bourgeoisie" had now become the principal contradiction in China. By midsummer the national bourgeoisie and capitalism itself were under siege. For months the owners of factories and shops became targets in a campaign against the "five evils"—bribery, tax evasion, theft of state property, cheating on government contracts, and theft of classified economic information. This campaign encouraged popular participation. Hundreds of businessmen killed themselves, and thousands underwent "self-criticism" before raging crowds who shouted abuses at them. Victims of these campaigns were forced to "confess" their counterrevolutionary thoughts and deeds under intense self-criticism sessions led by Communist cadre members who were sent to factories, businesses, and government offices to root out "petty bourgeois, counterrevolutionary thought." Initiated in 1952, the campaign against the national bourgeoisie brought all industry and business under the control of the government within five years. In this same period, peasants were forced or persuaded to combine their landholdings into agricultural cooperatives.

Realizing that his father had been right about the Communists, as Loh tells his story, he made plans for his eventual escape from China. To accomplish this he decided to play along with the Communists by participating in self-criticism sessions, not criticizing the regime even when he and his colleagues were encouraged to do so, and playing the role of an enthusiastic businessman to foreign delegates. In his book he tells of how he was provided for a day or two with a comfortable home and a wife and children as part of the show to persuade foreign visitors that all was well. Through these performances, Loh was able to convince party officials that he was a loyal supporter of the regime. He succeeded in escaping from China under the guise of claiming an inheritance from his departed father. He later came to the United States where he worked for the federal government as a translator and as a consultant to the House Committee on Un-American Activities. He published a number of books on Communist China, drawing from his experiences during the early years of the revolution. His story of his escape to Hong Kong, where he joined his family, makes for riveting reading.

The following excerpts capture the fear of those who came under scrutiny during the sessions of mass self-criticism. Those American anti-Communists who read *Escape from Red China* found in the book persuasive evidence of the totalitarian nature of the Chinese regime, its application of "mind-control" on a mass level, and the ability of the Communists to deceive. While some anti-Communists refused to believe that the Sino-Soviet split was real, there was no doubt that communism, whether from the Soviet Union or mainland China, remained a threat to the West.

🈺 When I entered the mill that fateful morning no one spoke to me, not even in answer to my greeting. For generations Chinese employees had always shown deep respect for executives and as long as the fiction of private enterprise under the new regime was maintained, the employees continued the old habit. Moreover, I had been friendly and informal with them so that our relationship had become close. Their sudden coldness therefore was a shock.

The Party Secretary was standing stiffly at attention with two rough-looking cadres in my office. He disregarded my greeting.

From *Escape from Red China* (New York, 1962), pp. 17–24, 120–125, 165–168.

"Loh, I have to inform you that henceforth you will not be permitted to leave this office until you have written out a full confession."

"Confession?" I stammered.

Visibly exasperated, the Party Secretary quoted me the official pronouncements about the Five-Anti Campaign.* It was as though a notorious criminal were being reminded by a judge of the laws he had broken. But the Party Secretary knew me, knew every detail of my activities in the mills and knew also that, under the control exercised by the regime, I could not possibly have committed any of the five sins in our mills. I simply could not believe that he was serious.

The Party Secretary did say that because of the Party's leniency, I was being granted three days to prepare my confession instead of one. But he warned me that only a full confession would be acceptable and that any attempt to hide my crimes would be dealt with severely. Then he went out, leaving the two tough tiger beaters to guard the door.** They watched me as though I were the country's number one enemy.

I sank down into the chair at my desk. I picked up a pen, but my hands were trembling too much to write. I know that I was terrified, but I was conscious mainly of confusion. I kept thinking that it was all a mistake. I sat for at least an hour, my head in my hands, trying to make my thoughts seem rational. For the first time, I knew the incredulous desperation of a campaign victim. . . . The simple truth was, however, that I still did not know enough about the mills' operations to have any idea concerning what I could confess.

*In 1952, the Chinese government launched a new mass campaign which became known as the "Five-Antis," and its stated objectives were to eliminate five major sins of the bourgeoisie: bribery, tax evasion, stealing government property, cheating on contracts, and stealing State secrets. The last "sin" referred to the act of discovering the government intention, for example, to buy up certain commodities and then to use that knowledge to make excessive profit. A number of businessmen had profiteered in this fashion during the Korean War, and up to now most businessmen were managing to make adequate profits despite extensive government controls. Prior to this campaign the government had launched the Thought Reform campaign to root out wrong thoughts among intellectuals but was in fact aimed at intellectuals themselves. This also coincided with the Three-Antis campaign to eliminate corruption among civil employees, although its effect was to eliminate old employees.

**During these mass campaigns the party used cadres called "tiger beaters" who entered business firms and selected "activists" whom they organized into teams of "beaters" to flush out the "capitalist tiger."

Later that morning some staff members entered and, without speaking or looking at me, put up some posters on the wall where I could see them from my desk. On the largest was a caricature of me. I was shown with the thick upswept hairdo that was then peculiar to young American hoodlums, and my tie was covered with dollar signs. This typed me as an American-educated capitalist. I was shown holding a paper marked CONFESSION, but the paper contained only an onionskin and a feather; this indicated that my confession dealt only with unimportant matters and evaded the important points. And I still had no idea what to confess. The other posters contained such slogans as CRUSH THE VICIOUS ATTACK OF THE CAPITALIST CLASS, SURRENDER, YOU VILE CAPITALIST, A COMPLETE CONFESSION IS THE ROAD TO SURVIVAL—ANYTHING LESS WILL LEAD TO DEATH.

Just before noon, technicians entered and installed a loudspeaker in one of the office windows. A few minutes past noon, it sputtered once and then burst into an ear-splitting racket. I gathered that a mass meeting of the employees was being held in the main dining hall. It went on for the entire lunch period. Most of it was a harangue against the unscrupulous capitalists. I realized that activists were working up the crowd to a frenzy, and now I was aware of nothing but fear. I did not know what might happen at the next moment.

When the mass meeting was over at 2 P.M., individual beaters took over the microphone to address me directly. They shouted abuse, insults and threats, and they admonished me constantly to make my confession full. Occasionally, the loudspeaker would cease, but before my nerves could loosen in the blissful silence, the shouting would begin again. At 5 P.M., I listened to another mass meeting and again felt the terror of unleashed mob violence.

At 6, the mill cook brought me a blanket, which he dropped on the floor, and a bowl of noodles which he put gingerly on the edge of my desk; he ran as though I were a dangerous animal.

I requested then to be allowed to go to the toilet, but my guards accompanied me. They would not allow me to close the door to the cubicle. Later, back in the office, my guards were changed for another pair of tiger beaters who stared at me with visible hatred.

When I tried to sleep, wrapped in the blanket on the floor, the guards would not allow the light to be turned off and they sat silently only a few feet away, never taking their eyes off me.

On the morning of the third day, a beater entered and ordered me to follow him to the Party Secretary's office. I had tried desperately to imagine what was wanted of me but had been unable to think of anything to confess.

As I walked through the building the employees jeered and called such insults as "capitalist swine," "unscrupulous dog" and "counterattack the vicious capitalist class." Those whom I passed closely spat at me and some tried to strike, but my guards prevented them. The employees who were loudest and most vehement in their insults were those with whom I had been the most friendly. At first, this cut me deeply, but then I realized that precisely *because* they had been friendly to me, they would be the ones threatened the most and for their own safety they would strain to show that they no longer had anything but hatred and contempt for a capitalist criminal like me. Oddly enough, this thought made me feel better. It was the first evidence I had had that the whole nightmare was being staged.

I entered the Party Secretary's office, realizing that this was the first time I had been made to come to him; previously, he had always maintained the pretense of my authority and had come to my office. Now he did not even rise from his desk. He held out his hand without looking up. "Your confession," he said.

"I am sorry. I have tried hard but so far I am unable to think of anything to confess," I said. I tried to sound calm but humble. "Perhaps it is because I am stupid—"

"Stupid!" he interrupted. "When the people ask you to confess you suddenly become stupid. Yet when you were exploiting the people you seemed to be very smart." He suddenly got up from his chair. I could see that he was trying to control what seemed to be real anger. Pointing his finger at my nose, he said, "You capitalists seem to think you can commit endless crimes against the people and pretend you have done nothing . . ."

"I want to confess everything, but I just don't know how," I answered.

The Party Secretary sat down again. "You had better stop pretending," he said. "I warn you, Loh, the people's patience has its limits. We will give you two more days, and if you do not have a full confession by then, we may not be able to prevent your arrest."

I spent two more days of torment—wearing the same clothes, going without shaving or washing, enduring the constant scrutiny of my guards and listening to the blasting loudspeaker while I wracked my brains for some crime that I might logically confess to. But it was still no use. When I was taken again to the Party Secretary's office I really felt I would not return. Although my failure infuriated the Party Secretary, however, he gave me one more chance: a full confession within 14 hours. I was in complete despair as I was escorted through the crowd of jeering employees back to my office.

An hour later, one of the accountants entered with his books. I was shocked, because no employee had been allowed to enter my office since the day of my detainment. The accountant banged an account book down on my desk and pointed to an inventory entry. "Did you ever realize where your property came from?" he asked. He tapped his finger against an entry which showed 30,000 gunny bags. Before I could answer, he had thrown open another old account book from the days of the Japanese occupation and pointed out a similar number of gunny bags. While I was trying to gather my wits enough to find meaning in all this, the accountant kept up a stream of accusations and questions—"How can you run a business if you do not know what is going on? How can you pretend to be blameless when you are guilty of stealing the people's property?" Finally I realized that these 30,000 gunny bags, which had been absorbed into our inventory in 1946, had originally come from the Japanese. Thus they should have belonged next to the Nationalists and then to "the people" under the present regime. This was my crime!

I felt a rush of relief. This was not because my danger was any less, but because this whole drama was being carefully staged, I thought I knew now the part I was expected to play. I wrote up my confession quickly and that afternoon I asked to see the Party Secretary to give it to him.

The Communist glanced at my paper briefly. Then suddenly

he wadded it up violently and threw it on the floor. "How dare you insult the people by pretending that you were guilty of such an insignificant amount?" he shouted at me. "I warn you for the last time, Loh. You will make a *full* confession or suffer the fate you bring on yourself."

Now, however, the Party Secretary's bluster did not frighten me as much, but I was depressed by the realization that my role was to be long and drawn out. I understood that my "confession" was to be squeezed out of me piecemeal. I was to play the stubborn hardened criminal while the Communists were clever, thorough officials who worked tirelessly in the people's behalf to uncover all my crimes. Back in my office, I had to endure another full day of agonizing suspense before the accountant appeared to point out another vague item which enabled me to confess to a further act of embezzlement. Six times my "confession" was rejected, and each time the number of my acts of embezzlement was increased. These crimes now totaled more than a hundred, and not one of them would stand up under even a casual scrutiny of the mills' affairs. The last felony, added to the list for my seventh and final "confession," was the most ludicrous of all. In 1950, the Communist authorities had submitted to J. P. [the mill manager] a contract which he had signed with them and which had stipulated that the mills were to grind 80 million carries of wheat into flour. The officially specified ratio required the mills to produce 65 carries of white flour for every 100 carries of wheat received; any amount of flour or byproducts milled in excess of the 65 carries was to be the firm's fee. The Communists now charged that the ratio should have been 70 carries of flour per 100 carries of wheat, and that originally the cadres had been unscrupulously lured into signing what was supposed to be an unfair contract. Thus, they charged that I owed "the people" for four million carries of flour. This amounted to JMP 800,000 (US $335,000). The casual way in which they repudiated a contract they themselves had submitted and signed was bad enough, but I could hardly believe that they wanted me to make myself culpable for an incident of this magnitude that had happened almost two years before I came to the mills.

Nevertheless, when the Party Secretary received my seventh

confession he remarked, "At last, I believe your confession is *relatively* thorough." He passed the papers around to his subordinates, who glanced at them and nodded sagely as though they also had arrived independently at the same judgment. "But the final verdict, of course, is with the masses," I was told. "You will now write out an expression of your attitude concerning your crimes."

By this the Party Secretary meant that I should "beg the masses for forgiveness," throw myself on their mercy and thank the Communist Party for its help in guiding me toward a true understanding of my evil and its consequences. I had read and heard the accepted "expression of attitude" often enough so that I was able to write one myself without effort.

A few hours after finishing it, I faced the climax of my "struggle." The tiger beaters propelled me roughly into the mills' dining hall, which was filled with every one of our employees. My entrance was the signal for a tremendous uproar. The screams of rage, the shouted slogans and insults, were deafening. I was made to stand with humbly bowed head before the small stage on which the Communist officials sat at tables. I had lost 13 pounds. I was filthy, unshaven and exhausted. My knees trembled with both weakness and fear. The shouting behind me was turned off suddenly. The Party Secretary rose and read off the list of the people's charges against me. When he finished, he commanded me to "face the masses;" I had to turn and bow with complete humility to the crowd. The shouting began once more.

When the noise was turned off again, the Party Secretary asked if anyone had accusations to make against "this capitalist." One by one, now, representatives from each of the employee groups—the old workers, the young workers, the electricians, the separate departments, etc.—came to the stage to denounce me. The worst accusations were made by those whom I had known best, but now I understood and sympathized with these people. I could see the pain in the eyes of some as they stumbled over their memorized speeches. Nevertheless, I listened carefully to the accusations, believing that in the stories they told of my evil deeds I would have a clue to my fate. All of the accusations, however, were only of crimes associated with my class. In a typical story, for example, an old worker said that ten years previously his wife had been ill and he had begged the manager for 5 yuan for medicine. He had not only been refused, he had been temporarily fired from his job, and his wife had died. He now pointed dramatically at me. "You thieving unscrupulous capitalist," he shrieked, real tears on his face, "my wife's blood drips from your hands."

Another old man occasioned the moment I remember clearest. He mounted to the platform, bent and feeble. He paused for a moment, his eyes closed, trying to remember, I think, his prepared speech. "Mr. Manager . . ." he began. All the others had addressed me only with epithets, of which "capitalist dog" was perhaps the mildest. Decades of habitual respect for "the management," however, prevented the old fellow from addressing me in the new unfamiliar terms the tiger beaters had taught him. He got no further with his speech. Two beaters jumped up to the platform, grabbed him by the shoulders and shoved him toward the stairs. The old man stumbled down them and would have fallen if members of the audience had not caught him. The look of pain and confusion on the old man's face haunts me still, and at this moment I came the closest to breaking down completely.

The beaters covered the awkward moment by leading another outbreak of slogan shouting.

The accusations took almost three hours. Thereafter, I was made to mount the platform. I read my confession in a weak voice. Then I begged the masses to forgive my sins and to give me one more chance to serve the people. I also thanked the great Communist Party which, under the wise and benevolent leadership of Chairman Mao, had instigated this great campaign. Because of the campaign, I had learned to recognize the evil in me and thus had a chance to make a new man of myself before it was too late.

When I finished, the Party Secretary again addressed the crowd. "Can any of you bring to light further crimes committed by this capitalist?" he asked. I sensed that this was the climactic moment for me. If the authors of this drama intended my role to be tragic, an actor or two from the audience would now accuse me of crimes that had not been specified for me to confess. I closed my eyes and held my breath.

But the masses were mute. Finally, the Party Secretary said, "I assume, then, that the masses regard the confession of this capitalist as relatively thorough." He cautioned the crowd, however, to continue to look for further of my misdeeds which would necessitate reopening my case.

The Secretary turned to me. "Loh, you have confessed the sins you committed and you have promised not to commit such sins again," he said. "Do you mean this? Are you sincere?"

"I am completely sincere," I said. The Secretary turned back to the crowd and raised his hand. Finally, I would know my fate. "I now declare," he said, "that the great Five-Anti Campaign for our mills has been completed with 100 percent success." This was answered by a burst of joyous cheering from the crowd. I was too dazed for a moment to realize that it was over and that I was free. Of course, I owed the government JMP 1,200,000 which I did not have, but at least I had been spared sudden death from a policeman's bullet or slow death from labor reform. An hour later, I was home. I shaved, bathed, drank a bowl of soup and went to bed for ten hours of sleep.

✳   ✳   ✳

In December 1953, the authorities suddenly announced the so-called "General Line." And from then on the fate that the regime had in store for us was no longer in doubt.

"The General Line and the General Task for the Transitional Period," we were told, would be to complete the "foundation for a socialist society." This was the first time that the word "socialism" had appeared as an aspect of official policy. Previously, whenever the question had been raised as to why socialism was not mentioned in the Common Program, the answer had been that socialism was too remote for consideration. In the present period, we were supposedly building the New Democracy which would need to be perfected before the plans for socialism could be made. Now, however, Mao announced that we *had* been building toward socialism since October 1, 1949. This was such a complete contradiction of what had been stated previously that much of the material published on policy during the past four years had to be withdrawn from circulation. Meanwhile, the top leaders were making marathon speeches to proclaim and explain the new Line.

Now began the tiresome effort of attending endless meetings on the subject of the General Line. It is important to understand that from the beginning of the regime, the entire population had been divided into groups which were subdivided into "mass" organizations. Every person was forced to belong to a mass organization of his group. Thus, for example, professors had to join the Educational Workers Union. Students had their own union. Every peasant belonged to a branch of the Peasants Association. Housewives came under their respective Residents Associations, which were divided into district, street and lane branches. Normally, everyone was made to attend meetings of his organization once a week, but during special campaigns the number and length of the meetings increased greatly. At the meetings, the pretense was scrupulously maintained that the regime's current policy was discussed by the people. The inference was that through discussion the people arrived at their own conclusions about the policy.

Actually, however, the Communists introduced their own conclusions in advance. Thereupon, the people went through the motions of discussing the policy; they praised it and finally gave in their "unanimous support." No one was allowed to avoid giving his comment, which might have to be rephrased many times before the organization officials were satisfied. The individual's response, behavior and attitude were under constant scrutiny. If he earned the disapproval of the officials, the other members of his group were made to turn on him; the others feared the same treatment if they did not.

Thus, although the individual belonged to a group, his greatest danger came from the group—from the only people who normally would be expected to understand, help and protect him. The result was that he knew the terror of being utterly alone and vulnerable in a hostile society. In the neighborhood where he lived, the census police kept a constant check on his movements. In his place of employment, the Communist officials ensured that he made an adequate contribution to the regime. But the control over his behavior, exercised by the officials of his mass organization, was absolute. The meetings therefore were a fearful strain.

At the same time, they were stultifyingly dull, and the idea of the number of them you would have to attend down through the years made the future difficult to face. I can remember only one amusing incident associated with these meetings. At a lane meeting in 1954, an old servant of ours was made to express her opinion on the draft of the new Constitution. The poor woman was senile and illiterate. In the Shanghai dialect, the words for "constitution" and "magician's trick" are pronounced the same. To the old woman, the whole discussion seemed to concern "supporting the new magician's trick." Finally, she managed to say, "During my seventy-three years I can recall having seen only one magician's trick. The People's Government which is now about to perform a magic trick, therefore, has my support. I am determined to witness it." The cadres were furious; no one dared to laugh, but the officials sensed the ridicule of the others. In punishment, the meeting was not allowed to break up until, hours later, the old lady had been taught to say something acceptable about the Constitution.

I belonged to two mass organizations. One was the Democratic League which I had joined while still at the university. It was for intellectuals. It was Communist-sponsored and -controlled, but was intended to create the impression that the regime democratically permitted political parties other than the Communist one to function. After going to the flour mills, I had joined in addition the local branch of the All-China Federation of Industry and Commerce, a front organization which had replaced the old Chamber of Commerce. In December 1953, when the authorities presented the new policy of the General Line for "discussion," I had to attend meetings on this subject sponsored by both organizations. We learned that private trade, industry, agriculture and even handicrafts would be taken over gradually by the State. Henceforth, the Party policy toward private enterprise would be to "utilize, restrict and remold." Private enterprise would be fitted into the framework of the overall national economic plan. The present owners eventually would become "self-supporting laborers." Meanwhile, pilot projects would be set up as models from which we could learn what to expect.

Most of us expected the worst. We were confused only by the fact that the regime appeared to be trying to warn us in advance, whereas their usual tactic had been to cover up their real objectives with false promises and assurances. Some took this new approach to mean that the regime had learned its lesson from Five-Anti and now was attempting to be honest with us; they hoped that our fate might be no worse than the authorities described it. Others, however, felt that the regime considered us so beaten down that elaborate deception was no longer necessary.

Charlie [a manager of the factory] and I had our first premonition of what the regime now planned for us at a mass meeting for prominent businessmen addressed by Shanghai's mayor. After describing the meaning of the General Line for the Transitional Period leading toward socialism, the mayor said, "You national capitalist friends are now approaching your first and most important barrier—the socialist barrier. It will not be easy to cross . . ."

All we had gone through previously, we were to understand, had been nothing. Only *now* were our difficulties in preparing for the "first barrier" beginning. I remember the look on Charlie's face. He had been badly shaken by his experience in Five-Anti, but now I saw him sink into utter hopelessness. I think my feelings were the same. The mayor added that although we would have to manage the climb over the barrier ourselves, he would see that no one died in the attempt. He reminded us that the Party was always ready to extend us help and advice. Our past experience with the regime's "help and advice" allowed us no illusions about our new status.

The fact that our status had changed drastically was immediately apparent in my job at the mills. The Communists were openly contemptuous of me as well as of the workers. With me, the Party Secretary began a kind of cat-and-mouse game designed to humiliate and demoralize me to the extent that I would never for a moment forget the power held over me.

By this time, the mills were operating entirely on a fee basis. The authorities sent us wheat and paid us a set amount to grind it into flour. In early 1954, however, the fee was lowered and the amount of wheat sent to us was cut until our labor force had only five or six days of work a month. Nevertheless, we had to pay the workers for full time, and we were not permitted to dismiss any of them. Our income now would not cover our payroll, but we were not permitted to go out of business. The whole situation was blamed on my evil capitalist ways; all I could do was to apply for bank loans and hope for a change.

Thus, in addition to the dishonesty of the life I led and the degradation of the job I was doing, I also was made to act out a pantomime on the evils of capitalism. I spent most of my time pretending I was a businessman engaged in the private enterprise of applying for a loan. While I humbled myself before the arrogant Party Secretary who acted as Manager and ran the bank, the Party Secretary who ran my mills knew whether I would get the money, but I did not. On the days when he knew I would return empty-handed, he would have the workers stage the sort of reception he considered best calculated to demoralize me. Sometimes I would face their scorn and derision as though I were a stupid and miserable failure. Again, I might contend with their sorrow and pain as though I were a heartless brute whose indifference was responsible for their children's hunger. And worst of all, I might face their unleashed fury as though, because of my criminal greed, I denied them their hard-earned pittance; many times I feared that the mob of my workers would get out of the cadres' control and that I would be thrown bodily into the river. Nevertheless, at the last minute the bank always provided just enough funds to put off the crisis for a few days; frequently the amount I received covered only the payroll — without my own salary.

*   *   *

The "Elimination of Counter-Revolutionaries" [launched in early 1955] began with an all-out propaganda attack on a well-known writer named Hu Feng. He had been pro-Marxist since the 1930s and had been one of the early members of a Communist front organization called the Left Wing Writers Group. The authorities, however, wanted writers to serve only the workers, peasants and soldiers. To this end, writers were subjected to such strict control that they either gave up in despair and merely turned out uninspired propaganda or they made the effort to retain their individuality. Those of the latter group were generally the older and long-established writers, and they always were in more or less open conflict with the authorities.

Hu Feng was an outspoken member of this group. He believed, for example, that political indoctrination for writers could be profitably abolished and that certain literary magazines should be exempt from Party control. Worse, he apparently led a group of like-minded writers and attempted through concerted action to persuade the authorities to his viewpoint. Party policies, however, were to be implemented—never questioned—and even the hint of united opposition to them was sure to bring swift retaliation.

Thus people at group meetings throughout the country suddenly found themselves denouncing Hu Feng and his clique. Next we found ourselves examining his ideas and looking for any similarities between them and our own. Finally, we were engaged in a full-scale campaign to uncover any "counter-revolutionary" thinking among the fellow members of our particular discussion groups.

The Elimination of Counter-Revolutionaries was not as brutal as Thought Reform had been, but it followed a similar procedure. Everyone classed as an intellectual prepared an autobiography that began at the age of eight and concentrated on the ideas he had had during his lifetime. Each paper, then, was studied by the other members of the author's group who searched for evidence of past unacceptable ideas. Generally, the cadres allowed most of the autobiographies of a group to be passed with only token criticism and warnings, but they chose from each group one or two "heavy points" who received concentrated attention. A heavy point endured pressure from his fellow group members to confess the "real truth" of his past thinking. The suffering of this unfortunate was intended as an object lesson for his companions, who would thus be discouraged from harboring unacceptable ideas. In my discussion group, to my dismay, I found that I was made the heavy point.

No matter what I wrote in my autobiography, my companions rejected it. And with each rejection, the scorn, insults and threats they heaped on me grew worse. During the day in my office at the mills, I faced much the same from the workers. No one who has never lived day and night as the focal point of such vilification and hatred can understand the effect it has. I could think of nothing but the paper I was having to write and rewrite endlessly. I was long past caring what I confessed to; I only wanted desperately to discover what the Communists expected of me.

At the same time I did not expect to be accused and punished as a counter-revolutionary. In my case, no real evidence of unacceptable thinking existed; moreover, I had given every indication that I supported the regime and endorsed Party policies. I remembered the case of my friend Professor Long who, during Thought Reform, had broken under pressure and had confessed to crimes of which the authorities later exonerated him; nevertheless, because he had collapsed he had been regarded as being "unable to stand up to the test of political purity." Thus I guessed that I was merely being tested, and my only real fear was that, through some unwitting mistake, I might fail to pass.

✳   ✳   ✳

I can recall the moment when living in Communist China became intolerable for me. It was at 11:05 P.M. on July 7, 1954. The night had been stifling in Shanghai, and rain had fallen earlier. When I came out of the Democratic League Building into Bubbling Well Road, the wet streets seemed to make the air too thick to breathe.

I was exhausted. I had just been to the third meeting in six days of my Communist-sponsored political discussion group. After a long day in my office at the flour mills, the physical effort of attending these meetings was bad enough, but the strain was worse. The smallest error—a mistaken response, a wrong gesture, a slip of the tongue—could mean catastrophe. People who live with fear eventually lose their awareness of it, but the tension remains and has serious effects. What bothered me most was constant fatigue. I desperately needed more rest in order to stay sufficiently alert for the continual struggle to survive.

In this, however, I was no different from the others in the crowd I joined that night in Bubbling Well Road. As always, I was surprised to find so many people still up at this hour. In the old days, of course, the streets had been crowded at every hour. Neon signs would have been garishly bright, and the people would have been dressed in many different styles and colors. They would have milled about, some moving quickly and others slowly. And above the traffic sounds, their voices would have been heard, chattering, calling, cursing, shouting, laughing.

But now no one spoke. The only sound was the shuffling of thousands of feet. Everyone moved at the same tired pace. Everyone had the same worried look and wore similar drab clothes. The only light came from the street lamps that made dim yellow pools at regular intervals along the wet pavement. Occasionally a motorcar swished by, arrogantly important.

Like me, the others still up had been to the grimly serious political meetings and were intent only on getting to bed.

I had gone the few paces to the corner of Gordon Road, however, when I suddenly came alive. Moving toward me out of the shadows was a face I knew better than any other. It belonged to Li-li [his former girlfriend]. I had not seen her for two years, but she was seldom out of my thoughts. Even in a shapeless uniform, she was beautiful. From Li-li I had learned how close it was possible to be to another human being; I think that neither of us was ever really complete without the other.

And now we found ourselves unexpectedly face to face. The pace, the time and the crowd were forgotten. We were aware only of each other. The moment lasted an age in which was concentrated all the anguish and bliss that knowing Li-li had meant.

But then the moment was gone. Li-li vanished into the crowd. I felt sharp pain as I realized she had made no sign of recognizing me. I knew that she had felt my presence, but not one muscle had betrayed it; her pace had not faltered, her facial expression had not changed, and no light had come into her eyes.

I was struck then by another realization that was even worse. During that moment of awareness with her, I too had completely hidden my feelings. Not even the most sharp-eyed observer would have suspected that Li-li and I had ever met.

What made this seem so shocking was not that under the Communist regime our romance had been thwarted. Lovers can be kept apart by many circumstances in any society. Moreover, I knew that the Communists were indifferent to our feelings; they were concerned only with how we acted. Li-li and I that night reacted instinctively. Each of us feared that recognition might expose the other to danger. The instinctive reaction made me realize that the Communists, simply by applying constantly the stimulus of fear, had acquired such complete control over us that our actions could be made to deny our most natural and decent inclinations.

At home that night, I tossed and turned for hours on hot damp sheets. Having faced the fact that the Communists completely controlled my behavior, I considered fully for the first time just how I was being made to behave. At this point, I perceived how much I had been deluding myself about the Communists' intentions, for when I saw myself clearly as they had remolded me, I was filled with loathing and horror. I felt that if I were ever again to become a self-respecting human being, I would have to be free.

By all logical reasoning, however, my chances of getting away from Communist control were nil. An unsuccessful attempt would mean the end of me. Nevertheless, just before dawn rain fell again and for a moment a cool breeze refreshed my room. I made up my mind. Thereafter, every thought I had, every action I took, every word I spoke would be toward an objective: to devise and implement a successful plan to escape.

*   *   *

[Through a clever ruse in which Loh pretended he had to return to Hong Kong to receive his father's estate, the government allowed him to leave mainland China with the expectation he would return with his inheritance. He did not. —ED.]

· 7 ·

HAROLD WILLIAM RIGNEY

A Priest's Tale About Faith in Hell

FATHER WILLIAM RIGNEY'S moving account of his four years in a Chinese prison in the early 1950s revealed in lurid detail the persecution of Christians in Communist China. Although *Four Years in a Red Hell* (1956) lacked the literary quality of Elinor Lipper's prison memoir, Rigney's book conveyed an uncompromising religious faith that allowed him to endure mental and physical torture by his captors.

Arrested in 1951 as an American spy, Rigney spent fifty months in the Communist prisons of Tsao Lan Tzu Hutung and Tzu Hsing Lu. Despite physical torture, sleeplessness, hunger, and fear of death, he refused to confess to being an agent of the U.S. government or to admit that his religious order, the Divine Word Missionary Organization, was under the control of the U.S. government. From his experiences he concluded that Chinese Communists were worse than Soviet Communists. Quoting the words of an emigré Russian who had witnessed the Bolsheviks in power, Rigney told his readers, "The Chinese Communists employ a subtlety in their tortures, unknown even to the Russian Communists. The Russians line prisoners up and shoot them, sometimes mowing down masses of them with machine guns, but the Chinese Communists do worse. They use refined, cunning tortures of which the Russians are ignorant and which are worse than death."

Rigney's account of his prison experiences found a large readership in the United States, especially among Roman

Catholics. His arrest and imprisonment sparked a massive letter-writing campaign by American Catholics. More than 65,000 letters written by Catholic schoolchildren were sent to President Eisenhower calling for Rigney's release. Letters from more than 300 Catholic school principals demanded that the U.S. government intervene in his case. Television and radio programs about his imprisonment were broadcast across the nation. Prayers were said on his behalf in Masses. Marguerite Church, James Murray, Charles Boyle, Melvin Price, and John McCormack spoke on his behalf from the floor of Congress. Senator Paul H. Douglas of Illinois submitted a concurrent resolution calling for his release. The campaign was taken by Roman Catholics to parishes in Canada, Africa, the Philippines, and Europe. After he was released following this public campaign, Rigney's book became widely read by American Catholics and the general public.

Educated at the University of Chicago Divinity School and ordained in 1937, Rigney had come to China to serve as rector of the Roman Catholic university in Beijing (Fu Jen Catholic University of Beijing), a school of 2,500 students, most of them non-Christians. As he writes in his memoir, he was given the appointment of rector "not because of great scholarship, which I do not have, or a rich background of experience in China, which I do not have, but because I was an American, an ex-commissioned officer and chaplain, fresh from the U.S. Army, with a Doctor of Philosophy degree in Geology." Although a modest man, Rigney was a man of courage, the kind of man needed to head an American university under attack by the new government.

Although only a small percentage of his students were Roman Catholic, Rigney organized the student body against Communist agitators within the university who in late 1946 initiated a series of strikes and street demonstrations. All of this, he later wrote, was "'criminal' according to the Communists: 'crimes' against the 'people' of China, 'crimes' of sabotage of the religious reformation movement in the New China." In 1950, Fu Jen was officially taken over by the Communist government, and Rigney was ordered home by his order's superior general in Rome. Before he was able to leave, he was arrested as a spy.

Throughout his book he conveys a strong spiritual faith that resonated with his Christian readers. His words were intended to inspire others in the struggle against atheistic communism. Concluding, he asks what he has learned from his experiences. He answers that physically he has lost much, but spiritually and educationally he has profited: "Although throughout my imprisonment I was unable to celebrate the Holy Sacrifice of the Mass, to receive Our Blessed Lord in Holy Communion, to visit Our Blessed Lord in Blessed Sacrament, to pray my Divine Office—all losses of inestimable spiritual value—I did suffer with my Divine Savior. I was also granted a deeper insight into the bitter sufferings of Our Blessed Lord in His Holy Passion." His message was clear to his readers: if Christ could endure suffering for the salvation of humankind, little was it to suffer in combat with the Communists.

Rigney reiterated a theme common to gulag literature—the Communists could not be trusted. "I have learned," he said, "that Chinese Communists are not to be trusted. This holds for all that brood of vipers from Mao Tse-tung who betrayed China to the Kremlin, from the smooth suave Chou En-lai who has deceived and is still pulling the wool over the eyes of many outstanding statesmen and politicians in many parts of the world, on down to the last received member of the party who is every inch an unthinking puppet, dancing to the hideous tune of his masters, who in turn are controlled by the Kremlin." He concludes by warning against complacency of "a slumbering, self-satisfied, overconfident free world." The Communist conspiracy was real and needed to be combated by a people willing to defend their cherished liberties.

His words inspired thousands of average Americans who were to join the fight against the Communist threat at home and abroad at the height of the cold war.

On October 12, 1950, Fu Jen was officially "taken over," better confiscated or stolen, by the communist government of China.

On October 19, 1950, I received a cable from my Superior General in Rome, ordering me to return to the U.S.A.

On the following Monday, I applied for my exit permit. This was necessary in order to leave China.

Day after day, week after week, month after month, I called at the Bureau of Foreign Affairs of the Peking Police for my exit permit but was always told, it had not come through.

In the previous August 1950, I had applied for a renewal of my residential permit but this was denied me — I was not allowed to live in China.

So, from October 23, 1950 until my arrest, I was not allowed to live in China and I was denied the permission to leave China.

Such inconsistencies are common in communist China.

I was informed by a friend of mine in November, 1950, of a way of escaping from Red China. This friend gave the name, address and telephone number of a person who could and would smuggle me out of China.

All I had to do was to present myself to this person, tell him my name and the name of my friend, and in an hour or so, I would be on my way out of communist China.

I thanked my friend for this kind offer but declined to avail myself of it.

This was because I wanted to wait until the release of Father Peter Huengsberg, S.V.D., of the Fu Jen University staff, who had been arrested on September 29, 1950. I expected him to be released any time, and I wanted to be around when he returned from prison so I could help him leave China.

Then, too, I thought that if I were smuggled out of China, all who knew me would be in danger of being punished by the communists.

As time went on, I was more and more avoided by those I knew, until finally, I was practically deserted by all.

No one visited me.

Hardly anyone recognized me on the street.

From *Four Years in a Red Hell: The Story of Father Rigney* (Chicago, 1956), pp. 21–23, 25–28, 56–58, 86–89, 90–99, 100–104, 137–140, 155–157.

Usually, if a Chinese who knew me saw me coming, he or she turned and went in the opposite direction, or simply refused to look at me, on passing.

Friends and acquaintances destroyed all their photographs that featured me—destroyed all evidences, as letters, recommendations, books, indications of ever having known me, spoken to me or received any benefit from me.

I was abandoned.

Staff members and students of Fu Jen, many of whom I had helped, now turned against me, accused me to the police, requesting my arrest, in order to save themselves.

Yet, I understood and forgave them because I knew these good people were under great pressure at the hands of the communists, forcing them to act against their conscience.

*   *   *

July 25, 1951, was a day when a decision was to be reached whether or not the cease-fire talks at Kaesong, Korea, were to be resumed. I had felt unwell and consequently taken a rather long rest after my noon dinner. At about 3:40 P.M., I arose, with the intention of listening in to the "Voice of America" broadcast at 4 o'clock, to learn whether or not the ceasefire talks in Korea were to be resumed.

As I started to dress, I was startled by the sound of many men running near my living quarters. I looked up through a window and saw the top of a helmet dart by. Alarmed, I looked out of another window and saw many policemen in helmets with tommy guns surrounding my residence. A group of about six of them formed in a line, about 50 feet from the entrance of my residence, in battle formation, with their rifles pointed at the door and windows of my cabin-like residence. I then knew that what I had been expecting for twenty months, since the communist armies occupied Peiping, February 1, 1949, and especially for the last ten months, since the "People's" government of China had taken over Fu Jen University, was about to take place—I was to be arrested.

I dressed as fast as I could. A policeman looked in my bedroom and saw me. He then went to my door and beat on it demanding that I open it, which I did. In a moment my living quarters were filled with armed Sepo (Security Police). Two of them seized me by the arms while other policemen made a hurried search of my bedroom and toilet. As I had only my shorts, pants, shoes, and socks on, a shirt was quickly gotten from my bedroom and given to me to put on. A silver medal of the Blessed Virgin Mary on a silver chain, a gift of my brother, hanging around my neck, was taken off. I was then handcuffed with my hands behind my back. A policewoman showed me a cardlike paper and spoke in Chinese, then in English, saying, "You are arrested as an American spy." To this I could only wryly smile. Another policeman took my picture.

I was arrested!

My brain was flooded with thoughts and conjectures. I thought the Korean cease-fire talks had been called off, that a state of declared war existed between Red China and my country, the U.S.A., and as a consequence I was being arrested by the communists in retaliation against the U.S.A. I thought I might be taken out and shot as hundreds of Chinese had been since the beginning of the year. I also thought that I might be questioned and given rough treatment for a few hours or days and then deported, like other missionaries, as Bishop de Vienne of Tientsin. I was in a daze. I did not know what was in store for me.

I was then led out to the entrance of the compound where I lived, and ordered to stand there, facing a group of what seemed like 40 or 50 little children of the parish catechism school with their teacher. These little children knew me and loved me very much. Whenever they saw me, they would run up and surround me, holding my hands and arms, all laughing and talking at the same time.

Now it was so different!

These little creatures had evidently been drilled by the communist police to gather where they did and clap, approving my arrest. Children of lower primary school age, they were too young to hide their emotions.

I shall never forget that scene!

Handcuffed, I looked at them. Their little faces were distorted and torn by strong conflicting emotions: fear of the cruel communist police; love and sympathy for me, in chains. The poor little creatures were all crying. Some faintly clapped their little hands. Under inhuman pressure, they were forced to act against their finest, deepest, noblest sentiments. My brain was full of thoughts. I thought of what I had heard, how the Chinese communists had forced children to sign death petitions, requesting the execution of their fathers, and wives of their husbands. My heart went out to these tortured little children before me. Their evident sympathy for me consoled me. I blessed them, making a little sign of the cross with my right hand, handcuffed behind my back, and I thought that I needed no further proof or demonstration of the intrinsic malice of communism that so distorted, so twisted and so worked to destroy the finest, the noblest, the deepest sentiments in the hearts of little children!

My picture was taken again and I was then ordered onto a jeep, an American-made jeep, with 3 or 4 police guards. The rest of the Sepo boarded a truck. I was then driven in front of Fu Jen University, where all could see me in disgrace, in chains, being driven away by the dreaded Sepo. We turned south on the busy Hsi Szu Pai Lou Ta Chieh to the next street south of Hsi Szu Pai Lou, where we turned east to Ts'ao Lan Tzu Hutung, near the National Library. The jeep stopped at No. 13 of the hutung before a high red gate and blew its horn, signaling to the guard to open the gate. As I looked at the gate, I thought of the words Dante placed over the gates of hell: "Abandon all hope ye who enter here."

The gate slowly opened.

The jeep drove in. I was ordered out and placed in a little room. I wondered what was next. Was I to be shot? Was I to be deported immediately? Was I to be questioned then deported? In about 5 minutes a policeman came, removed my handcuffs and ordered me into a little nearby office where I was searched and my rosary, watch, fountain pen, Sheaffer pencil, knife and money were taken away from me. A list of these articles was then written up and I signed it first in English, then in Chinese. Lastly my fingerprint was added.

I was then led to a dark, damp corridor in an old one-story building, to Cell No. 10.

The heavy wooden door was opened with a clang of the iron

bolt and I was ordered to enter. The door was then slammed and bolted with a bang.

I was in prison!

*   *   *

During my first sixty days and nights of imprisonment, I had two full nights of rest. In the latter part of these days, my physical reserves were at an end.

I was subjected to the nerve racking of long court sessions during the night as well as the day. I was exhausted from lack of sleep. I was tortured by a gnawing hunger; I was covered with bodily dirt and weeks of unwashed perspiration. My one and only set of clothes, that were literally falling to shreds, were infested with lice. My ankles and wrists, sore and bleeding from the fetters and handcuffs I wore, were in extreme pain. My legs and arms were swollen from these shackles. Often, especially in the long night court sessions when I perspired profusely, I was tormented by thirst. I had never cared much for tea, but often as I was plagued by thirst, as the judge quaffed cup after cup of tea, serving himself and the recorder and interpreter, my mouth watered in vain, for a cup of tea. I thought that if I ever would become a free man again, I would drink tea, a gallon of tea. I had been subjected to endless humiliation and insults.

In this state of wretchedness I was called out of my cell one night around 9:45 P.M., the time for retiring. There was nothing unusual about such a call. But this call opened up an unusual experience for me, unusual even for my Ts'ao Lan Tzu experiences.

The Sepo guard directed me to a room in a courtyard adjoining the courtrooms.

The male interpreter was there. He told me to sit on a soft sofa. This was unusual treatment—apparent kindness. He then began to talk to me in soft, unctuous words, explaining how I could help myself by confessing my crimes. Such would lead to clemency on the part of the government. The court had dealt harshly, it is true, with me, he explained, but I would experience a bountiful generosity on the part of the government if I would only confess. It would not take long, only about an hour of confessing to clear up my case. Why be so obstinate? The government did not want me to suffer but to enjoy life. I was only harming myself by being stubborn, preventing the government from showing how benevolent it could be.

So he went on for about one hour. I, struggling to keep awake, told him I would like to clear up my case but I had no crimes to confess.

He was a little ruffled by this but continued his cajoling line. I was favorably impressed by his "kindness."

I was then led to the courtroom and told to sit down.

This was unusual.

Formerly, for weeks, I was obliged to stand at attention during my court sessions. This night, however, the judge magnanimously told me to sit down.

I saw cats and dogs running all over the courtroom. Cats were jumping in and out of the wastepaper basket at the side of the judge. After a few questions put to me by the judge, my delirious brain could fully function no more.

I went to sleep.

All I remember is that I said "Yes" to many questions the judge put to me. How long this went on, I do not remember. It stretched out into the hours.

Finally, I came to.

I opened my heavy eyes and raised my nodding head to look at the judge and the cats I saw jumping in and out of his wastepaper basket.

A fear suddenly came over me. "I have admitted too much. I have confessed too much," I thought.

Then I said, "What I have said tonight must not be taken as true and valid unless I confirm it."

The judge called the session ended and ordered me to return to my cell.

As I arose and walked to the door, dragging along my fetters with my hands handcuffed behind my back, the interpreter quickly picked up the red fingerprint inkpad, seized my right index finger, rubbed red ink on it and pressed to this finger the lower right hand part of the paper with the questions of the night put to me by the judge and my answers.

My fingerprint was on this paper. Whatever I had said that

evening was unsigned but bore my fingerprint forced from shackled hands. It made an impressive document for an international court, or for one of the deluded or deluding communist sympathizers from the western world (many of whom wear the garb of a clergyman, or carry the title of a barrister at law, a scientist, a politician), visiting Peking.

I was much disturbed by this forcing a fingerprint from me. I was certain I had incriminated myself, while I slept from sheer exhaustion or had been put into a trance.

The "kindness" of the interpreter and the judge were only deceptions of cunning communist court officials to trick me into a false confession. I knew from past experiences and reliable testimony that communists are never to be trusted. Their words mean nothing. Only their deeds can be accepted. Yet, I had given them my confidence, in a sleeping condition, and I feared they had led me into a false confession.

The judge opened my next session on the following night with words like these: "Last night you confessed very well. You were honest for a change. You confessed that you led a conspiracy to assassinate Chairman Mao Tse-tung. This is the most serious crime committed in China since the liberation."

*   *   *

The fetters I wore cut deep into my ankles. My leather low cut shoes were ruined by then. For a day or so I protected my ankles by wrapping my pants around my ankles under the fetters. These pants were strong U.S. army pants, which I had worn in the army during the Second World War. The fetters cut through this tough cloth, stained with my blood. When the judge saw this protection of my ankles, he ordered me to remove my pants from beneath the fetters and keep them removed. My bare ankles must not be protected from the rusty, rough, dirty, iron fetters.

My feet and legs swelled up. My feet swelled so much it was impossible to put on my shoes. There was a discarded pair of old worn-out Chinese cloth shoes in the cell. The chu chang [cell boss] gave me these to wear but they soon fell to pieces, and I went to court in my bare feet.

My arms and hands swelled up from the handcuffs.

These fetters and handcuffs became painful.

From them I learned the meaning of "wretchedness."

Seven times I was handcuffed with my hands behind my back for times ranging from one day to seven days and nights. The first time was a few days after my arrest. I forget the reason the judge gave when he ordered them on.

I ask the reader to use his or her imagination in judging and understanding the torture of having your hands handcuffed behind your back. Aside from the pain of the rough, dirty, rusty iron cutting into your skin and flesh, every time you move your hand, there are other sufferings: humiliations, insults you undergo too delicate to write or talk about. This is especially the case regarding acts associated with urination and bowel movements.

You cannot bathe yourself. You cannot wash your face. You cannot comb your hair if you have long hair. You cannot scratch yourself when the lice bite.

If you wear spectacles, who cleans them of the sweat, dust, and grease that collects on them?

It is most difficult to sleep, on the hard wooden kang.[*] You lie on one arm. This is painful. Every position you take, lying down is painful.

How can you eat?

The first time I was handcuffed, the chu chang ordered a cell mate to feed me. Later I had to eat unaided the best I could, like a dog. My wo tou was thrown on the kang[*] with curses, then placed above the stinking urine bucket by Lu, the chu chang, and I was obliged to kneel at the side of the kang, over this stinking urine bucket which was under the kang, and eat my wretched wo tou, like a dog.[**]

Creatures, cellmates who claimed to be human beings, subjected me to these indignities. Chu chang Lu, the ex-Kuomintang colonel, was the leader in all of this, in his efforts to carry out the or-

---

[*]A wooden bed on which all prisoners in the cell slept.

[**]Wo tou was three or four ounces of a poor grade of corn which prisoners were given daily. This was mixed with water without salt or any leaven, shaped like a thimble and steamed. Prisoners were also fed pai tsai, a soup made of water and a little Chinese cabbage with no meat.

ders of his new communist masters who also claimed to be human beings—but perhaps I am wrong, misjudging the Chinese communists. There are no human beings according to Marxist communists. A human being is a spiritual animal, but Marxist communists deny spirituality to men. Therefore, they deny that we are human. We are only two-legged, upright walking brutes.

We do not have souls.

We do not have spirituality.

We are not human!

The idea of being "human" is just so much bourgeois, imperialistic, religious rubbish, according to the prophet Karl Marx.

The last time I was handcuffed was in punishment for refusing to accuse Father Joseph Meiners, S.V.D., and Professor Dr. William Bruell of being Gestapos. The former had been on the staff of Fu Jen University and had manifested much zeal in developing the Legion of Mary at Fu Jen.

The latter was an efficient teacher of chemistry, who had remained at his post as head of the Department of Chemistry of Fu Jen University, until the communists forced him out. When the judge accused Father Meiners to me of being a member of the Gestapo and asked me what evidence I knew to substantiate this, I said, "I know of no fact to indicate or prove that Father Joseph Meiners is a Gestapo, and personally I do not believe he is one."

At this, the judge blew up into a rage of fury, shouting, pounding his desk, cursing me, calling me a liar and the like.

I held my ground, in spite of all the abuse dealt out to me.

Then the judge accused Professor Bruell the same as he had Father Meiners, and I replied in a similar manner.

Again the judge fell into a tantrum.

This went on over Father Meiners and Professor Bruell for some 3 or 4 hours throughout the morning session.

I was then handcuffed with my hands behind my back.

The heaviest fetters had already been placed on me. These weighed around twenty pounds.

It was so difficult to try to sleep lying down that I sat up.

The nights were cold and my blanket was wrapped around me but every night it soon unloosened, and I became very cold.

For seven days and nights, I wore these handcuffs. My wrists and arms were very much swollen.

When these handcuffs were removed, as usual it was very painful to bring my arms around to their normal position, or in front of me. Especially it was difficult to lift them up. It took two or three days of practice to lift them above my head.

For several months my wrists were numb.

Men, prelates, priests, brothers and women—yes, nuns, the most sensitive of creatures, underwent these unspeakable indignities!

Then there were the fetters.

The pain of these instruments of torture became more intense day by day. Each step was agony as the horrible, heavy, rough iron ground back and forth into my flesh.

I would have preferred being shot to walking fifty feet in fetters.

And the sadistic judge called me back and forth, three or five times a day to his hellish court which was about 300 feet away.

I got blood poisoning from these filthy fetters and would have died, but the communists wanted me to live. I was of more value to them alive than dead. A living prisoner can confess. A dead one cannot.

So my fetters were removed this time and some two dozen penicillin injections or what was told to me was penicillin were administered to me.

It is easy for the communists to kill a prisoner without the formality of shooting him. Fetters, exposure to cold, starvation are some of the means at their disposal to do away with prisoners.

I remember one night while slowly making my way to the court in the excruciating pain of these fetters, with a cruel Sepo guard at my rear, cursing and shouting at me to move faster. In utter abandonment I prayed the only prayer I could think of and utter: the words of Our Blessed Lord on the cross, I began to understand for the first time! "My God, My God, why hast Thou forsaken me?" Matthew, XXVII, 46.

* * *

"Who were the F.B.I. spies in the Divine Word Society in the U.S.A.?" asked the judge in a court session, one day in November.

I loved the Divine Word Mission Society to which I belong, but I never realized how much I loved it until the communists calumniated it, accused it of being a spying organization.

The Divine Word Mission Society, a spying organization? Outrageous!

The court asked me to write the history of the Divine Word Mission Society. I did this, describing how a pious, German priest, the Venerable Father Arnold Janssen founded this society in 1875, to train foreign missionaries and conduct foreign missions. The court was very angry because I did not write that Father Arnold Janssen was a spy who founded a big espionage organization which he called the Divine Word Society. The judge also claimed that St. Mary's Mission Seminary, Techny, Illinois, U.S.A., was a spy training center.

St. Mary's Mission Seminary, a spy training center? Outrageous! I had studied there eleven of the fourteen years I spent preparing for the priesthood and loved this beautiful spot very much. I had been ordained a priest there. Now the communists maintained that it was a training center for spies!

Such utter rubbish!

The court, however, continued pressing me to confess what members of the American Provinces of the Divine Word Missionaries were F.B.I agents. Then one night after retiring time, when all the cellmates were in bed, Lu was called out of the cell. I had been transferred to Lu's cell, where he was chu chang. Wang was also in this cell.

In a few minutes Lu returned and ordered Wang and me to get up. He then told me through Wang as interpreter that he had just been called out by my judge, who had instructed him to press me to name the American Divine Word Missionaries who were F.B.I. men. The judge further stated that there would be no sleep for anyone in my cell this or the following nights until I confessed.

So there I was, sitting up shivering in the cold of a November's night in Peking, keeping the rest of my cellmates awake.

I told Wang and Lu that I knew of no American Divine Word Missionary who was an F.B.I agent. They insisted that there were many. We carried on like this for one or two hours. Then, I considered, for me to keep all my cellmates awake night after night was no small matter. So I said I knew some American Divine Word Missionaries who were F.B.I. men and after about an hour, listed some members of the Divine Word Missionaries outside of China, out of range of the Chinese communists.

With this we were all allowed to sleep.

Furthermore, my fetters were removed and I was allowed my first hot bath in four months.

What a relief it was to have those heavy fetters removed! My ankles were sore and full of wounds from these and especially from the first pair of medium-sized fetters that had cut into my skin and flesh. It was three months before my ankles healed, because walking kept the wounds open. The bath was another great relief for which I had longed, for many months.

*   *   *

In the winter of 1952, in cell 6 of the North or B Compound, I discovered that one of the Chinese cellmates, prisoner Lee, was a Catholic priest. Lee and I were allowed to converse together a little in Latin. However, by agreement, we spoke together only when necessary or in urgent cases. We followed this policy for our own protection. Since we were both priests, talking together often and over long periods would only invite punishment. Father Lee, however, often interpreted for me in the cell, using Latin.

I wanted to receive the sacrament of penance, to go to confession. I had not made a confession since July 1951. No religious ministrations were allowed in this prison. So I bided my time, waiting for an opportunity when unobserved I could confess.

After about two weeks my opportunity came. It was a Sunday afternoon. Four cellmates were playing cards with a homemade set of cards. Father Lee and I were sitting close together watching the game. I opened by talking to Father Lee in Latin about card playing. I did this so if afterwards anyone should ask what we had been talking about, we could say we had spoken about the card game.

Then I asked Father Lee if he would hear my confession, since I had not confessed for seven months.

Father Lee said he would. I then made a short confession and the pious priest folded his hands as in the confessional box, closed his eyes in prayer, and quite openly made a sign of the cross as he absolved me. Anyone watching us would have certainly seen we were up to something religious, something unsocialistic, uncommunistic.

I was greatly relieved and thanked this good priest. God bless him!

With the confession over Father Lee said, "Be careful, the fu chu chang (assistant chu chang) is watching us."

This was no sooner said than the fu chu chang shouted at us, demanding to know what we were talking about. Father Lee said that we had been talking about the card game which was true. I had first spoken about the game in preparation for just such a question.

A few days later Father Lee was moved from my cell. I missed him very much. The very presence of a fellow priest was a consolation, even if I hardly ever spoke with him.

*   *   *

A few weeks after this, in the end of the Lenten season, Father Yuan [a colleague at the Fu Shen University—ED.] was suddenly brought into our cell. We immediately recognized one another but gave no indication of this.

Father Yuan was ordered, for some reason or other, to leave his cell and join our study classes on this one particular day. He sat near me as I sat near the wall on the edge of the kang, in isolation.

The hour passed, then came our second or last meal of the day around 4:30 P.M. After this we filed out to the latrine.

We went to the latrine twice a day. The first time was about an hour after rising. Outside the cell as we filed along, keeping silent, we were supposed to keep our heads down, with eyes directed to the ground, observing no one else. I kept my eyes down when in view of the Sepo guards, otherwise I took in all the other prisoners I could, to see who were in prison with me, who were in fetters or handcuffs, etc.

On this particular day, some prisoners asked and received permission to collect their clothes which they had hung up in the morning to dry. The others, excepting Father Yuan and me, were detained for some reason or other. Consequently Father Yuan and I returned to our cell.

No sooner were we in the cell than Father Yuan whispered to me in Latin, "Let us give one another conditional absolution. This will stand for our Easter sacrament of penance."

I agreed.

Conditional absolution is given in cases of emergency when a penitent is unable to confess, such as when a large number of soldiers are about to go to battle, in an accident, etc.

Soon the class period opened. I again sat just behind Father Yuan. After about half an hour, I gave him a gentle poke in the back, as I signaled I was about to give him absolution. I noticed the head of the good, pious Chinese priest bend slightly lower and I absolved him. Then I waited and noticed he turned a little towards me, with his right hand hidden under his left arm. I then prayed an act of contrition as he gave me absolution making a sign of the cross with his hidden right hand. So Father Yuan and I received our Easter sacrament of penance in 1952.

About this time I noticed on a few occasions a foreigner among the prisoners. He was of middle age. "He must be a priest," I thought. There was that indefinable characteristic about him that is common in a priest. So one day as I came on him, squatting in the open latrine, I raised my hand and made a little sign of the cross as I gave him absolution. In a moment's time I noticed his hand go up as he made a little sign of the cross, and his lips uttered an absolution for me.

In Ts'ao Lan Tzu and the work prison where I was from September 21, 1954 to July 13, 1955, I gave absolution daily to all the disposed Catholics, and my blessing to all the rest of the prisoners as we gathered, hundreds together, to go to the latrine, or at general assemblies when 4,000 or 5,000 prisoners gathered together. I also did the same to my cellmates at night on retiring.

                        *   *   *

So I could multiply accounts of such priestly doings.

God bless those stouthearted priests, Chinese and foreign, and there were many of them, as well as brothers, sisters and Catholic laymen in Ts'ao Lan Tzu and Tzu Hsing Lu prisons, most of whom were thrown into prison for no other reason than that they promoted the Legion of Mary, opposed the separation of the Church from the Bishop of Rome, the Pope, and the like, while they were charged with outrageous, exaggerated crimes.

As I saw these priests, brothers, sisters and Catholic laymen, many in chains, I often thought of the words of Our Blessed Lord:

"Blessed are they who suffer persecution for justice's sake, for theirs is the kingdom of heaven.

"Blessed are you when men reproach you, and persecute you, and, speaking falsely, say all manner of evil against you, for my sake. Rejoice and exult, because your reward is great in heaven; for so did they persecute the prophets who were before you." Matthew V, 10–12.

"When will Easter be this year?" I asked myself in early 1952.

From my arrest on July 25, 1951, to the end of the year, I observed the outstanding feasts: The Assumption of Our Blessed Lady, August 15th; The Nativity of Our Blessed Lady, September 8, which is the anniversary of the foundation of the society of the Missionaries of the Divine Word (S.V.D.); St. Michael's, September 29; St. Teresa of Lisieux, October 3; St. Francis Assisi, October 4; St. Francis Xavier, December 3; the Immaculate Conception, December 8; Christmas; and Circumcision, January 1st.

All these are immovable.

There were many movable feast days approaching, all reckoned on the date of Easter, which changes, year for year: Ash Wednesday, Passion Sunday, Palm Sunday, Holy Week, Easter, Pentecost, Corpus Christi, Trinity Sunday.

Easter is the first Sunday after the first full moon following the vernal equinox, which is March 21st.

I dared not inquire the date of Easter. So I asked the date of the coming Chinese New Year, usually at the end of our January or the beginning of February. This is a new moon. A full moon is on the fourteenth day following. So I calculated Easter from the Chinese New Year. From Easter, I calculated the entire liturgical period from Ash Wednesday to Trinity Sunday.

In the best manner I could I lived this liturgical period. Since I fasted every day in Ts'ao Lan Tzu, there was no difficulty in perfectly observing the Lenten fast. I commemorated the beautiful feasts, especially Ash Wednesday, Holy Week, Easter, Pentecost, and Trinity, with special meditations and prayers.

Each year in prison, I fixed the Easter and worked out the movable feasts of its period, observing these lovely days.

*　　　*　　　*

"Sign and fingerprint this," the judge said as he threw back to me the statement I had written.

I had been called to a court session with a strange judge who spoke English. He had asked me about the Catholic students of Fu Jen University. My reports about them were not incriminating. The judge, as usual in such cases, was angry. After all, he was not so much interested in a true statement about these good Catholic students as he was in getting grounds, true or false, to persecute them, to destroy the Catholic faith in them, to turn them on their former teachers at Fu Jen, to turn them against their bishops and priests.

After about two hours of fruitless questioning, he ordered me to make a written statement there and then, in the courtroom.

I sat on a bench before a small tea table and began to write with the steel pen and ink, on the cheap manila paper provided by the court.

It seemed difficult to write.

"I must write," I thought. I exerted unusual effort to write. "I must write something." So I wrote, abbreviating many words ordinarily not abbreviated.

"Let me see what you have written," the judge said as I finished.

"Write this over!" he shouted after glancing at the statement and throwing it back to me, "and write clearly. I cannot read this."

So I sat down again and copied my statement, making efforts to write clearly and without the unconventional abbreviations I had used. On finishing, I handed my statement to the judge. He took it and looked at it.

"Sign and fingerprint this," he said as he threw my statement back to me.

I signed in Chinese and English as usual.

Then I did a very strange thing.

Raising my finger in the air, I went through the motions of rolling my right index fingertip as if the ink pad were suspended in the air.

"This will do," I thought, "this is all make-believe anyway."

Then I rolled my fingertip on my statement, next to my signature, and returned the statement to the judge who was absorbed with a book or some paper.

He took one glance, grew angry, threw first my statement back to me, then the inkpad at his side, shouting, "Fingerprint this! I told you to fingerprint it!"

In bewilderment, I then properly fingerprinted my statement.

On my way to my cell, a fear came over me, a new kind of fear I had never experienced in my life.

"What have I done?" I thought. "Lifting my hand in the air and rolling my finger for ink that was not there! This is not the way a normal man acts! Can it be that I am losing my mind?"

I feared to answer this question.

Then I remembered back 38 years to the days when I had studied Shakespeare's King Lear in my preparatory seminary days. King Lear realized he was losing his mind. I remembered a footnote stating that often a person losing his mind realizes that he is going insane.

This memory frightened me more.

On returning to my cell, I took my place on the kang in a corner of the cell, where I sat, that day in January 1954, two years and six months after my arrest, and reviewed my conduct in the court-room.

The cellmates told me in those days that I spoke in my sleep as I had never done before.

It was difficult for me to make up my mind to do anything. Often I sat in my corner, an isolated prisoner, especially despised and persecuted by the other cellmates, unable to arouse myself to get up, for instance, and walk to the other end of the cell to look for my notebook which I had left there.

One of these days, the members of the cell were ordered to prepare for a bath. The other cellmates quickly got their soap, if they had any, and a little towel that served for a wash rag and after being wrung for a towel.

I sat there, on the edge of the kang, motionless and indifferent.

"Rigney, do you have your towel?" the English-speaking cell-mate who was allowed to speak to me in English, asked me.

"I am prepared," I said.

When we were ordered to leave for bath, I joined the cell-mates, without soap or towel.

In the bathing pool, I simply splashed water on myself for a few minutes, then went to the room where our clothes were heaped on the floor. I was wet and shivering from the January cold. In this condition I dressed and returned to my cell, walking about 1000 feet.

I was happy that no one saw that I had had no towel, else I would have been tou chenged by all the cellmates for not taking one.* The cellmates took every opportunity they could to contradict me, shout at me, tou cheng me, the American imperialist, the Catholic priest.

Several incidents as the above occurred. For some of them I was punished when I should have received kindness. Teng, the chu chang, however, was too selfish to forego an opportunity to advance himself at my expense.

On another occasion I was given a paper, a report to write for

---

*Tou cheng is an indoctrination method in which victims are surrounded and ha-rangued until a confession of politically incorrect thought and behavior is made.

the court. I could hardly write, my hand was so unsteady. But I
wrote out the paper and handed it to the English-speaking cellmate
to be translated into Chinese.

At one glance he said, "Rigney, your handwriting is terrible!
How can I read it! You never wrote so poorly before."

"That is the best I can do," I said in a feeling of utter helplessness. I felt for all the world as though I was breaking, going to
pieces, losing my mind.

Around this time, I drew the conclusion: "I am losing my
mind."

Then I resolved to make the greatest effort I could, to hold myself together, to save myself from going stark mad as others had.

"I will not let these cellmates goaded on by the cruel, inhuman communists, ruin me. I will disregard them." I resolved and I
begged God to help me.

So with this resolve, supported by all the effort I had, and a re-
doubling of my prayers, I faced the future.

In a few days, I felt I had gotten hold of myself, with God's
help I had won. I had saved myself from going mad. The cellmates
said I no longer talked in my sleep. I was able to act, to decide and
carry out my decisions.

I was saved.

                    *   *   *

"I hope that son of a b—— is shot," said chu chang Tito to activist
Wang one cold day in the winter of 1953, as these two worthies returned to the cell.

They had been called to attend a big tou cheng of four or five
prisoners, in the prison "hall." The shouts of the tou chengers could
be faintly heard in my cell. They sounded like heinous cries from
some distant inferno.

Both Tito and Wang related to the rest of the cellmates the details of the tou cheng. They were evidently proud and elated for
having been called to participate in it. And, of course, the lesson of
the tou cheng must be brought home to all prisoners, especially the

stubborn, unreformed ones. Each gave full details of the events: how the prisoners had been brought forth separately, accused, denounced, and ordered to confess.

Some confessed and were dismissed, without further punishment. Two failed in their confession and the zealous activists demanded that they be shot. Each was handcuffed and shackled and led away to solitary confinement.

The prison officer concluded by telling the activists that the government appreciated their zeal and would consider their requests to shoot these two stubborn prisoners.

Tito and Wang each emphatically repeated their hope that the "People's" government would shoot these two prisoners—unreformed, stubborn, reactionary prisoners.

The other cellmates vied with one another in loudly voicing their agreement with Tito and Wang.

"Shoot them! Shoot them!" they shouted.

I remained silent, horrified at the thought that these two poor wretches were facing death at the hypocritical, cowardly request of their fellow prisoners!

"What is on your mind, Rigney?" Tito asked. "What do you think about this tou cheng? Do you agree with the rest of this cell that they should get shot or do you sympathize with them?"

"Yes, I feel sorry for them," I said, unable to hide my sympathy. "I do not like to have any prisoner shot. I hope the government will not shoot them."

"That only shows, Rigney, how reactionary, unreformed you are! You will be among the next to be so tou chenged, I can assure you, and I hope the government shoots you!" Tito shouted.

For weeks Tito repeatedly predicted that I would be publicly tou chenged.

The prison authorities, he said, were preparing for more such tou chengs for such prisoners as me.

Then one day I was called out and lined up with a few prisoners of other cells. I was resigned to a public tou chenging with the activists, including Tito and Wang, who accompanied me, demanding that I be shot.

It seems that there just is no end to the kinds of tortures to which the Chinese communists submit their prisoners.

We were marched over to the "hall," a big room, with the bare ground as the floor. Some one hundred prisoners were present.

A name was called out. A frightened, pale prisoner arose or was forced to arise and, in a daze, made his way to the front.

It seemed all hell broke loose. Most of the hundred prisoners sitting on the ground burst forth in screams and howls, cursing, abusing the poor wretch, who was forced to stand with his head down.

Every so often, an exceptionally zealous activist, throwing all shame and self-respect to the winds, arose, rushed up to the accused victim, waving his fist in his face and shouting, "Ti tour (Down with your head!)," seized his head and jerked it down.

The accused made several efforts to confess but the crowd shouted him out. Sometimes a large part of the crowd jumped to their feet crowding around him, carrying on like so many madmen.

At last, after about an hour of this, the officer stepped forward, put handcuffs and fetters on the accused, and led him away.

Then a second name was called and a rather short-sized, frightened man of refined features arose and walked before the howling mob. He went through quite the same ordeal as the first.

Wang at the end shouted to shoot him, and several times rose to his feet shaking his fist, yelling accusations and curses.

This prisoner was also put in chains and led away.

On returning to our cell, Wang said that the second accused was Wu, his brother-in-law. Wang was hoarse from his shouting at his own brother-in-law, shouting even for his execution.

I had refrained from all this shouting and as a consequence was subjected to much questioning by Tito. At the end I had to write a paper, expressing all my thoughts about these awful ordeals.

I wrote that I did not like them and felt sorry for the accused.

A year later, similar tou chengs were held again. This time Wu, who had suffered eight months in handcuffs and fetters, was among the mob and to my disgust was one of the most zealous activists accusing, cursing the two victims.

Again I was obliged to explain why I had showed such sympathy and lack of interest in these tou chengs.

I wrote in detail about how I felt sorry for the accused and how hypocritical I thought the other prisoners acted in accusing the two victims.

I wrote that Our Blessed Lord must have dealt with just such a scene when he came on the woman who had been taken in adultery, being accused and about to be stoned to death, and how he wrote on the sand, "Let him without sin throw the first stone."

But I thought that these two victims for whom I had so much sympathy in a few weeks would be activists like Wu, accusing others.

So the folly went on in Ts'ao Lan Tzu.

*   *   *

Many Catholics, including priests and brothers, were arrested that summer of 1954. They were dealt with harsher than the other prisoners. I remember one brother, who was cruelly beaten by the acting chu chang, Judas, a "progressive Catholic," who was a tall, well-built six-footer. The brother, a brave and stouthearted Chinese, took these tortures with outstanding fortitude. Several times Judas, in a fit of uncontrollable rage, seized the chain of the brother's fetters and with all his might, jerked them up and down: the sharp edges of the rusty iron fetter bands dealt painful blows on the sensitive bones of the shins and feet, causing bruises and drawing blood.

The brother in agony stretched out his legs and clinched his jaws, bearing the pain.

On one occasion, I seized the arm of Judas crying, "Stop, you will break his bones. You are not allowed to beat prisoners." He stopped but what he reported about me to the prison officer, I never heard. It undoubtedly contributed to my further detention and sentence in prison, while most of the other foreign priests were released in the spring and summer of that year of 1954. Such actions as I had done were dangerous and usually brought punishment for both the doer and the one protected or defended.

In 1952, beating of prisoners was forbidden by the prison, but it seemed the officials granted many exceptions since this brother was beaten many times. On one occasion, Judas stamped on the brother's feet so hard that I thought he broke the bones of the poor brother's foot arch.

Judas defended the Ke Hsing Huei [pro-Communist Reformation Committee consisting of a few renegade Catholics collaborating with the Red government] of the Pei Tang [North Church or Cathedral] of Peking and tried without success to induce the brother to support it.

Later a prisoner, Brutus, came to our cell to conduct the tou chenging and breaking down of the brother. On several occasions Brutus beat up the brother, dealing him hard blows in the face. The other cellmates, excepting *me*, joined in the beating. Judas told them if they did not beat the brother, they were not on the side of the communist government.

To stand by and witness such brutality and tou chenging hour after hour, day after day, dealt out to a helpless prisoner, was always a mental torture for me. And I witnessed such for over four years.

Judas was accustomed to hum Catholic hymns and parts of a mass in my hearing. I showed no reaction. Judas had shown his colors and I was on my guard against his provocations.

Had I joined his humming, or led off on a religious discussion, he could, and certainly would, have immediately reported me as spreading subversive propaganda, trying by means of religious appeals to wean "progressive Catholics" from the bosom of the government, etc.

Shortly after, the brother was moved to another cell and a young Chinese priest was brought in.

Judas and the other cellmates pressed him as they had pressed the brother to support the Ke Hsing Huei.

To strengthen this brave young priest and to clarify before the "People's" government my stand, I asked a prisoner to translate for me to this young priest. "Is the Ke Hsing Huei united to the Bishop of Rome, the Pope?" I asked.

"No."

"Then since the government guarantees freedom of religion in China, we Catholics are free to support or not support the Ke Hsing Huei. To support the Ke Hsing Huei would be separating from communion with the Pope and this would be denying our Catholic religion since union with the Pope is essential to Catholicism. Therefore, we Catholics are not bound to support the Ke Hsing Huei. For my part, I do not support the Ke Hsing Huei. I am a Catholic and am resolved to remain a Catholic. If I supported this committee, I would be changing my religion. The government declares I am free to select my religion, and I choose to be and remain a Catholic."

A few days after this, I was sentenced.

*   *   *

[Father Rigney's imprisonment ended in 1955 when his case became publicized through the efforts of his sister, Mrs. Mary Anne Hanley, and Father Ralph Wiltgen, S.V.D., who was assigned by the Divine Word Missionaries in the States to work for his release. This mobilization finally pressured the Chinese government to release Rigney after 50 months in communist prisons. —ED.]

· 8 ·

JOHN MARTINO

Prisoner in Paradise: A Cuban's Tale

JOHN MARTINO, an American held prisoner from 1959 to 1962 in Cuba, confirmed what anti-Communists in the United States had been saying all along: Fidel Castro, who had come to power in 1959, was a Communist, aligned with the Soviet Union; his regime was repressive; and Cuban prisons had been created for political prisoners. Martino's prison memoir, *I Was Castro's Prisoner* (1963) gained wide circulation in anti-Communist circles with its detailed account of his three-year incarceration.

American anti-Communists found much to like in the book. Martino wrote in a direct style that pulled no punches. He provided graphic details of the brutal nature of the Castro regime, the kangaroo courts, the mass executions, the attempts at constant "brainwashing" of prisoners, the corruption (and sadism) of many Communist officials, the government's involvement in cocaine trafficking, and Castro's betrayal of the revolution. His account of William Alexander Morgan's execution showed how Castro misled his followers.

Morgan, born in Ohio, joined Castro's guerrilla army fighting in the Escambray Mountains in 1957 against the Batista regime. By the time the Batista government fell in 1959, he had risen to the rank of major in the rebel army.

When it became apparent that Castro's government was headed toward communism, Morgan began distributing anti-Communist material to villagers in the Escambray Mountains. As a result, Morgan and his close associate, Major Jesus Carreras Zayas, were arrested and accused of being counterrevolutionaries. Martino describes the final months of Morgan's life in the La Cabaña prison. In February 1961, Fidel and Raul Castro came to the prison to see Morgan marched before a firing squad. His hands were tied behind his back, and a man in the shadows of the lights beamed on him shouted out, "Kneel and beg for your life." Morgan replied, "I kneel for no man." Two bullets in each of his knees brought him down. At that point a sharpshooter put two bullets in each of Morgan's shoulders before he was finally shot to death.

Morgan's death presented an image of crucifixion and of betrayal, a theme that runs throughout Martino's book. Especially poignant are his descriptions of American officials in Cuba who are described as incompetent and naive. Throughout his trial and imprisonment, Martino says, American embassy officials did nothing to help him. One official, he writes, told him that the embassy did not wish to make Martino into a "diplomatic issue" that might jeopardize the opening of new diplomatic talks with Castro. In the end, only his wife's petitions to the Cuban government eventually freed Martino, in the fall of 1962. Martino explains that he had no inkling of the motives prompting his release.

By 1963, when Martino's book was released, the American anti-Communist movement felt a general sense of betrayal itself. As soon as Castro assumed power, American anti-Communists had warned that Castro was a Communist and would align Cuba with the Soviet Union. And, they had expressed fears that the Soviet Union would place nuclear missiles in Cuba as a means of blackmailing the United States into diplomatic submission. These warnings appeared well before the Cuban missile crisis of 1962 and even before John F. Kennedy's election to the presidency. But these admonitions appeared to have fallen on deaf ears. Moreover the Bay of Pigs invasion in 1961 revealed to anti-Communists the moral turpitude and perfidy of the Kennedy administration. "Was the administration just incompetent, or were there insidious forces at work within the administration?" anti-Communists asked.

Whatever the answer, anti-Communists felt increasingly

isolated as they came under attack by journalists, academics, and politicians for political extremism. The Fulbright Memorandum, written by Democratic Senator William J. Fulbright of Arkansas in a private letter to President Kennedy, warned of extremist propaganda being used in the U.S. military to educate American troops about the nature of communism. Under Kennedy, the Pentagon revised its educational programs to present a more moderate view of communism.

Equally worrying to the anti-Communist movement were the inroads of the left among student circles. Fidel Castro and Ché Guevera were emerging as romantic heroes among many of the youth. The sociologist C. Wright Mills, in his widely read *Listen Yankee: The Revolution in Cuba* (1961), portrayed Castro as a nationalist reformer who had been driven into the arms of the Soviet Union when the United States decided to defend American corporations in Cuba from nationalization by the Cuban government.

Thus the American anti-Communist movement felt embattled as never before. Soviet expansion was just ninety miles from American shores; the Kennedy administration seemed incapable of defending the national security; and American youth were being led astray by those who sought to romanticize Castro. As if this were not enough, American anti-Communists were being denounced as extremists, paranoids, and anti-intellectuals.

Under this onslaught, anti-Communists continued to study and promote such books as John Martino's. Upon his return, Martino joined the anti-Castro forces. Martino, who had once worked for mob chief Santos Trafficante (a fact he conveniently omitted from his memoir), threw in with the Cuban exiles. After the Kennedy assassination, Martino emerged as one of the many figures who popped up among the Kennedy conspiracy theorists by claiming that Oswald had been framed by anti-Castro forces. Martino died in 1975, but in 1994 his wife Florence Martino told the author Anthony Summers that on the morning of November 22, 1963, her husband had told her, after receiving numerous phone calls, "Flo, they're going to kill him. They're going to kill him when he gets to Texas." Who phoned him, she did not know.

In the summer of 1959, a group of Americans asked me to fly to Havana to bid on installing automatic totalizing machines for the Oriental Race Track and flood lighting for night racing. I agreed to go to Cuba and look into the situation.

On the afternoon of July 23, I called Rafael ————, a Cuban friend who was connected with the track, gave him my flight number and asked him to meet me at Havana airport that night. As I was packing, I decided to ask my thirteen-year-old son, Edward, if he would like to come along.

"That would be fine, Daddy. I have never been to Havana." While Edward and I were at the Miami International Airport buying our tickets, Jorge Hernandez, a Cuban friend whom I hadn't seen for several months, approached me.

"I have been looking for someone who is going to Cuba," he said. "Could you do me a favor?"

"What is it?"

"When you go to Havana, would you call Mrs. Sofia Cisneros—here is her phone number—and tell her that Mrs. Rodriguez has had her operation and is convalescing well."

I suppose I was preoccupied with the problem of the race-track totalizers. At any rate, it didn't occur to me that it was strange that Hernandez should camp at the airport waiting for a potential messenger, when he could have telephoned or wired Mrs. Cisneros. Not suspecting that the message was in code or that I was involving myself in Cuban revolutionary politics, I took the slip of paper with the phone number and agreed to deliver the message.

My friend, Rafael, met us at the Havana airport that night and we drove to the Hotel Comodoro where Edward and I checked in. While the three of us were having dinner, I telephoned the Cisneros house. A man's voice answered and identified itself as Manuel Cisneros. He established the fact that I was John Martino of Miami Beach and that I had a message for his mother. He said she was not at home and asked me to call back in twenty minutes.

I tried again after dinner. Manuel Cisneros said he had been in

From *I Was Castro's Prisoner: An American Tells His Story* (New York, 1963), pp. 12–21, 44–50, 59–62, 66–68, 185–189, 191–193, 207–215, 260–264.

touch with his mother and they would appreciate it if I could drop by the house with the message around nine-thirty.

"There is nothing confidential about the message," I said innocently. "I can give it to you over the phone."

"My mother would prefer to receive it from you in person, so she can thank you."

"Unfortunately," I said, "I must drive to the race track immediately."

"Splendid. My house is on your way."

The trip seemed to me quite unnecessary, but there was no graceful way out of the situation. Cubans carry politeness to excess and they can easily be offended by our brusque American way of doing things.

When we drove up to the Cisneros house, I told Rafael that my errand would not take more than five or ten minutes and suggested that he show Edward the dog track, which was right around the corner.

"Won't you sit down," Mrs. Cisneros said when I had given her the message. "I will get coffee ready."

"That is very kind of you."

She excused herself and disappeared into an adjoining room. As I sat down to wait for the coffee, the front door burst open and four men in civilian clothes, armed with Tommy guns, plunged into the room.

"Don't move," their leader shouted in barely adequate English. "Hands up. Everybody here is under arrest."

Mrs. Cisneros returned to the drawing room and we were searched. The police took my money from my wallet, counted it and returned it. They removed my wallet and hotel key. The leader explained in his gimpy English that they had been ordered to surround the house and arrest everyone in it. We would now have to wait. I had better drink my coffee.

I explained that my son and my friend are at the dog track and didn't know what had happened to us. This made no apparent impression on the policeman. He began to ply me with questions, asking me how I liked Miami, how I liked Cuba, what I thought of Fidel Castro and how many times I had been here.

"If I do any talking," I replied, "It will be when I am taken to the police station and told why I am being held."

We waited for an hour and three quarters. Then more police came in, bringing with them two persons they had evidently just arrested—a woman with blond hair and an old lady. We were put into two cars and driven to another part of town. The cars parked beside a building; five of the guards entered it, taking the blond woman with them. We waited another quarter of an hour.

Then an extraordinary thing happened. Three more cars arrived, carrying fifteen more civilian policemen who were also armed with submachine guns. To my astonishment, they disarmed and arrested the policemen who had taken us into custody.

All this occurred in the middle of the street at a time when most of Havana was outside enjoying the night air. Consequently, there was a crowd around us and a great deal of speculation and argument as to what was happening.

We were ordered back into the cars at gunpoint, whereupon the motorcade took off and soon was racing at breakneck speed through the streets of downtown Havana. Our destination was the central police station. Once inside, we were taken to the confidential bureau, which served in the early days of the Castro regime as the secret police headquarters.

"Gringo, you are going to see a friend of yours," one of the guards said, spitting the epithet at me so that I could read the hatred on his face. "You are going to see the Chief of Police."

In this as in other matters, the police were mistaken. I had never met Efigenio Almeijeiras Delgado, Chief of the National Revolutionary Police under Fidel Castro, but I did know something about him. During my three years in Cuban prisons, I would learn a good deal more and, on my return to the United States, I would take the trouble to distinguish between rumors and cold facts.

Incredible as it may seem, Almeijeiras was a professional petty thief, who used to operate under the name of "Tomeguín." (This is the name of a small Cuban bird with a pronounced beak which is in the habit of picking up other people's property.) In the winter of 1949, then-Lieutenant Esteban Ventura Novo, Chief of the Robbery Division of the Cuban Bureau of Investigation, picked up

"Tomeguín" Almeijeiras. He was charged with mugging women
and with purse snatching. It appeared that "Tomeguín" and his
gang operated in the Fraternidad Park opposite the Hotel Manhat-
tan. In addition to snatching purses in the park and on city buses,
they stole car batteries and peddled drugs. Almeijeiras was a marihuana user. Since it was his first offense, Castro's future Police
Chief drew only 60 to 180 days.

When he was released from prison, he resumed his former occupation, but changed his area of operations to the Vedado district.
He used to snatch the purses and handbags of women who went to
the Calixto García Hospital to visit the sick.

He next came to the attention of the police when he got into a
fight with a hospital cook, after which a friend of the cook am-
bushed him and shot him in the leg. This was his baptism of fire
as a revolutionary. He was later charged with being a member of a
gang which beat up people, for hire, in the city of Havana. Finally,
the files of the municipal court of Puerto Padre in Oriente
Province, which no doubt have been since purged of the entry, con-
tain a record of the conviction and sentence to sixty days in prison
of Efigenio Almeijeiras Delgado and Armando Cubria for ped-
erasty. The two homosexuals were caught in flagrante in a private
house.

Additional light on Police Chief Almeijeiras was cast by Alex
Rorke, an American news photographer who was arrested in Castro
Cuba. On the Celebrity Table program of radio station WRCA
(New York) for November 16, 1959, Rorke characterized Almeijeiras
as "a dope addict and a murderer," adding that "he murdered his
own wife." I have no corroboration of the charge of murder and report it for what it is worth, if anything. However, Almeijeiras' career
as a marihuana user, drug peddler, petty thief and sexual deviate
was confirmed to me by several different sources during the years I
spent in Cuban prisons.

Almeijeiras was part of the criminal element which was attracted to Fidel Castro and to Castro's program of invasion and revolution. He was wanted by the police, had no stake in the existing
social order, no loyalty to anything, and everything to gain by violent political change. As I shall point out later, all during his adult

life, Fidel Castro has had an affinity with the underworld, associated with criminal elements and perpetrated crimes. The relationship of the professional criminal class and of dope addicts and pushers to the Castro movement is a phase of our contemporary history which has been ignored by the correspondents.

Almeijeiras trained with Castro's forces in Mexico and was one of the 82 men who landed from the *Gramma* on December 2, 1956. Of these invaders, all but twelve were either killed or captured by the Batista forces. Almeijeiras was one who survived. That made him one of the immortals of the Cuban Revolution.

I was taken into a large office crowded with policemen. Almeijeiras was a mulatto with a brutish and rather stupid face. He wore a straggly goatee. As I entered the room, he greeted me: "Mr. P———, we have been waiting for you. We expected you last night."

I flushed with anger as nobody had ever called me that before. Suddenly, I was aware of someone advancing on me from the side. As I started to turn around, I felt a hard blow on my mouth which knocked me down. I was lying on my back on the floor, looking up at the ceiling. There was the taste of blood in my mouth and I felt sick at my stomach with anger. The police sergeant who had hit me was a powerfully built man who must have weighed about 210 pounds. My own weight at the time was 150.

I got up from the floor and found a chair. I tried to dissociate myself from what was happening to me, to imagine that I was a bystander. I knew that, if I lost my temper, I could be beaten to death here in the police station. That had happened before in Cuba.

They ordered me to take off my clothes and, while I sat naked in the chair, went through the routine of searching my pockets and linings, counting my money and taking my wallet, my ring, my watch and the rest of my jewelry, which they then returned to me.

"All right, wise guy, where is your pilot's license?" I gave Almeijeiras a blank look. I have never flown a plane in my life. "You know what I am talking about. We know you are a pilot. We know all about you. Where is the license?"

"You must be out of your mind," I told him. "You have got the wrong man. You have my wallet, my driver's license, my credit cards. They will tell you that I am John V. Martino of the Neptune Electronics Company and of Miami Beach."

"That's what you say," the sergeant who had hit me remarked. "You are a Yankee pilot. You are a gunrunner. You're part of the counterrevolution and you have been hired to drop propaganda leaflets on Havana. You are also in charge of the squads that burn the sugar cane in the fields."

I spoke to him in a calm, reasoning tone:

"It is very easy for you to check on who I am. All you have to do is call the airport. They will confirm that I came in by Pan American flight tonight."

The police sergeant apparently had not thought of that. He began by ordering me not to tell him how to do his job and then asked where my plane ticket was.

"It is in my coat pocket, the coat I left in my hotel room. You have the room key. Why don't you go get it?"

They ignored that. Phones were ringing and there was a great deal of bustle and disorganized commotion. About half an hour later, they brought in Edward, who seemed to be taking the experience calmly. I was not allowed to talk to him and they took him and my friend, Rafael, into separate rooms for questioning. Meanwhile, the officer who had arrested Edward and Rafael had turned over my suitcase and the papers I had left in my hotel room to Almeijeiras and his assistants. After going through these documents, one of the police officers turned to me:

"These papers are all false. Why don't you tell us the truth?"

"How can you say they are false?" I asked him indignantly. "All you have to do is check their authenticity with your own Department of Immigration. Moreover, I want to phone my Embassy."

This touched off a minor explosion.

"You don't have to tell us what to check and what not to check. You Americans are all alike. The minute you get into trouble you yell for the American Embassy. Well, you are in Cuba now. And it isn't the way it was before when Ambassador Smith was here. We are the bosses of Cuba now and we are going to make you Yankees do what you are told."

At about half past two that morning, I again asked them to call the Embassy for me. I reminded them that they were holding my son who was only thirteen years old.

"Is that so?" the sergeant asked in fake astonishment. "But he knows all about gunrunning and he knows who you are."

When you are exposed to this sort of stupidity, it can be really exasperating. You are blocked by a wall of stubbornness which cannot be penetrated. I was in the hands of a police department which was being run by a dope pusher and petty crook and which was staffed by cops who acted as if they had learned about police methods from the silent movies.

They finally put me into a cell and I was able to snatch a few hours sleep. The next day, July 24, was devoted to asking me questions, the same questions over and over again. Relays of interrogators alternated with each other, some who spoke English, some who spoke an unintelligible jargon and others who didn't pretend to any English at all. I was supposed to fall into a trap and contradict myself, after which my fabricated story would supposedly collapse like a house of cards. They showed me a photograph of a pilot in a U.S. Army Air Force flying suit, standing beside a plane. They told me that was me in World War II. The resemblance between me and the pilot was only superficial; I had never seen him in my life.

"Please call the Embassy," I said at one point. "You are holding a boy and a sick man. At any moment, I may have an attack and need a doctor."

"When we finish with you, you are going to need much more than a doctor" was the reply.

＊   ＊   ＊

In Cuba, there is nothing resembling our grand jury procedure. The prisoner is taken before a judge who reads the charges. The prisoner is then permitted to make a statement. The judge then has seventy-two hours to decide whether he is to be held for trial or released because of insufficient evidence. If the prisoner is held for trial, he is confined in the Castillo del Principe, one of the worst holes in the Western Hemisphere.

I was taken before the judge of instruction. Nobody was pres-

ent from the Embassy; in fact, he and I were alone. He handed me
a piece of paper and said in English:

"Here is your confession. Sign here."

I looked at him in amazement. I denied angrily that I had confessed to anything.

The judge shrugged his shoulders.

"Read it anyhow," he said.

My so-called confession stated that I, John Martino, had come
to Havana three times by clandestine means. I was employed by the
counterrevolution to serve as a courier and smuggle people out of
Cuba illegally by plane. On my last trip, I had come to smuggle the
family of Colonel Esteban Ventura out of the country. I was also a
gun runner, an agent of the Batista exiles in the United States and a
counterrevolutionary.

When I told the judge that the document was a tissue of lies
and that I would not sign it, he shrugged again, rummaged in his
desk and showed me a sheet of paper about six inches square. Had I
ever seen this paper before? I said that I had not.

"Let me read you the accusation." The judge said that the
paper was the $100 bond of a counterrevolutionary organization
known as the White Rose (*Rosa Blanca*). It was signed by the treas-
urer of the group, the former Cuban Senator, Rolando Masferrer.
He said that I was known to be the head of the American branch of
the White Rose. The bond had been found in my pocket when I
was arrested.

I told him I had never seen this so-called bond before and that
I would not sign a false confession. Sitting there, I remembered that
he had said the bond had been found in my pocket. Yet it had never
been folded or creased. I made a mental note of this discrepancy,
which was to prove important in my defense.

*   *   *

The prison of El Principe, where I was to spend the next fourteen
months, is on a hill overlooking the central park of Havana and the
monument to Jose Marti. The Reina Mercedes Hospital is on one
side and the Palace of Justice on the other. As in the case of Atarés,

the Castle is surrounded by a dry moat with a drawbridge and there is only one entrance. El Principe is about the same age as Atarés, but considerably larger.

The entrance to El Principe is flanked by the fingerprinting department, on the right, and the *requisa*, or room where prisoners are searched on reception, at the left. There are twenty-five *galeras*, or partially underground cells, each of which sleeps 65 to 100 men, and which face a central, star-shaped patio. On top of the Castle and set apart from the prison is the infirmary which faces the central park and commands a view of Havana.

The Castillo del Principe is run by the Ministry of the Interior which supplies the guards. There is also an Army garrison, which is entirely independent of the Interior Ministry.

When I was there, the Castillo housed between 2,500 and 3,000 prisoners and was overcrowded. As a general rule, the inmates were serving short sentences since, in theory at least, those who had perpetrated major crimes were shipped out to the Isle of Pines. However, the Administration of El Principe was flagrantly corrupt and long-term prisoners with influence or money found ways and means of staying there, thus remaining in Havana and enjoying the privilege of having visitors three times a week.

The worst thing about El Principe was that each *galera* had a chief and second-in-command and these men were almost invariably hard-core criminals, serving fifteen to thirty years for murder. Almost always, they were men who had served on the Isle of Pines and, through political connections, had maneuvered their transfer to El Principe.

The prison had a grapevine of informers. The stool pigeons in the prison received such benefits as extra food and were allowed *pabellmi*. This is a system in the Cuban prisons whereby a man is allowed to have his wife visit him every week or so in a special *galera* outside the prison, where they can be alone for a couple of hours. Naturally, while these women are supposed to be wives, this is not necessarily the case. Prisoners, who are unmarried or tired of their wives, will pay to have girls sent up to see them.

In El Principe, it was easy to buy anything you wanted. Marihuana cost fifty cents a cigarette. Morphine, cocaine and heroine were available, not to mention seconal, nembutal and other drugs of that sort. Cocaine is very popular in Cuba.

The prisoners fell into two groups—those who had money or connections and the poor prisoners who had nothing. The first group had steaks and other delicacies brought in from the outside and cooked them on their small electric stoves in the *galeras*. The poor prisoners had to subsist on the inadequate and deficient regular prison fare: coffee, milk and roll in the morning; a lunch around ten of rice and *malanga,* a root which is the traditional diet of hunger in Cuba, and in the afternoon around four o'clock, supper of rice and perhaps black beans or a stew. All this food was served cold, including the coffee.

In most *galeras*, there was a group that ran the card and dice games, another group that controlled marihuana and a third group that sold the more expensive drugs. All this went on with the knowledge of the corrupt guards under the Ministry of the Interior.

The prison is a place where nobody dares to talk. Everybody knows what is going on, but even the doctors and nurses in the infirmary are afraid to tell the truth, because they may be framed and sent to the Isle of Pines. Deportation to the Island—and hence, as a rule, death by hunger, mistreatment, violence or medical neglect— is the dread that permeates the prison constantly like a miasma. The stool pigeons are motivated by fear of the Isle of Pines as much as by greed. The existence of the Island makes everyone, or almost everyone, try to curry favor with the authorities.

There is a prison store, but it is run by hardened convicts. Constant disagreements and knife fights occur about the amount of money spent by prisoners there. Most of the hard-boiled prisoners carried knives, or even machete blades, slipped inside their trouser legs. Since there was no death penalty for common crimes, a man serving twenty or thirty years for murder had nothing to lose by killing again.

Another bad thing about the Cuban prisons was the institution of amnesty. Whenever there was a change in administration, there would be an amnesty and a large proportion of the prisoners would go free. I have talked to men in El Principe who had been sentenced half a dozen times for the same sort of crime. I know men who have committed murder, been released by amnesty, and have then committed a second murder.

To the outside observer, El Principe seemed quiet and orderly, but inside it despicable assaults on young boys and other depravities were the rule. The evil was below the surface. There are workshops there, but nobody works. It is a community of depraved men, run by those who are worse than the rest. The hard-core, long-sentence, degenerate criminals have one visible trait in common—all of them are tattooed. They have the run of the prison because the administration depends on them to know what is going on. They are very dangerous men.

Every three months or so, the garrison in the prison changes, but the guards from the Ministry of the Interior stay. Once in a while, there is an attempted shakeup. The judicial investigators arrive, but the guards and informers have been forewarned and El Principe appears to be a model prison.

*   *   *

Shortly after I entered El Principe, the direction of the prison was turned over to two of the worst human beings I ever had the misfortune to meet—Lieutenant Enrique Kammerer Perez and Captain Herman Marks. One of their first acts was to deny all medical attention to the prisoners regardless of their condition. . . .

Herman Marks had joined Fidel Castro in the Sierra Maestra. He had a record of thirty-two arrests in the United States, including one for rape. In the Castillo del Principe all the guards hated him. At that time they were *guaiiros* from the hills and comparatively decent people.

The hatred grew when he had seven prisoners bayoneted to death in a *requisa* (or search) in 1960. In one of these cases, a man's back was slit open so I could see his bloody, exposed lungs.

There was also the time when *some* of my friends were being held in the *capilla*, or death cell where men are placed to await execution. Instead of being simply kept there a few hours or being held overnight, they remained in *capilla* for 163 days. Every day or so, Marks would go into the *capilla* and point at one of the men:

"Tonight, they are coming for you."

Once when the wife of one of these men came to visit him, Marks told her that her husband had been shot the day before. It was his idea of a great joke. As it happens, that man is alive today.

A man called de Leon, as I recall the name, asked Marks to give him the *coup de grace* in the heart, instead of the head, as his body was to be sent for burial to his eighty-year-old mother. The American captain promised to do so. However, after the firing squad had done its work, he pumped five .45 caliber slugs into de Leon's face, changing it into a shapeless piece of meat. The body was sent to the boy's mother and, when she opened the casket, she died of heart failure.

After Marks had bayoneted seven men in El Principe, he was transferred to the Isle of Pines and a full investigation of his conduct was started. Instances of his brutality and sadism came to light and there were increasing suspicions that he had been stealing funds from the prison. Accordingly, he escaped in a small boat with a female American writer and eventually turned up in the United States. On April 10, 1963, the United States Court of Appeals ruled that Marks, who was stripped of his citizenship, could not regain his nationality and that the U.S. was free to deport him. The American Civil Liberties Union then announced that it would ask the U. S. Supreme Court to review the decision and stay deportation. Aliens are commonly deported to the port from which they came. In Marks' case, his lawyer argued, "he would be killed if he returned there." The Marks story was apparently nearing an ironic finale.

*   *   *

[Martino tells of his experiences in various prisons, including the La Cabaña, before he is transferred to the infamous Isle of Pines. In this prison he witnessed the execution of William Morgan, an American who served Castro as a spy and agent-provocateur before being accused of plotting against Castro. Martino also informs readers of other former supporters of the regime who were sent to prison. In this section he describes the brutality of the prisons.— ED.]

The prisoner is thrown into one of these [a torture cell] naked. It is so small that he must stand up and can barely turn around. There are enormously powerful lights in the ceiling and the heat is almost unbearable. The victim is kept in the hot room until he has had all he can stand and then is put into a similar cell, which is air-conditioned and is kept at near freezing temperature. This treatment is continued, alternating heat with cold, until the victim loses consciousness or confesses.

They also apply mental torture. One method is to take prisoners from the prison to one of the beaches. The men are tied to stakes and told they are about to be executed. A firing squad is assembled; the commands are given; the only departure from realism is that blanks are fired.

In most of these cases, there is no physical torture in the sense that victims were not touched. At the time . . . about 15000 prisoners were being held at G-2 (Secret Police) headquarters in Havana. Among them were women and children. They were given the physical and mental torture of the *cabanitas* [secret police] to make them confess. Those who did break down and confess generally ended at the *paredón*.

The questioning was done by teams of interrogators who repeated their questions and charges hour after hour. The prisoners who were recalcitrant would be put back in the hot and cold cells for hours and then brought back again for questioning.

There were also G-2 "farms" — in reality, isolated houses — out in the country, where men were taken for more severe torture. Few people ever returned from these farms and hence it was not easy to find out what happened there.

One case we knew about was that of Jorgé Diaz. He was blindfolded and taken at night from G-2 headquarters to one of these torture farms. Here he was imprisoned for six or seven months with no toilet paper of any sort.

When he was brought to us, he was unable to walk and his buttocks and anus were a festering mass. We had to wash him with boric acid and, by doing that continuously while he was with us, we improved his condition about 50 per cent. Then he was shipped out to the Isle of Pines and we never learned what happened to him.

He said that six men had been taken with him from the G-2 to the torture *finca*. He was the only one brought back to Havana. On the return trip, the guards were joking about how one man had died of heart failure, another for a different reason and so forth. In short, all had been tortured to death or allowed to die of neglect.

"When we were Rebels with Fidel Castro in the hills," Diaz once said, "we used to talk about how the Batista people would run red hot irons up women's vaginas. This was propaganda, of course. But in the G-2 farms, they actually do this to women and they also run hot irons up the anal openings of men. Whenever this is done, a human being is killed."

I have seen men come back from the *fincas* whose fingernails had been torn out. There was a man who had had all the bones in his fingers smashed with a gun butt and there was another whose legs had been stretched so much to make him confess that he couldn't stand up.

A man named Segundo Prieto was kept in the hot box in G-2 headquarters and made to look into the bright light until he lost his eyesight. He is now in La Cabaña and hopelessly blind. Another man, who is now serving time on the Isle of Pines had his testicles twisted off on a G-2 torture farm. He was able to stand the agonizing pain because he is a student and practitioner of yoga.

In the G-2 farm, the torturing is usually done by Negroes. As for the Rebels who fought for Castro in the hills, almost all of them are whites and are considered unsuitable for this ghoulish business.

The supervision and direction of the tortures is in the hands of Russians. These men are generally either police officials or physicians. They never touch the victims themselves, but they give the orders for torture and decide when it is to be interrupted. They also handle the interrogations and inject sodium pentothal, the so-called truth serum.

Outside of the specialized machinery of torture to induce confession, sadistic treatment and callous neglect tends to be the rule.

For example, a former corporal in the Cuban Army under Batista [the former dictator of Cuba before the revolution], named Adolfo Caballero, was sentenced to serve three years on the Isle of

Pines for allegedly having mistreated Rebel prisoners. When he was sent to the Island, he was a very powerful man, slightly over six feet tall, weighing perhaps 210 pounds. On the Isle of Pines, he got into trouble during one of the *requisas* [search of the cell by the jailers] and was put into an isolation cell and left there to die.

At the last moment, he was transferred to La Cabaña and became one of our cellmates. The ex-corporal was all skin and bones. He could hold no food. His eyes were glazed. He would cry like a baby and ask for his wife and children.

During the three years he had been on the Island, he had never received a letter and did not know whether his family was alive or dead.

While Adolfo was dying in our cell, a male nurse, Manolo Blanco, who was serving four years for having tried to leave the country by plane, became furious at the fact that nothing was being done to save this man's life. The turnkey, who was also a decent human being, was persuaded to help Blanco to carry the dying man on his mattress into the prison office. There, the two put up a successful fight to have Adolfo admitted to the Military Hospital. But it was too late. Adolfo died there the next morning. For this act of mercy, Blanco was sent to the Isle of Pines and the turnkey became a military prisoner in La Cabaña.

Another case of callousness was that of fourteen elderly, retired monks, who lived in a monastery in the Havana area. Because of Castro's fierce hatred of the Catholic Church and of religion in general, I suppose, these old men were arrested and thrown into *Galera* 12, which was supposed to house forty prisoners and already had 180.

These monks naturally had no beds and it was raining very hard. The oldest, a man of ninety-two, had to sleep on a tiny ledge by the open grating, exposed to the rain, and, when the morning came, he was dead. I should add that, after four weeks of prison, the aged monks were released. When they left, all the prisoners cheered them.

✽   ✽   ✽

Conditions were abominably bad in the prison and I kept getting sicker and weaker. I could not keep my food down and was passing a lot of blood. I stayed in my bed as I could scarcely manage to walk. My weight dropped steadily.

Father Dario Casado was finally released and enabled to go to the United States, where he joined the faculty of Villanova University. This was a great relief to me as I knew he would keep his promise to look up Florence and the children in Miami and my mother in Atlantic City. They would have definite word that I was alive.

When I asked Father Casado how Castro and his Communists had managed to conquer in a Catholic country such as Cuba, his answer was that Cuba is only nominally Catholic. "I would estimate that only 30 per cent of the Cubans who call themselves Catholics have been baptized and confirmed," he told me. "Moreover, while most of the colored people know of God and of the Virgin, they devote themselves to the worship of various saints and use voodoo practices in their worship. They are not Catholics in the true sense. Catholic doctrine does not guide and restrain them and, for the most part, they are too ignorant to understand it."

The members of the Catholic youth organizations, however, were of very different fiber. Many were students. All understood the doctrines of the Church. Religion played a guiding role in their spiritual life and made them implacable enemies of the Communist dictatorship.

The Castro regime evidently recognized that fact. In the late summer of 1961, we had a special *requisa*. The objects of search this time were not weapons, but religious objects. The guards seized all the medals, rosaries, holy pictures and Bibles they could find, piled them in the middle of the patio and, in the presence of the prisoners, set fire to them. The new rule was that no prisoner could possess any religious article and that no more rosaries or prayers could be said.

This did not stop the young Catholics, who by this time constituted a large proportion of the prisoners. Instead of saying rosaries openly in the mornings, we would place men at the *galera* door at night and say the rosaries clandestinely, as the early Christians in Roman catacombs must have done. As before, prayers were invariably said for the men who were executed. The guards knew of these religious practices and many of them fiercely disapproved, but they were unable to stop them.

Carlitos Gálvez, a boy who had set fire to El Encanto [a department store], used to come to my *galera* at least once every day to talk about American jazz. He had worked in a music store and had become a fan. In September, he was called up for trial. Like the others, he shaved and dressed very carefully for this occasion. The reason for this was that the judges and the militiamen in the audience looked filthy. Their shirts would be open and their shoes half laced. They had no military bearing or discipline. The prisoners, by contrast, went to trial with their hair cut, their faces shaved and scrubbed and their clothes as neat and clean as possible. They sat up straight and preserved a military bearing. This contrast was one that the Rebels resented.

Carlitos came into my *galera* the morning before the trial and sat on my bed, while his friends came to say goodbye. We were all sad because there was no doubt of his fate.

"I don't know why all of you look so gloomy," Carlito said. "After all, I am the one who is going to be shot. The only thing I am sorry about is that I didn't have time to burn down the Palace of Justice and the Ministry of Communications building."

He had had these two additional acts of sabotage carefully planned when he was arrested. That night, they took him back from the trial and executed him two hours later.

We could see that the dictatorship was preparing for a new American invasion. Anti-aircraft guns were mounted on the prison walls and the dry moat was filling with tanks and artillery. Outside in Havana harbor, tanks, military trucks, field pieces and anti-aircraft guns called *cuatro bocas* [four mouths] were being unloaded almost daily. All this new material was of Russian or Soviet-satellite origin.

At the same time, around October, we learned from the grapevine, from our visitors and our lawyers, that the Communist Party was openly taking over all across the island. They were running the trade unions, the cooperatives and the industries, supported by hordes of fellow travelers and a substantial group of for-

206 JOHN MARTINO

mer Batista people with administrative know-how who had jumped
on the bandwagon.

*　　　*　　　*

Roberto Riveroni [a fellow prisoner] introduced me to a young
friend of his, known as the Checo. This man was violently anti-
American and an old-line Communist Party militant. He was in
prison because he had had a personal dispute with Ché Guevara
when the latter headed the Cuban National Bank. He was very
friendly toward me. As all Communists in Cuba did, he assured me
that he was anti-American merely in the sense of being opposed to
the trusts and imperialism; he had nothing whatsoever against the
American people.

One day, he told me that he had heard a good deal of discussion of my case. He did not want to arouse my hopes, but there was
a good chance that I would be set free before very long.

"Moreover," he said, "the Communist Party has a fine plan for
the political prisoners, but the Party is having trouble with Castro.
This is partly because Fidel Castro tends to follow the line of Red
China. He is strongly opposed to freeing political prisoners and he
is equally opposed to putting them to work. He wants to keep everyone under lock and key and subject them to the worst tortures
imaginable. He seems to have limitless hatred for everyone who has
turned against him or opposes him."

"What do you Communists propose?" I asked.

"It is not convenient for the Party to have so many Cubans in
prison. Do you know that there are from 100,000 to 150,000 political
prisoners on the island? And with our large Cuban families that
means that over half a million people—about a tenth of the population of Cuba—have a member of their immediate family in prison.
These people hate Castro and the regime. They will hate him as
long as these conditions continue."

"Castro should have figured that out," I said.

"That is the trouble, Martino. Castro doesn't figure things out.
He doesn't think. He does whatever comes into his head. We have
fine leaders in the Party, men like Juan Marinello, Blas Roca and

Lázaro Peña. We are trying to make him see the light. You see, Martino, many things have been done wrong in Cuba and the Communist Party is trying to correct them."

"Why are you telling me all this, Checo?"

"Because I have plans for you. We are going to need you."

"I am an American. I am not a Communist. And I have nothing to do with the problems of Cuba."

"That is where you are wrong, Martino. You are part of the Cuban situation now. Things are going to get better for you, because you can be useful in the new plan."

"What plan?"

"A school will be opened in La Cabaña to give the prisoners a chance to learn to read and write, to study and to do many things."

I looked at him in amazement:

"Checo, you know who these prisoners are. They are doctors, lawyers, university students. They don't need you to teach them how to read and write."

Checo waved this objection aside:

"The school is just the beginning of the plan. Pretty soon, everybody will be called into the office and they will fill out questionnaires. They will ask you about your social and class background, why you are in prison, whether or not you have been tried, how many years you have to serve, about your wife and your relatives and their social origin and whether—if you had a chance— you would be willing to be integrated into the new society and to go to work. In that way, many men will go free.

"Now as to the school. The teachers, in many cases, will be drawn from the prisoners. I will head what we call the Communist Party nucleus of the school. We will pick the teachers and try to sell the idea that the men should go to school in all the *galeras*. We will show them that the school is a way toward freedom."

"How will that work, Checo?"

"The prisoners will show their good intentions by signing up for the school. After they have worked in the school and been under observation for one or two months, they will be passed out of the prison compound and will live beyond the walls in *Galeras* 24 through 28."

"Then what?" I asked.

"There they will have better food, better beds, a canteen where they can buy what they want and visits three times a week. They will be allowed to wear civilian clothes. But they will have to study, to work hard."

"Study what, Checo?"

"Socialism. After they have mastered the elements of Marxism-Leninism and after three months in the outside *galeras*, then the ones who pass that test will be sent to farms. There, they will work and study under close observation for another half year. The ones who pass that test will go free under provisional liberty."

"What is going to stop them, once they get their provisional liberty, from going right back into counterrevolutionary activities?"

"You don't understand," he replied with a condescending smile. "After they have eventually been set free, they will go on the streets. But with one proviso. A member of their family or the neighborhood Committee of Defense will have to guarantee that these men will not engage in counterrevolutionary activities, because, if they do, they will go back to prison, another ten years will be added to their sentences and reprisals will be taken against their families."

"What will stop these men from going to a foreign Embassy and getting political asylum?"

"Well," he said, "that is where the family comes in. A member or two will be held responsible and they will go to jail in place of the man who was set free provisionally and escaped."

"Checo, you have worked out quite some plan."

"It is not my plan, Martino. It is the plan they *use* in the Soviet Union and elsewhere in the Communist world. It is going to be put into effect here. I will be in charge and my assistant will be a good friend of yours, Alejandro Martínez Sáenz, the Nicaraguan."

"So he is in the act too? That doesn't surprise me." Martínez Sáenz was a Nicaraguan revolutionary who had had trouble with Ché Guevara. He was one of those people who kept assuring me that he was just a nationalist, not a communist.

I told him I didn't think the plan would work. He would have trouble trying to force the prisoners to accept it.

"You will see," Checo replied. "They will be called into the office, one by one. Those who reject the plan will not just be sent to the Isle of Pines. They will be put in a concentration camp where they will have to work with pick and shovel at forced labor. You will find out where you come in later," was his parting shot.

The Communist faction put two men into each *galera* to sell the school plan to the prisoners. However, of 1,289 prisoners in La Cabaña at the time, only sixty-seven men attended the opening classes of the school.

Shortly before the school opened, Checo came to me to urge that I be its English teacher.

"We are against the American system," he said, "but not against your language. Furthermore, if you join the school as a teacher, you will have the biggest class in the school."

"Why is that, Checo?"

"Because you are an American and many of the prisoners will follow you."

"Checo, the answer is no."

"But you teach English right now in the *galera*, don't you?"

"That's right. I teach my friends who want to learn the language." I had acquired a dictionary and a first-grade reader and I had been teaching José Cabañas González, General Sánchez Gómez and a few of the others. Checo argued that, if I could teach English in the *galera*, I could do the same in the school. In return, I would get better food, fresh milk, medicine and a chance for freedom.

"Checo," I said, "you know I am an American and not a Communist. You also know all about my case and that I am innocent. I don't *see* why I have to sell myself to get out of prison. Moreover, if jail is good enough for my friends, I will stay here until I die."

"It is up to you," he said, shaking his head.

Soon the attempts at persuasion were resumed. This time the agent was a boy, Cesar Fuentes . . . He came to the *galera* to tell me that he would be the German teacher in the school and that, if I cooperated by teaching English, I would have a good chance to go free. I repeated what I had said to Checo.

"If you don't cooperate," Fuentes said, "remember you have a good chance to be sent to the Isle of Pines. They are setting up these schools all over Cuba and in all the prisons. When they take men from the Isle of Pines to go to the schools, there will be room there for a few hard heads from La Cabaña."

That afternoon, the prison was in great excitement because the sixty-seven men who had decided to join the school had been told that, if they did so, they would be beaten up.

Alfredo Montoto came in.

"The chief of the prison says it is very important for you to join the school, because you are looked on as one of the leaders here. Everybody respects you and, if you join, there will be no trouble. The rest will follow the lead of an American."

"In other words," I replied, "I am supposed to be a symbol of the United States. If an American goes to school to become a Communist, it will break the morale of the rest. They will feel the United States has thrown in the towel."

"That is one way of putting it," he said.

I repeated that I would not do it. When he asked me what I would do if the chief forced me to go at gunpoint, I replied that I was a prisoner and would yield to force, but that the chief would merely be making trouble for himself.

"I am sorry to say this," Montoto replied, "but you are going to be shipped out together with a lot of other troublemakers."

The school stayed open exactly thirteen days. On the night of April 23, 1962, as the students were going to school after the dinner hour, a riot started in the patio. The prisoners ganged up on the students and teachers and mauled them for about a quarter of an hour.

The prison director took a machine gun and fired over the heads of the prisoners. He then ordered all men back to their *galeras*.

When they had returned the prisoners to their cells, including those who were bloody and beaten, the guards took the students with them and went from *galera* to *galera*. The students were ordered to pick out the men who had attacked them.

What followed was one of the most terrible sights I have ever seen. They opened up *Galera* 17 and took out six or seven men who had been accused of taking part in the riot. The guards lined up in two files facing each other. They made these prisoners run the gauntlet between the two files and, as they did so, about twenty-five guards on each side jabbed them with their bayonets and clubbed them with their rifle butts. As the guards battered them, the men tried frantically to reach the safety of the office before being clubbed off their feet.

They repeated this *galera* by *galera*. The entire bloody process took nearly four hours. By night, 167 men had bayonet wounds. Some also had broken ribs and cracked skulls.

About ten that night, we were all ordered back into the patio, including the sick. Four machine guns were pointed down at us from the roof. The chief, who had fired wildly into the patio with his .45 during the disturbance, now spoke over the public address system:

"If there is another riot in the prison, if anybody tries to stop the school, if any of the prisoners tries to beat up the students, *then* I *will kill everybody.*"

The prisoners who had run the gauntlet were being patched up in the office. Afterwards, they were put in an underground *galera*, held incommunicado and fed on bread and water. Later, they were given a special trial for starting a riot in the prison and sent to the Isle of Pines.

The night of violence ended around two o'clock and early in the morning I was called to the office and, for the first time, met the chief of the prison face to face. He asked me to cooperate with the school and again I refused.

"We are going to take care of you troublemakers," he said.

At that moment, Franco, the officer of the day, intervened in my favor. I have no idea why he wanted to help me.

"Do you know the story of John Martino?" he asked the chief.

"I don't want to know his story. He is another American. He is an enemy of the Revolution."

"Why don't you go into the office and look at his dossier," Franco replied. "There is an order from the tribunal that he must not be removed from La Cabaña Fortress."

The chief asked Franco why he was defending me. The O.D.

replied that he was pointing out what was in the Martino file so that the chief would not get in trouble with the tribunal.

"All right, take him back to the *galera*. I will see why they don't want to send him to the Isle of Pines. But he must go out of this prison, because he is the source of a lot of trouble here, because he keeps telling the prisoners that some day the Americans will come and free them."

"I don't know where you got that information," I told him. "It is false, but I suppose it is useless for me to try to argue with you."

"I know everything that goes on in the *galeras*. I know you are always talking politics."

After the riot, they suspended all visits and locked us in our *galeras* again.

That night, when the school opened, the students were escorted out *galera* by *galera*, but, instead of sixty-seven men, only forty-two went to the school.

That morning at three o'clock, we had another *requisa*. This one lasted for ten hours.

Because of the riot, there was an investigation of the prison by high officials of the G-2. It was rumored that Ramiro Valdéz was taking part in the probe personally.

The *galeras* were opened again. Three new guards were brought in. From now on, they would be the only ones allowed inside the prison area and in contact with the prisoners. These men were ardent Communists, who had just returned from Russia. The chief of the prison was removed and a young man of about twenty, whom we knew only as Pepe, took his place.

Three or four days after the change in administration, they announced that the school was closed. The 100-odd men who had been held in the underground *galera* on bread and water, were brought back. The water was turned on again. They explained that the whole thing had been a mistake and that the plan for a school had been shelved, as far as La Cabaña Fortress was concerned, because we were too vicious and incorrigible and had no real desire to go free.

*   *   *

Around this time, they brought Luis Alfaro, the leader of the students who had staged the January 1961 hunger strike, back to La Cabaña from the Isle of Pines. I was surprised to see him. He came in with a group of six other boys.

"You must have good connections to get off the Island," I said.

"No, we are returning from the so-called rehabilitation farms."

I was shocked. I told him he was one of the last people on earth I would have picked to turn collaborator.

"You have to try to get out of prison one way or another," he replied, "but these people turned out to be too smart for me. We are running up against Russian methods here."

He told us that, when they were on the Isle of Pines, all the men who wanted to be rehabilitated were put in *circular* 3, which was known to the prisoners as Moscow. He said that, at the time he left, there were about 15,000 to 20,000 prisoners on the Isle of Pines, that conditions were indescribably bad, that they suffered most from the water shortage and lived in a morass of human excrement. Tuberculosis and fungus were slowly killing the prisoners and it was a place worse than death.

Very cautiously, he had gotten together a group of men who had no ties and no family in Cuba and who were willing to do anything to escape to the United States. They decided to join the school, take part in the rehabilitation program and, at the first opportunity, try to escape.

"How many prisoners on the Island would you say have joined the school?"

He gave me a wan smile:

"About 300 or 350."

"Out of fifteen to twenty thousand?"

"It was very dangerous to join the school," Alfaro explained, "because, unless your group really knew your plans, you had an excellent chance of getting killed. Eight or nine men had been killed in the prison because they wanted to join the school and become collaborators.

"It was dangerous in two ways. To keep from getting murdered, you had to let a few people know your real purpose. But if too many knew or the wrong people knew, the authorities would find out and you would be put in punishment cells or sent to torture farms. We lived in an atmosphere of suspicion, fear and terror. Everyone looked on me as a traitor, a traitor to the other prisoners and to the cause of Cuba.

"We finally convinced the political commissar and his five assistants that we were sincere. We joined the school and studied there for three months. Then they moved us from *circular* 3 (Moscow) to one of the outside *galeras*, which was much safer.

"There they buttered us up. We had lessons and studied Marxism-Leninism ten hours a day. Living conditions were much better. They gave us plenty of water and we even had clean beds.

"After two months in the outside *galera*, we were sent finally to the farm in Pinar del Rio.

"Now, Martino, do you know who ran this farm?" I shook my head.

"He was one of your *paisanos*. Yes, an American. His name is Stanley Mitchell and he is the boss of the rehabilitation farm. He does all the political screening. He is a brilliant man. In fact, he is so brilliant that we wound up back here in La Cabaña Fortress. They gave us another ten years yesterday."

Luis Alfaro was moved to the farm with a group of thirty other prisoners. They were met by Mitchell, who lived there with his wife. He was affable, always smiling or laughing. He spoke Russian, Spanish and English fluently.

According to Luis, Mitchell is about forty-five and originally from California. In World War II, he had claimed to be a conscientious objector, but his claim had been rejected and he had been compelled to go into the Army.

He deserted, was caught and sentenced to serve two years in Leavenworth. There he became a Communist. He traveled to various parts of the world to learn about Communism and studied the Soviet system. After working in the United States, he was sent to Cuba by the Comintern after Castro took power. He was put in charge of setting up rehabilitation farms in Pinar del Rio Province.

"What were conditions like on this farm?" I asked.

"They make it very inviting for you, John. You get clean bunks and good food. You wear blue pants and light blue shirts."

"The same uniform as the guards wear?"

"Yes. There are thousands of Russian and Chinese technicians around, Martino, large numbers of them in Pinar del Rio. They are supposed to be working on farms, but I guess you heard that there are missile bases being built all over Cuba—particularly in Pinar del Rio.

"These Russians wear blue pants and light blue shirts also. This is the new uniform in Cuba for the workers. The workers in factories and in the militia are to wear the same uniform.

"To get back to my story, we thought we had this man, Mitchell, fooled. We even had permission to go to the adjoining village twice a week with only one guard. We were getting visits and money from friends. Finally, they sprung the trap on us."

"What was the trap?"

"We were doing light work on the farm, tending chickens and that sort of thing. One day, Mitchell got the six of us and five others together. He told us we were all honor prisoners. He had decided to allow all of us to go home and visit our families in Havana the following Saturday and Sunday. He said that we were on parole. We were honor-bound to be back at the farm on Monday.

"This was just the opportunity we had been waiting for. We had made all our plans to go into hiding in Havana and then try to get to the United States. But we made the same fatal mistake everybody else makes."

"What was that?"

"One of my group had been on the other side all the time. Mitchell and the G-2 were completely informed about our plans. We had arranged to meet some people and escape in a boat. I had spent $2,000 of my own money to arrange the getaway for the six of us.

"We went to the rendezvous point and stepped into the boat. Then, one of my men pulled a gun on us. We waited there with our hands up until other members of the G-2 arrived. And here am I, Luis Alfaro, the leader of the students, the man who thought he was so smart, right back in La Cabaña."

"You mean, Luis, you never suspected that this man was an agent?"

"How could I? I handpicked the men myself. The terrible thing is that this is what is happening all over Cuba.

"I will never underestimate the Communists again. These men are determined and dedicated. Can you understand a man allowing himself to be sent to the Isle of Pines so he can work there as an informer among the prisoners? These informers suffer the same way we do. They go through the *requisas*. They thirst. They live in filth and feces. They have to endure everything we do. But there it was, when the chips were down, this man belonged to the G-2."

Luis is a man of strong character. Yet, in the middle of his story, he broke down and cried. He became so hysterical, we had to send for the doctor. I realized that it was the hard core of dedicated Communists that enabled Fidel Castro to do the seemingly impossible.

Once the Checo had said to me:

"You know, Martino, the difference between a Communist and you people who believe in democracy? We work twenty-five hours a day at being Communists. The ruthless dedication of our people—especially the young ones—is something frightening to see."

                    *   *   *

[After three years in prison, Martino was finally released in September 1962 through the persistent efforts of his wife, who finally convinced authorities that a mistake had been made. —ED.]

· 9 ·

DOAN VAN TOAI AND DAVID CHANOFF

A Tale of Mistaken Identity in Vietnam

AS FRENCH PROFESSOR Jean-Louis Margolin astutely observes in his essay "Vietnam and Laos: The Impasse of War Communism," in *The Black Book of Communism: Crimes, Terror, and Repression* (1999), "Admitting the damage caused by Communism in Vietnam is today still an anathema to many Westerners, who took a stand against French colonialism and American 'imperialism' in the area and found themselves in the same camp as the Vietnamese Communist Party."

The war in Vietnam led to reconsiderations of America's struggle against communism. Many Americans simply could reconcile dropping bombs on the Vietnamese with the claim that the United States was fighting for democracy. Bombing people to bring democracy did not make much sense. And claims of fighting for democracy were belied by the corrupt government dictatorships of South Vietnam.

Moreover, in fighting against the Viet Cong insurgents and the invading North Vietnamese, the United States appeared to have placed itself on the side of defending European colonialism and imperialism. Surely, it was argued, the United States itself had been formed in anti-colonial struggle against the British. While few critics of the war really saw the Communist leader of Vietnam, Ho Chi Minh, as the "George Washington of Vietnam," large numbers of Americans concluded that involvement in this war that could not be won was not worth the effort, communism or no communism. Communism, their argument went, was not monolithic; not every Communist leader was under the control of the Soviet Union; and while anti-colonial struggles for self-determination used the rhetoric of communism, the real issues were agrarian reform and economic development in nations such as Vietnam.

By late 1968, polls showed that the majority of Americans wanted out of Vietnam with a negotiated settlement. The final withdrawal of U.S. troops came with the signing of the Paris peace treaty in January 1973. On April 30, 1975, the South Vietnamese regime fell to the North Vietnamese army.

The Vietnam War left the nation's confidence in itself and in its foreign policy shaken. In light of the war, policymakers, politicians, and the military undertook a reevaluation of cold war interventionism. While not fully retreating into an "isolationist" foreign policy, the United States in the 1970s remained leery of military intervention and divided over how best to confront Soviet communism.

The publication of Doan Van Toai's *Vietnamese Gulag* in 1986 caused considerable excitement in the United States. It appeared during President Reagan's second term, just as the Soviet Union was undergoing a crisis of confidence and while U.S. confidence in America's role in the world was being restored. The book allowed supporters of the Vietnam War to declare, in effect, "See, I told you so. North Vietnamese Communists are just as cruel as any other Communists." While this was a minority view, Doan Van Toai's memoir assured its readers that the war in Vietnam was not simply the good guys (Vietnamese peasants) versus the "bad guys" (American troops). Perhaps, there had been something worth fighting for in Vietnam.

Vietnamese Gulag chronicles the repression that followed the Communist victory in 1975. At first the North Vietnamese proclaimed a "policy of clemency" for the approximately one million officials and soldiers who had served the Saigon government. Within months, however, the Communist government announced a reeducation campaign for these groups. They were sent to reeducation centers with the promise that they would be occupied for only a couple of days or at most a month for officers and high-ranking officials. The days turned into seven or eight years. The last survivors of these programs did not return home until 1986, eleven years later. From 500,000 to 1 million individuals were sent to these camps. Although large numbers of these people were students, intellectuals, and Buddhist and Catholic monks, many of them had supported the National Liberation Front (the Viet Cong). Doan Van Toai was one of these people arrested in these round-ups because of a mistaken identification.

The camps varied in their treatment of prisoners. "Difficult" individuals were sent north where conditions were especially squalid. Detainees were fed poor-quality rice, often only seven ounces daily. Doan Van Toai describes a universe that shared many of the characteristics of Chinese prison camps, though conditions were worse. Often seventy to eighty prisoners were placed in a cell built to accommodate twenty. It was common for people to take turns standing by the one small air hole. Torture and executions were common but hidden by officials.

Vietnamese Gulag provided gripping insight into the harshness of the Vietnamese Communist regime. Although the regime began to liberalize in 1986, when large numbers of political prisoners were freed and camps closed, in South Vietnam arrests continued among political intellectuals and peasants. American policy toward Vietnam and the American perspective on communism might have changed as a result of the war, but to many readers of *Vietnamese Gulag*, communism had not changed and never would—in Vietnam or China, Cuba or North Vietnam—until those regimes collapsed under their own weight.

🔣 On the evening of June 22, 1975, less than two months after the fall of South Vietnam, there is a concert in Ho Chi Minh City, formerly known as Saigon.

From *The Vietnamese Gulag* (New York, 1986), pp. 11–21, 22–24, 185–189, 312–314.

Vietnam's National Orchestra has come here from Hanoi. At
8:00 P.M. it will perform at the Grand Theater—formerly the home
of South Vietnam's parliament. For the past week it's been impossible to get tickets. Ages have passed since the southern capital has
heard a classical concert played by a real symphony orchestra. I'm
thirty years old, and I've never heard anything but third-rate bands
featuring electric guitars and syrupy songs with the most astonish-
ingly affected lyrics. American ersatz. As for traditional Vietnamese
music, it's been killed off by the war.

But that evening I'm at the Grand Theater, thanks to some
Communist party friends who are repaying a favor. The Vietnamese
National Orchestra isn't the Berlin Philharmonic. But for the first
time I am enjoying a true professional orchestra, over a hundred
musicians, live. I'm amazed. So this is one of the luxuries peace has
to offer, this peace I have never known.

The orchestra has just finished a Beethoven concerto. I am in
heaven. The master of ceremonies now announces that a ballet performance will follow. That's when I notice the four *ho dois* (soldiers) in their green uniforms at the end of my row.

One by one they are taking away the people sitting between
me and the aisle, and talking to them. The *ho dois* are obviously
looking for someone. When my turn comes, one of the soldiers
leads me to the lobby. I'm curious about what they want, but calm.
In the lobby there are maybe ten more soldiers, all from the North,
to judge by their accents. One of them, very young, eighteen at the
most, shouts at me, clipping his words, "Is your name Toai?"

"Yes," I say. I'm about to add "why?" but before I can, he takes
a step forward and slaps me. Then one of the others holds him
back, and I'm quickly surrounded and hustled up the stairs toward
the manager's office on the second floor. As I'm being rushed along,
struggling to keep my balance, I remember when I raced up these
same stairs five years ago at the head of several hundred university
students—members of the Saigon Student Union. We were about
to take over the National Assembly building, to demand that a number of our imprisoned comrades be freed. That episode had earned
me a stay in President Thieu's jails.

The Communist party and the NLF certainly know all about

my antiwar activities as a student leader.* They know that even though I had never formally joined either one of them, I was always their ally. What could they possibly want with me now? In the manager's office I'm forced to stand in front of a North Vietnamese Army lieutenant. While *ho dois* on both sides pin my arms, the lieutenant stares at me and asks,

"Are you Ngo Vuong Toai?"

I suddenly understand. Now I know what's wrong. About ten years ago, Ngo Vuong Toai was president of a small anti-Communist student organization that was a front for the Thieu government, and probably the Americans as well. It was commonly known that the NLF had condemned him to death, and in 1966 they tried to assassinate him. Toai had been wounded in the stomach and had barely survived. Afterward he left his little group and went to work directly for the government, in the well-guarded offices of the Ministry of Information.

Obviously there's been a misunderstanding; I'm being mistaken for this other Toai.** "No," I tell the lieutenant. "I'm not Ngo Vuong Toai. I don't have anything to do with him. I'm Doan Van Toai. I was vice-president of the student union. I fought against the puppets. I worked for the Front. I've been in jail for it. Now I'm working with the PRG Finance Committee.† You can verify everything with Colonel Nguyen Ngoc Hien and with the Association of Patriotic Intellectuals."

I take a certain pride in listing my titles and credentials. I watch for the effect, waiting for the apology I so richly deserve. The lieutenant is obviously embarrassed. He's been told to arrest a cer-

---

*The National Liberation Front (NLF) was a political umbrella organization founded in 1960 to direct the insurgency in South Vietnam.

**In Vietnamese the family name comes first and the given name last. But there are relatively few family names, and so the given name is most often used for identification. Nguyen Van Thieu (given name, Thieu), South Vietnam's political strongman from the mid-sixties until 1975, was known as President Thieu. North Vietnam's defense minister, Vo Nguyen Giap, was General Giap.

†The Provisional Revolutionary Government (PRG) was founded by the insurgency in 1969 to challenge the Saigon regime for recognition in international forums as South Vietnam's true representative government.

tain Toai, who was supposed to be at the concert. Apparently he has the wrong man.

But while I watch him trying to decide what to do, something else occurs to me. How did I happen to be in the very row he was told to search? Is this really just a simple misunderstanding? Somebody who knew I was at the concert has to be involved. What are the chances that the *ho dois* would know exactly where to find me, yet mistake me for Ngo Vuong Toai? Not so good, I think.

Meanwhile, as far as the lieutenant is concerned, my person matches all too well the individual described in his orders. Or at least I'm not so bad a fit as to be dismissed out of hand. So he reacts as any policeman would. "Not the right Toai? Maybe *so*, maybe not. Take him in and we'll check it out."

Outside the theater, I'm ordered to climb on the back of a Honda motorcycle, and accompanied by two other Hondas, we speed off to the police headquarters on Tran Hung Dao Boulevard. I haven't given them a bit of trouble. Although I'm beginning to have some doubts about what's really happening, I'm still convinced it's a misunderstanding that I'll be able to clear up quickly. Several years earlier I had read the first volume of Alexander Solzhenitsyn's *Gulag Archipelago*. I vividly remember chapter 2, entitled "Arrest." Even in the Vietnamese translation, the writing was dazzling, memorable—though I had dismissed the substance of the book as propaganda. But now the words come back to me, the thoughts of someone who's just been arrested. "Who, me? What for?" "It's a mistake, they'll clear it up." But that was in Russia. Who knows whether things like that really go on there? Anyway, this is Vietnam, the new Vietnam.

At police headquarters I wait in the hallway, guarded by three *ho dois*. I listen as the lieutenant discusses my case with the duty officer. The lieutenant is trying to unload this potential embarrassment on the officer. This may not be the Toai he was told to arrest, but he's not sure. "We'd better keep him." But the duty officer doesn't want any trouble, doesn't want to be saddled with the responsibility of arresting the wrong person—someone who might be able to cause problems. But the lieutenant says, "Look, you'll have even more problems if you don't lock him up and he turns out to be the right guy."

The discussion goes on forever, until both men suddenly realize it's already eleven o'clock. That puts an end to it. At this hour
there's no way anybody can disturb a higher-ranking officer to resolve the matter. Better to lock up the prisoner until tomorrow,
when they can ask someone what to do.

So I'm pushed up to the desk.

"You are Doan Van Toai?"

"Yes, Doan Van Toai! Not Ngo Vuong Toai, the one you were
supposed to arrest. I protest this treatment. I demand . . ."

The duty officer cuts me off with a wave of his hand and says
loudly, "We'll clear it all up in the morning. Right now, you're
under arrest."

"Under arrest!" Now I'm beginning to get excited, raising my
voice. "That doesn't make any sense. I'm not Ngo Vuong Toai. I
never collaborated with the puppets. I was a student opposition
leader. I spent time in jail. Can't you understand that? This treatment is unacceptable!" By now I'm shouting. "How can you arrest
me? What am I supposed to have done?"

The officer has been drumming his fingers on the desk, not
looking at me. Now he raises his eyes and says in a formal tone,
"You are accused of suspicious acts."

"Me? Suspicious acts? What suspicious acts? Who has denounced me? I demand to see the liar who denounced me!"

Already I know I don't have a chance. Any more discussion
with this low-level nonentity is useless. It doesn't make any difference to him that he might be jailing an innocent man. I'll have to
explain myself to somebody else, somebody in charge. Meanwhile,
this individual is reciting a catechism to me.

"If the revolution decides to arrest someone, it has its reasons.
If a mistake is made, that will be acknowledged. Be patient and wait
for the revolution's judgment. While you wait, you'd better keep
your voice down."

I start to protest again, but my heart's not in it. This representative of the revolution has decided I should be locked up. So I'll be
locked up. If I keep shouting, they'll beat me. That's pretty clear.

A *ho doi* removes my belt and searches my pockets, taking my
wallet. It's ten minutes before midnight, according to my watch,
which I glance at as the *ho doi* pulls it over my wrist. Then two of

them push me down a hallway with doors on each side, cell doors. The air is heavy, stale with the smell of unwashed bodies. Snoring comes from behind the doors. I have the feeling that the place is full.

That's my first surprise about prison. During the war the NLF often declared it would eliminate prisons. After victory, Le Duan, the Communist party general secretary, personally visited Thieu's famous tiger cage cells in the Con Son Island jail. Looking at the symbols of the southern regime's repressiveness, Le Duan declared: "We will transform the jails into schools!" Yet this place seems full. The prisoners here must be some of the thieves and traffickers who operated so blatantly during the last weeks before the old regime died—the dregs of a Vietnamese society corrupted by war. I feel humiliated at being here with such people, ashamed to be associated with them in any way. I'm relieved when the *ho dois* shove me into an individual cell that boasts a bare cement bench to sleep on, a toilet hole, and a faucet.

I lie down and try to stay calm, to control the feelings that are boiling up inside me. Above me, behind a vent in the ceiling, a light bulb throws off a weak glare. The prison's nocturnal sounds come alive, just as I remember them from my previous stays in Thieu's jails: the sighs of the sleeping prisoners, the padded footfalls of the guards, who watch you through the peepholes while they remain unseen. I tell myself, "Tomorrow I'll clear everything up. Then they'll let me out." I fall asleep repeating that.

Morning wake-up is an insistent, raspy voice coming through the cell door's eye-level peephole. "What the hell do you think you're doing? Sleeping? What's your name? Don't you know you have to be up at six and straighten your bed?" (I'm using my rolled-up pants as a pillow and my shirt as a half sheet.)

With a free man's logic I try to answer the voice, this prison system that already possesses me as a spider possesses a fly caught in its web. "But I don't even know why I'm here."

"You don't, huh?" rasps the voice through the peephole. "No, I don't. I was mistaken for . . ."

I'm interrupted by a humorless laugh. "Ha, ha! If there weren't any reason, ha, ha, why have they brought you here? Listen, you weren't up on time, you don't eat."

And the peephole shutter closes. No breakfast. I lie on the cement bench staring at the ceiling, until a few minutes later the voice is back, louder this time. "Prisoner, didn't I tell you to get up? You think you're going to sleep all day? Lying down is forbidden! You sit, or you stand."

I sit up. What can I do? I look at my hands and listen to the noises. I begin pacing the cell, three steps one way, three the other. The prisoner's domain is quickly measured. Prisoner! Several times before I was a prisoner. But not exactly like this. Being a prisoner under Thieu was like being a celebrity. Outside, my family and friends were doing everything they could for me; politicians were challenging the government; newspapers were denouncing the repression of the students. Dozens of foreign correspondents were covering the whole affair for papers all over the world.

Suddenly I feel chilled. My isolation comes home to me and begins to settle in. Nobody knows I'm here. Even when they find out, what can they do? Hire a lawyer? There are no more lawyers; there haven't been any since liberation. Nor are there any political parties. The newspapers are gone too, and the foreign correspondents. Vietnam is cut off from the world. Before, the demonstrations and protests had an international audience. But now there's only the party. The party runs the new Vietnam. Maybe that's not so bad, for the job of reconstruction. But for a prisoner . . . I can feel the walls around me getting thicker, heavier. I am alone here.

Not quite. There are certainly others. Signals are coming at me from neighboring cells. "Psst, newcomer." "You . . . in cell five." "Hey, newcomer." I ignore them. Why should I talk to thieves and profiteers? I'll wait. The duty officer had to submit my case to someone in charge. Soon enough they'll realize there's been a misunderstanding.

Meanwhile, I wait, in this cell where one has no way to measure time. The only light is from the weak bulb set into a vent in the ceiling. Under the bulb a fan turns, one of those old-style colonial fans left behind by the French.

Finally, the shutter opens. I rush to it. A woman's hand sticks in a large bowl of "red rice," as we call it, a coarse rice that's usually fed to the pigs. "Wait a minute," I shout. "I want to see someone in charge!"

On the other side of the shutter a girl's face stares at me—she can't be more than eighteen. She looks at me apologetically and whispers, "I can't do anything for you." Then loudly: "Talking is forbidden, prisoner." Later I learn that she too is a prisoner, being used as a servant. Her boyfriend had been arrested with a gun in his possession. Unaware that he was in trouble, she had gone to his house and was taken herself.

Ravenous, I begin to shovel the rice into my mouth with the plastic spoon they've given me, but there's sand in it, or some kind of grit. This rice meant for pigs seems to have been picked up from the ground.

Later in the day a second bowl appears at the shutter, the same red rice with lots of sand and a little salt. This time I discover a trick. If I run some water into the bowl and stir, the sand collects on the bottom. It's disgusting, but at least now I can swallow it. A few days later a guard tells me the sand is there for a purpose, mixed in "so prisoners will think of their mistakes while they eat."

Night comes—I can tell from the coolness in the air circulating through the ceiling vent. I'm beginning to worry. No one has tried to talk to me all day, except for the raspy-voiced *ho doi* and the girl servant. And the prisoners in the nearby cells whom I'm still ignoring, though they're very persistent. "Hey, you, newcomer! Young man! You in number five!"

How do they know I'm a young man? With my ear pressed up against the shutter crack I can hear their stage whispers clearly, calling me, telling me who they are, talking to each other. If I lie flat I can hear even better through the wide space under the ill-fitting metal door. I can even see a little through it, and through the crack between the door and the frame on the hinge side. "He's a young man . . . looks like he's educated . . . maybe an official." Little by little I realize that these voices don't belong to criminals. Most of them seem to be Saigon army officers.

Still I keep quiet. I don't want to do anything that might jeopardize my imminent release. But what are all these army people doing here? As far as I know, there have been very few arrests since liberation. Another night goes by, then day. The conversations go on, though now the voices have stopped trying to draw me out. I am beginning to understand that I was wrong. There obviously have been arrests, lots of them. But it's all been done so quietly, without disturbing the general public feeling of relief that the war is over.

During the day two bowls of red rice appear at the shutter. While I eat, I read the inscriptions on the cell wall, most of them dating back to the former regime: "Down with Thieu!" "Down with the Americans!" But others are more recent. One says, "I am Nguyen Tu, a reporter for *Chinh Luan*.* I was arrested on May 2d. I am seventy years old. Better to die than to stop writing."

May 2d! Nguyen Tu was arrested two days after liberation. What happened to him after he left this cell? Another message has no date. It says, "Nothing is more precious than independence and liberty"—Ho Chi Minh's most famous saying. Is it the defiant statement of some prisoner of the Saigon regime, or the bitter irony of a more recent guest? In any case, during the fifty-two days since Saigon's fall, at least several people have occupied this cell. One of them has written in large letters, "Down with communism"—a sentiment that wouldn't have made any sense two months ago.

I too scratch a message on the wall with a sliver of stone I've found on the floor: "Doan Van Toai, thirty years old. Former vice-president of the student union. Previously arrested by Thieu as pro-Communist. Arrested again June 22, 1975, 9:00 P.M. Don't know why. Am not against communism. Am against those who misapply it." Mine is the longest statement on the wall, even longer than Nguyen Tu's.

That night I am overwhelmed by the injustice I'm suffering. I can imagine the anxiety my mother and father are feeling, and my wife and three little boys, the oldest of whom is four. Luckily, I'm in

---

Chinh Luan was a right-wing newspaper, one of the thirty or so Saigon dailies the Thieu government allowed to exist. After liberation the number of dailies fell to two.

good health. I begin to do a little yoga. A few stretches, then some relaxation exercises to help me fall asleep.

*   *   *

From day to day new prisoners arrive, sometimes women with little children, sometimes peasants from far-off provinces. Squinting through the crack, I catch glimpses of them as they walk by. (Later on my food port was left open occasionally, as it was for most of the longtime prisoners.) Some have their hands tied, and bloody feet. Some are blindfolded. The next morning they ask, "Where am I?"

On my "street" in Tran Hung Dao Prison I see two Buddhist monks and a Catholic priest led by, chained hand and foot. I see Thai, Chinese, and Cambodians. I also see four white prisoners dressed in black Vietnamese pajamas. I hear that one of them is the French owner of the Brodard Cafe on Rue Catinat, the gathering place of intelligentsia and reporters. The others are said to be Americans on their way north.

Day merges into night and night into day. Asleep one night, about a month after my arrival, I am startled awake by the sound of my door slamming shut. A guard has pushed someone into the cell. He's sitting on the floor near my bench. He speaks to me in a low voice. "Where are we? Which jail? Is there any water?"

I point to the faucet. "You'll have to use your hands, I don't have a glass."

"Can you help me?" he says. "My hands . . ."

I look at his hands and see that his left wrist is handcuffed to his right ankle and his right wrist to his left ankle. The poor man can't stand up, or get himself out of his awkward, knees-drawn-up position. I help him to sit on the bench, then bring him water in my cupped hands. He drinks thirstily, then thanks me. I'm dying to ask him questions, but I have to be cautious. Why have they put him here?

He looks to be about fifty. He speaks with the sharp sibilants of a northern accent, and his refined speech contrasts with his miserable physical condition. He looks emaciated. He hasn't shaved in a while, and he certainly hasn't bathed. His body gives off a pungent smell. He asks when I was arrested.

"A month ago. How about you?"

"Two months ago." Until now he's been in jail in Saigon's Third District.

"What did you do before?" I ask.

"Dean of the law school," he says. I can't believe it. Flabbergasted, I look at him more closely: "Are you Professor Thong?" I blurt out.

"Yes. Do you know me?" "I was one of your students." Of course I know him. This filthy, emaciated man, grotesquely hunched up on the bench, is the brilliant Professor Thong. The way he looks, it's no wonder I didn't recognize him at first. But he is indeed my former professor, one of Vietnam's best-known lawyers. I introduce myself, adding, "I was sure you left before the fall."

"I wanted to," he says. "But I couldn't desert my old mother. Besides, I thought they wouldn't go after a law professor. You can see that I was wrong. They accused me of being a CIA spy. They tortured me. But I don't have anything to confess."

Professor Thong tells me that almost all the law school faculty was arrested, and the school itself shut down. "It's like the French Revolution," he says. "They used to say that the republic doesn't need learned men. Now our revolutionaries are saying that Vietnam doesn't need any lawyers. And no judges either. What do we need any of them for when the party decides what's legal and what's not?"

We talk for hours.

Early in the morning a *ho doi* takes Professor Thong away. Where, I don't know. That evening another one comes in with handcuffs and trusses me up like the professor. "Asshole [*lo dich*]," he growls. "You can't be trusted, can you!"

I can see it coming. They're letting me know that Professor Thong has told them what I've said to him, that it's because of his tattling that I'm chained up like this. They want to make me angry at him, so that I'll tell them myself what he has said to me. It's a standard technique.

Sure enough, two days later I'm taken out of the cell to an interrogation room. Apparently, Professor Thong has made some accusations against me, based on what I told him. I play dumb. "I don't understand. I only gave him some water. We talked a little, then I fell asleep. What can he have said?"

The *can ho* (official) is disappointed. But he doesn't give up hope that I'll tell him something interesting about the professor. I'm kept chained for the next two weeks. Twice a day my handcuffs are unlocked, for five minutes at a time. Sometimes a little more if the guard's in a good mood. My ration of sandy rice is cut in half. I can't get to the faucet. Instead I'm given two cans of water a day, about a liter and a half—for drinking, washing the rice, and washing myself. My body begins to itch all over. It's agonizing. I didn't have any idea how well off I was before.

After they remove the cuffs I'm kept in cell five for another month and a half. Eating the sandy rice, doing yoga, exercising my memory. Once they decide I won't say anything about Professor Thong, there are no more interrogations. I am left alone. My only connection with life outside cell five is the guarded whispering under the door, and the occasional glimpse of prisoners arriving or departing. The universe consists of six square yards of cell and a handful of people locked up near me, whose faces I do not know. That and a hallway where *ho dois* and sometimes prisoners pass quietly. Night and day are the same. I develop the impression I am living underground, among ghosts. In spite of the discipline I impose on myself, I feel that I am drifting away, as if a gauzy veil is settling over my mind.

*   *   *

From midday of April 30, Saigon's streets were filled with *ho dois* in green uniforms, column after column marching by, shouldering their Chinese-made AK-47s. The NLF fighters wore floppy bush hats; the northerners, colonial-style pith helmets. The bush bats were swamped in a sea of helmets.

T-54 tanks rolled in, flying the NLF flag, half red, half blue, a yellow star in the center: Vietnam's two halves, united in a single purpose. A young Saigon architect—a student activist during Diem's time—hitched a ride on the first tank, then rushed up to the roof of Doc Lap Palace to unfurl another Vietcong flag. The first revolutionary troops inside the palace, though, were northerners; the tanks were from the North's 203d armored brigade, the infantry sitting on top of them from the 116th regiment. With eighteen other divisions in and around the city, it was apparent that the entire northern army had come south.

Since General Duong Van Minh had ordered all southern soldiers to lay down their arms, the revolution's army just walked into the city. A few ARVN paratroop units fought on briefly at Tan Son Nhut airport. Here and there, some snipers took pot shots at the marching *ho dois*. Other than that, the city was ominously quiet, clothed with apprehension. Most people locked themselves up inside. Watching furtively from their windows, they saw the last southern soldiers throw down their arms, then strip off their uniforms, leaving little piles of clothing on the sidewalks. They saw the last looters scurrying by with goods of every imaginable sort, "liberated" from American offices, warehouses, and villas.

There followed a period of surprised mutual inspection, the Saigonese eyeing the Communist soldiers, the *ho dois* gawking at the citizens and the city. The Saigonese were nonplussed, staring at these invincible jungle fighters. For years, competing propaganda had created myths about them. For some, they were ferocious monsters, for others, heroic liberators. For everyone, fearsome warriors. And now, here they were: tired, sallow-faced, thin young men, staring in bewilderment at the wonders around them.

If the Saigonese were surprised by what they saw, the *ho dois* were flabbergasted. Twenty-one years had passed since the country's division, and most of these victors had passed their entire lives on an exclusive diet of Marxist ideology and northern propaganda. Shaped by nineteenth-century doctrines of class struggle and imperialist oppression, they were incapable of comprehending the reaction of the society they had suddenly walked in on. After years of inhuman sacrifice, they had now triumphed over the crushing evil that was enslaving their southern brothers. Everything in their experience told them to expect the glory and honor due saviors. Saigon's streets should have been awash with joy and adulation. It should have been the Parisians pouring out their hearts to the Free French in August of 1944, or the Hanoi citizenry embracing Ho Chi Minh's guerrillas in August the year after.

Instead, they found themselves camping in nearly empty streets watched by apprehensive eyes. The Saigonese were reserved and wary, curious certainly, but also a bit contemptuous. The *ho dois* couldn't understand it.

Another thing they couldn't understand was the fairy-tale wealth of the place. All of them had grown up in the most desperate kind of Third World poverty, and many had been living for years like wolves in the forest. In Hanoi a watch or radio was a major purchase, bicycles were a luxury, a refrigerator or television an inaccessible dream. Now they found themselves in Ali Baba's cave. Saigon's shop windows and markets were choked with transistors, stereos, cameras, refrigerators, televisions—all the paraphernalia of a modern consumer society.

Although they had been warned about these seductions—"poison encased in sugar pills"—they walked the streets with their eyes popping, buying up everything in sight, preyed on by happy merchants and streetwise children who quickly learned to exploit their simplicity. They were especially fascinated by digital watches, the "one-pilot" kind that showed the date and the "two-pilot" model that showed the day also. Men who had never heard of flush toilets became the proud owners of the latest Western and Japanese technology.

The Saigonese observed all this with wonder, and at times hilarity. They watched as young *ho dois* chopped down city trees to make their cooking fires in streets and courtyards, and sometimes indoors, when they failed to grasp the principles of the electric or gas ranges. Hundreds of stories made the rounds about the deprived *ho dois'* encounters with the new and strange. Nothing was too improbable. Hot-water indoor showers were an amazement to them (as they were to me when I first encountered them), and a neighbor who had several adolescent soldiers quartered in her house described how one of them had gone into the shower and scalded himself—then jumped out, yelling in alarm, "My nguy!" (American puppet), sure that he had been booby-trapped. Another puppet booby trap was the toilet, a sparkling clean container of water evidently meant for washing vegetables (but why was it so low?). Then with a swirl and roar the precious greens were gone.

But though the stories may have been humorous, there was a serious side to them as well. Many of the more thoughtful revolutionaries found themselves infected, not by decadence, but by disillusionment. Assaulted by the visible realities of southern life, the simplified Marxist caricatures that had informed their vision for two decades began to come undone. Nothing illustrated this disaffection better than my friend Hoang Van Liem's encounter with his father, a revolutionary cadre since the French war. It made Liem laugh and cry at the same time.

His father was one of those who had left for the North after Geneva, hoping to return in two years when elections reunified the country. As the years went by, he never lost hope that he would one day be reunited with his family. Meanwhile he had risen through the ranks and had even been sent to Moscow for advanced training. There be had bought a transistor radio and a watch, treasures that he would present to his son when the glorious day came.

During the same years Liem had been able to attend school and had become an electronics technician. He made a decent if modest living for himself working in the Con O battery factory. He had also gotten married, and had bought a small house not far from ours.

After liberation, his father had been sent to Saigon as a middle-level administrator. Immediately he began searching and before long had found Liem's address. With the Russian watch and transistor in his pocket, he located the house, but blanched when he saw that the address belonged to a private home. He couldn't believe his son lived in such a place. Finally he rang the doorbell and was greeted by a woman who assured him that it was indeed Liem's house and that she was Liem's wife. The answers she gave to his questions removed the father's lingering doubts, and he sat there in silence, refusing to touch the tea and oranges she served, waiting for his son to come home.

When Liem's father saw him pull up in front of the house in

his Dalat (South Vietnam's version of a subcompact), his worst suspicions were confirmed. My friend's wife met her husband at the door and told him about this extraordinary visitor. As her words came out, Liem rushed into the living room, his arms opened to embrace the father he had not seen in twenty years and only vaguely remembered. But the man standing there shoved him back angrily. Taking the transistor and watch out of his pocket he threw them to the floor, breaking the radio into pieces. Then he spat out at Liem, "I've saved these for you for years, because I thought you were worthy of being my son. But I see you're a traitor to the country, and a CIA agent."

Astonished at what he was hearing, Liem managed to stammer out that he had never even worked for the Saigon government. What did his father mean about the CIA? But the older man was enraged, "You have a house, a television set, a car! . . . How could an honest person get such things?"

It took days for Liem to convince his father that in Saigon even a technician could afford such things. The revolutionary cadre had lived for twenty years with an absolute faith in what the party newspaper and radio broadcasts had told him. The reunion with his son and his observations of the city he was supposed to help administer were a shock from which he wouldn't recover. At Liem's house he immersed himself in books and back issues of newspapers and magazines. One day while I was visiting he murmured to me, "I've wasted twenty years of my life with those bastards." He was a broken man. They had stolen his life.

*   *   *

"Where to, Comrade?" asks the driver, turning his head slightly to glance at me.

"I'll tell you in a bit. Right now just drive around. I need some air."

I'm struck by the unreality of these words, or maybe it's their very reality that sounds so strange: "Where to?" "Just drive around." It's too sudden, this freedom. In my mind I'm still in Zone A marveling at the space, or maybe it's Zone C, gasping for breath at the peephole.

"Sure thing," says the driver, glancing back again. "You're awfully pale. All that office work, huh? I'm lucky; I get to spend the whole day outside, where the air's better. Of course it's even better than it used to be, now there isn't so much traffic. Any special direction you want me to go? Toward town? Away from town?"

This guy's a talker, but I find it soothing. Then I know why; he's living in the normal, everyday world, and who talks more about normal everyday things than cab drivers? The weather, the traffic, food, wives, girlfriends, money—all those things that do not exist inside, but are the stuff of life outside. I couldn't have chosen a better guide to reintroduce me to Saigon, a guide who addresses me formally no less, instead of the "hey you" I'm accustomed to hearing. And that business about the office is delicious.

On the other hand, his remarks about how clean the air is now that there's not much traffic ring false. In the old days the dream of every pedicab driver was to graduate to taxis. They coveted each hack that went by, no matter how broken-down. Maybe he thinks I'm some kind of threadbare *can ho* [beggar]. I'm wearing the clothes I was arrested in, good enough 863 days ago, but now the pants are ragged in the knees (and seat) where I wore holes in them and then managed to patch them clumsily. I remember that the northerners who arrived on April 30, 1975, didn't look much better than I do now. They weighed about the same, and their clothes had a notable drabness. Another laugh. Not only am I on the street, but I might even be a *can ho*.

Perhaps to confirm the cab driver's impression of me as a serious person, I take out the official papers Tu Tuan gave me and look at them closely:

The Central Office of the Investigation Section of the Public Security Department orders the release of:
Doan Van Toai, born in Vinh Long Province in 1946.
Reason for Arrest: [this space left blank]
Reason for Release: [this space left blank]

Doan Van Toai will report to the local offices of the Public Secu-
rity to regularize his status.
Copy to: People's Committee of Ho Chi Minh City.
By authority: Bai Hieu (Tu Tuan) Commander, Le Van Duyet
Prison

There it is. According to the only official document they have
ever given me, I was arrested for nothing and released for the same
reason. I reflect that in some ways I'm lucky. Hundreds of thousands are imprisoned even longer for even less. At least I had an active political life and an unfortunate streak of independence to
blame. But so many in prison don't even have that, and most of
those in the hard labor camps—the soldiers and civil servants—are
only pawns who were just trying to survive. Had they lived in Front-
controlled areas, they would have made their accommodations with
the Front; they would have been the revolution's cannon fodder
and petty functionaries. Certainly the bulk of them are less "dangerous" than I. And certainly in the disease-infested jungle camps their
fate is even worse.

· 10 ·

NIEN CHENG

A Kind of Torture:
A Tale from the Chinese Cultural Revolution

FEARING a loss of power as factions within the Chinese
Communist party called for economic reforms—an implicit and
sometimes direct criticism of the disastrous Great Leap Forward
campaign in the late 1950s—the aging Mao Zedong called upon
the masses to initiate a Cultural Revolution against "revisionists"
and "counterrevolutionaries" within the government. Thus began
one of the most traumatic events in the history of the Communist
regime in China. Mass campaigns led by radical students
denounced any deviation from Mao's revolutionary thought.
Artists, writers, and intellectuals were attacked. Ancient
monuments, art collections, and symbols of China's
prerevolutionary society were destroyed by zealous bands of Red
Guards, shouting slogans drawn from Mao's *Red Book* of
revolutionary aphorisms and slogans. Universities and schools were
shut down; traditional music and classical Chinese opera were
banned; books were burned. Musicians and artists had their fingers
broken for having played "anti-revolutionary" music. Writers,
journalists, professors, foreign-language instructors, and school
teachers were humiliated and publicly tortured to force
"confessions" of deviations from Mao's revolutionary thought.

In this great upheaval, which lasted from 1966 into the 1970s,
tens of thousands of people were sent to the countryside to work
with peasants in order to be "reeducated." Even Deng Xiaoping,
leader of the "reformers" within the party and the future leader of

China after Mao's death in 1976, was sent to work in a factory.
Other tens of thousands were sent to prison or labor camps. Red
Guard groups gained control of many provincial and city
governments, purging officials for political deviation. In the
enthusiasm of the Cultural Revolution, Red Guard factions
attacked one another for not being sufficiently "pure" in their
revolutionary thought. The mass hysteria that prevailed throughout
China wrecked the government and the economy. The exact
number of people who died as a result of the Cultural Revolution
is not known, but some estimates have placed the number of
deaths in the millions. During these years of revolutionary
upheaval, it was not uncommon to find bodies that had floated
from the mainland to Hong Kong. Order was finally restored by
the People's Liberation Army in the late 1960s, but the conflict
between radicals and moderates within the party continued well
into the late 1970s.

Scores of books, many of them written by members of the Red
Guard, later appeared in the West, recounting the atrocities
committed in the name of revolution. Nien Cheng's *Life and
Death in Shanghai*, first published in Britain in 1986, stands as
perhaps the most powerful indictment of the Cultural Revolution.
It quickly became a best-seller in Britain and later in America.
Unlike many of the books produced by the Cultural Revolution,
Cheng's memoir tells the story as a victim of the Red Guards. A
fluent English speaker who had worked with Shell Oil Company
in Shanghai, she was accused of being a British spy and sent to
prison. Because of her refusal to confess, she was placed in solitary
confinement for six and a half years. Following her release, she
continued to be harassed and intimidated as a former member of
the "bourgeois" class.

The book is both a story of the extraordinary courage of a
refined, well-educated woman caught up in the Cultural
Revolution, and a mystery story of sorts, as Cheng investigates what
happened to her only daughter who disappeared during the
troubles. Only gradually does Cheng learn upon being released
from prison that her daughter had been beaten to death by
overzealous Red Guards.

Life and Death in Shanghai revealed to Western readers the full extent of the tragedy of the Cultural Revolution. Cheng's riveting account revealed in graphic detail the "mindless humanity" of this era in Communist China. With the appearance of Cheng's memoir and other memoirs from the Cultural Revolution, readers in Europe and America discovered that life in China during this time was far different from what many of them had imagined. In the 1960s many leftists had romanticized Mao and the Communist regime in China. Within the New Left in the United States, Maoist groupings gained considerable influence. One Maoist party, Progressive Labor, was able to win control of the Students for a Democratic Society, a key student radical organization in the 1960s. The Black Panther party, a black nationalist group with chapters throughout the United States, declared itself to be a Marxist-Leninist vanguard party upholding the "revolutionary thought of Mao." Its meetings and demonstrations often began with readings from Mao's little Red Book. Intellectuals and writers were not immune from the enthusiasm generated in the West for the Cultural Revolution. In France, the existentialist philosopher Jean-Paul Sartre and the historian Michel Foucault declared themselves to be Maoists and were seen passing out Maoist revolutionary leaflets on the streets of Paris.

Of course, most intellectuals, students, and average Americans saw these demonstrations on behalf of Maoism as a kind of lunacy. Both liberals and conservatives denounced the Cultural Revolution for its violation of human rights, even though it was not until the 1980s that the full extent of these violations became apparent.

Anti-Communist conservatives had loathed Communist China since 1949. Groups such as the Committee of One Million lobbied to keep China out of the United Nations, to maintain diplomatic ties with the Nationalist government in Taiwan, and to refuse diplomatic recognition of Communist China. The need to isolate China diplomatically, economically, and culturally remained central to the core beliefs of the anti-Communist right in America. Thus many on the right were dismayed when the United

States ended its long-standing opposition to UN membership for the People's Republic of China, though the United States continued to support Taiwan's membership. Nonetheless, in October 1971 the UN voted to admit the People's Republic in place of Taiwan.

The worst moment for conservatives arrived when President Richard Nixon announced in 1972 that he would go to China to meet with Premier Chou En-lai and Communist party chairman Mao Zedong. During his visit the Shanghai Communiqué was signed, promising to normalize relations between the two nations. Nixon's China policy disappointed and angered conservatives, as did Nixon's support for détente and arms control with the Soviet Union.

Throughout the late 1970s and 1980s the Republican party, however, remained divided on relations with China, even after the collapse of the Soviet Union at the turn of the decade. The free-trade wing of the party supported trade with China on the belief that the introduction of capitalism would lead to political democracy. The situation in China, they argued, was analogous to the Soviet Union. The introduction of economic reforms in the Communist system there had eventually undermined one-party political control. Others within the Republican party saw China as an emergent military power and a direct threat to America's democratic ally, Taiwan. The rapid Chinese military buildup, especially its development of long-range missiles which threatened not only Taiwan but the continental United States, heightened these fears. The military crackdown on student protesters in June 1989 in Beijing's Tiananmen Square, in which hundreds of protesters were killed, followed by mass arrests and the executions of pro-democracy supporters, strained relations between the United States and China. Yet within a decade the United States had moved to favor China's entrance into the World Trade Organization.

🈳 "What do you want to say to the interrogator?" the guard asked me. "I want to ask him when he is going to clarify my case."

"He can't clarify your case for you. He just asks the questions and assembles the material. The government will make the decision about your case."

"When is the government going to do that? I've been here such a long time already. I'm not well, I need medical attention," I said.

"You are all right. We give you medicine and special food."

"I'm not all right. My condition gets worse every day. I have had several more hemorrhages recently and my gums are very painful. The sulpha drug I am obliged to take is bad for my kidney. I have only one kidney, you know. When I had my operation, the doctor warned me not to take too much sulpha."

The guard did not speak for a moment. Then she said, "The difficulty about your case is really your own doing. You have to stay here because you won't confess."

"I haven't done anything wrong. What am I supposed to confess? The interrogator has examined my whole life and my contacts with all my relatives and friends. By now the government should know all about me. How can anyone still think I am guilty of anything?" Frustration and disappointment made me raise my voice. But the guard merely closed the window and walked away.

During the past few months when I was going through many sessions of interrogation, I had gained a distinct impression that when my life and activities had been examined, I would be released. Now I could not understand what was holding things up. The guard had said that it was up to the government to make the decision. This made sense to me because it was the usual working method of the Communist Party. What I did not know was on which level of authority my case was to be decided, and why it was taking so long. If my hopes had not been raised, perhaps my disappointment would not have been so great. As it was, I was plunged into renewed despair and disappointment.

From *Life and Death in Shanghai* (New York, 1986), pp. 274–303.

The misery of my life in the winter of 1969–70 was beyond imagination. Looking back on those months of heavy snow storms, intense cold and constant physical pain, I marvel that I could have lived through it all. One day when I asked the guard to buy soap, I was given something that did not lather. The guard told me that soap was rationed and each person was allowed only one cake per month. When I requested permission to buy a little more because I had to wash my underclothes more frequently, the guard became annoyed and shouted, "When are you going to get rid of your capitalistic way of wanting more than other people? You are lucky to be allowed one cake per month. In many places the people are only allowed one cake per family."

The toilet paper made of melted-down rice straw was replaced by something even harder, made with old newspaper, string and old cloth; bits of these were clearly visible on the rough grey sheets stiff as a board. This substitute for toilet paper was rationed also. The codliver oil and vitamin pills I was allowed to purchase were often not available. A small lump of fat rather than meat often appeared with my rice. The severe shortages seemed to affect the guards as well. Several of them lost a good deal of weight and even the militant guards who used to stride in and out energetically now looked rather subdued and peaky. It was all too apparent that the country was going through another period of economic crisis that invariably followed each political upheaval.

The newspaper printed reports of peasants "voluntarily" reducing their already meagre rations and rural Party Secretaries offering to increase the quota of grain which the Communes sent to government purchasing agencies. This was a repetition of the hunger and shortages of the early sixties immediately after the failure of the Great Leap Forward Campaign. In such times of hardship, there were daily stories in the newspaper about heroes who increased production output and decreased their consumption of food and other commodities. However, half a sheet of the *Shanghai Liberation Daily* was still given over to articles of criticism of the "capitalist-roaders," who were also called "revisionists." The subject of contention now was Mao Tze-tung's military theory of the People's War against the capitalistic concept of the importance of military skill and modern weapons. Two ousted and disgraced military leaders, former Defense Minister Peng Teh-huai and former Chief of Staff Lo Jui-ching, were the main culprits. Daily newspaper articles read to us over the broadcasting system accused these two of believing that advanced weapons rather than men armed with Mao Tze-tung Thought were the most important factor in deciding the outcome of war. Since both men had been removed from office several years earlier and handed over to the Red Guards and the Revolutionaries for persecution, the continued campaign to criticize their viewpoint could only mean that their viewpoint was shared by others in the Party and military leadership.

Prolonged hardship and privation were eroding my mental power in a frightening way. The stalling of my investigation produced in me a deep feeling of despondency. Not being able to keep clean because of insufficient soap and toilet paper was demoralizing. Even the evidence in the newspaper of differences of opinion, or perhaps fierce debate, in the Party and military leadership failed to rouse me from lethargy. Every day I sat on the wooden bed, leaning against my rolled-up bedding, too tired and too ill to move.

In early spring, I again became ill with pneumonia and was taken to the prison hospital. There I made a slow recovery. When I returned to the No. 1 Detention House, just before May the First, the weather had become warmer. Even though living conditions continued to be extremely hard, the milder weather made life easier to endure. I felt I had somehow survived another crisis and been mysteriously brought back to life from the brink of death. When I was allowed outdoor exercise on a warm and sunny day and saw the young leaves unfolding on the plane tree over the wall, I thanked God for the miracle of life and the timely renewal of my own. . . .

One afternoon in January 1971, I was summoned to the interrogation room. The call was so unexpected that my heart was pounding with excitement as I followed the guard through the courtyard; I hardly noticed that a blizzard was beginning. At the door of the interrogation room, the guard suddenly gave me a hard shove so that I staggered into the room rather unceremoniously. I found several guards in the room. As soon as I entered, they crowded around me, shouting abuse at me.

"You are the running dog of the imperialists," said one. "You are a dirty exploiter of workers and peasants," shouted another. "You are a counter-revolutionary," yelled the third.

Their voices mingled and their faces became masks of hatred as they joined one another to go through the list of abuse that I had become familiar with during the Cultural Revolution. While they were shouting, they pushed me to show their impatience. I was passed around from one guard to another like a ball in a ball game. Trying to maintain my balance, I became dizzy and breathless. Before I could gather my wits together, suddenly a young male guard grabbed the lapels of my padded jacket and pulled me towards him. His face was only inches from mine and I could see his eyes glistening with sadistic pleasure. Then he bit his lower lip to show his determination and gave me a hard push. I staggered backwards and hit the wall. But before I collapsed onto the floor like a sack, he grabbed my lapels again and pulled me forward, and again, he bounced me against the wall. He did this several times with lightning speed in a very expert manner. All the time, the other guards continued to shout at me. I became completely disorientated. My ears were ringing, my head was splitting and my body was trembling. Suddenly my stomach heaved and I vomited. Water from my mouth got on the guard's hand and cuffs. He became furious. Pushing me into the prisoner's chair, the guard swore under his breath.

My heart pounded as if it was going to jump out of my throat. My breath came in gasps. I collapsed into the chair and, trying to recover my equilibrium, closed my eyes. Suddenly a stinging blow landed on my cheek. The voice of a female guard shouted, "Are you going to confess?"

Another sharp blow landed on my other check, while several voices joined in to shout, "Are you going to confess?"

I remained in the chair with my eyes closed and ignored them. That was my only way to defend myself.

Someone grabbed my hair from behind and jerked my head up. I was forced to look up and found all five of them staring at me expectantly. It seemed that they really expected me to change my mind simply because they had beaten me up. But then I thought, people who resort to brutality must believe in the power of brutality. But it seemed to me that these guards at the detention house were rather stupid not to know me better after watching me day and night for so many years. I knew, however, that they were merely carrying out someone else's orders.

One of the female guards was the militant young woman who had made trouble for me on many previous occasions. Now she said, "Are you going to confess or do you want more punishment?"

When she saw that I remained silent, she gave my cheek another smart slap, took my arms and draped them on the back of the chair on which I was seated. The young male guard who had pushed me against the wall grabbed my wrists together and clamped a pair of handcuffs on them.

"These handcuffs are to punish you for your intransigence. You will wear them until you are ready to confess. Only then will we take them off. If you confess now, we will take them off now. If you confess tomorrow, we will take them off tomorrow. If you do not confess for a year, you will have to wear them for a year. If you never confess, you will have to wear them to your grave," said the militant female guard.

"Think about it! Think about the situation you are in!" a male guard shouted.

"If you decide to confess now, we will take off the handcuffs straight away and you can return to your cell," another female guard said.

"What about it? Are you ready to confess? Just say yes and we will take the handcuffs off," another male guard said.

"Speak! Speak!" several of them shouted.

I looked at them all and said in a feeble voice, "I've done nothing wrong. I've nothing to confess."

"Louder! Louder! Speak louder!" they yelled.

Though I spoke in a low voice, each one of them inside the room had heard what I had said. Someone must be listening outside in the corridor. They wanted this person to hear my answer. From where I sat I could not see whether the small window behind the prisoner's chair was open. But I did notice the guards glancing in that direction when they were pushing me around.

I pulled myself together with an effort and stated in a clear and loud voice, "I'm innocent. You have made a mistake. I have nothing to confess."

I heard the small window behind the prisoner's chair closing with a loud bang. My tormentors waited a little while before opening the door to usher me out, perhaps to make sure the person outside had time to get out of sight. When I stood up, the militant female guard came behind me and put her two hands round the handcuffs to tighten them a few notches so that they fitted snugly round my wrists.

The blizzard was now in full force. Whirling snowflakes were falling from the darkened sky and the strong wind nearly knocked me over when I stepped out of the interrogation building. The guard said, "Follow me!"

He did not return me to the women's prison but led me in another direction into a small building in a corner of the prison compound. When he opened the door and flipped the switch on the wall to put on the dim light, I saw that the place was in an even worse state of neglect than the rest of the prison compound. A thick layer of dust covered the floor and the walls. When we moved down the corridor, cobwebs floated down from the ceiling. The guard unlocked a small door and said, "Get in!"

The room was very dark. I waited for him to switch on the light, but he just closed the door after me. Standing outside, he asked, "Are you going to confess?" When I did not reply, he snapped the lock and went away.

I stood just inside the door in total darkness, trying to make out where I was. An unpleasant odor of staleness and decay assailed my nostrils. Gradually I realized that the tiny room in which I was locked had no window. However, the door fitted badly; a thin thread of light seeped through the gap. When my eyes became accustomed to the darkness, I saw vaguely that there was a wooden board on the dusty floor and a cement toilet in the corner. Actually I was standing on the only space left, for the room was no more than about five feet square. Something soft dropped on my forehead. I was so startled that I experienced a moment of panic. With my hands tied at my back, I could do nothing to brush it away. I shook my head hard and it slid down my face to my jacket. Perhaps not many insects could live in this dark room, I thought. It must have been a cobweb from the ceiling.

My heart was still beating very fast. In spite of the unpleasant

plete isolation, time assumed a different meaning or had no meaning at all. I only knew that my legs felt stiff and my head ached. But
I refrained from moving as long as the guards continued to come.
When a guard switched off the light in the corridor on his departure, I thought they might have decided to retire for the night. But I
still waited for a while before standing up. It was not possible to
walk because there was simply no space and I was afraid to bump
into the dirty wall in the dark. So I shuffled my feet to try to restore
circulation to my legs. My arms ached from being held at my back
in the same position for so long and my hands felt very hot. I tried to
get some relief by moving my shoulders up and down.

After standing for a while, I sat down again. With my head on
my knees, I rested. Perhaps I had snatches of real sleep or perhaps I
just dozed while murmuring prayers. Then I would stand up again
to repeat my newly devised exercise. I felt very weak. My natural in-
clination was to move as little as possible but I compelled myself to
do the simple exercise, for I knew that was the best way to keep
going. In the past I had not suffered from claustrophobia, but there
were moments during the night when I felt myself getting tense. My
breathing became difficult and I had the sensation that the walls
were falling on me. To prevent myself from getting into a panic, I
would stand up quickly to move my body as much as possible in
that confined space. And I would breathe very slowly and deeply
until I felt calm again.

The best way for me to snap out of fear was always to take the
initiative in doing something positive. Even the simple act of just
moving my body around made me feel better immediately. If I had
just sat there feeling dejected and let my imagination run wild, I
could easily have become terribly confused and unable to cope
with the guards. Of course I was hungry and my throat was parched.
But when I thought of the cement toilet coated with dust and
grime, I was reconciled to not having any food or water that might
force me to use it.

The night dragged on very slowly. More and more I felt that I
was buried in a cement box deep underground. My hands became
very hot and uncomfortable. When I found it difficult to curl my
fingers into a fist, I knew they were swollen. My hands became my

smell in the room, I breathed in and out deeply and slowly to try t
calm down and slow my heart beat. When I felt better I sat down o1
the wooden board and tried to look round in the dark. I was relievec
not to see anything that suggested blood, excrement or vomitec
food left by previous prisoners. I was so tired that I put my head or
my drawn-up knees and closed my eyes to rest. The only compensa-
tion for being locked in a cement box, I thought, was that without
the window to admit the cold air and wind, the place was decidedly
warmer than my cell.

The handcuffs felt different from the others I had worn before.
I examined them with my fingers. Indeed, they were different,
much heavier and thicker, with a square edge, not rounded like the
others. My hands felt hot and my fingers were stiff. I tried to exercise my hands by moving them as much as the handcuffs allowed.

"Are you going to confess?"

The sudden sound of a voice startled me. Had the guard been
outside all the while or had he just come into the building? How
was it that I had not heard him?

There was really no point in exhausting what little strength I
had, so I did not answer him but remained where I was with my
head resting on my knees. I tried to take my mind off the present by
recalling beautiful scenes and pleasant experiences in the past. But
it was very difficult. The ugly reality was all too real and overpower-
ing.

Other guards came at intervals to ask me the same question. I
listened for their footsteps. Some came quite stealthily, while others
did not bother to soften their tread. When they opened the door of
the building to come inside, I could hear the howling wind and the
sound of the guards stamping their feet to get rid of the snow. I supposed they were told to come and see if I had succumbed to their
new form of pressure. Some of them lingered for a moment after
asking their question; others did not wait for my answer but left almost immediately after delivering their question.

Apart from the guards, there was no sound whatsoever. I must
have been the sole occupant of that building on that day. If there
were other prisoners, surely I would have heard a sigh or a moan
long ago.

I did not know how long I sat there. In a dark room, in com-

sole preoccupation and worry. I feared that the brutal and ignorant men, intent on getting what they wanted from me, might inadvertently cripple me. I knew that when a Communist Party official tried to achieve an objective during a political campaign, he went to excess to carry out his orders and ignored all possible complications. Trained to obey promptly by such slogans as "Wherever Chairman Mao points, there I will run," and fearful of the consequences of appearing hesitant or reluctant, he exaggerated everything he had to do. If the victim suffered more than was intended or was left a cripple, that was just too bad. I had seen this happen again and again. Hands are so important. If my hands were crippled, how would I be able to carry on with my daily life when the Cultural Revolution was over?

I pressed my fingers in turn. At least they were not numb. But I could tell they were badly swollen. I wondered how long I would remain manacled like this and how long I could live without food or water. Vaguely I remembered reading in an article that a human being could live for seven days without sustenance. In my present weakened state, perhaps five days, I thought. In any case, hardly twenty-four hours had passed. At that moment I did not need to think of the threat to my life, only the threat to my hands. What could I do to lessen possible damage to them? It seemed to me the swelling was caused by the tight handcuffs fitted firmly round my wrists which prevented proper circulation. When the militant female guard put her hands round the handcuffs to tighten them, she knew exactly what she was doing. If she had not tightened them but had left them as they were when they were put on, perhaps the state of my hands would not have been so bad now. The guard who first put the handcuffs on had not tightened them, so they were probably just instructed to put the handcuffs on, and no instruction was given to tighten them. In that case, a mild guard might be persuaded to loosen them a little. I decided to show my hands to the guard who would come in the morning, and request the handcuffs to be loosened.

When finally I heard the sound of a guard coming through the outside door and saw the thin line of light appear again around the door, I stood up.

"Are you going to confess? Have you thought over the matter?" It was the voice of a male guard.

"I would like to speak to you for a moment," I said.

"Good! So, you have decided to confess at last."

"No, no, it's not about confession. It's about my hands."

"What about your hands?"

"They are badly swollen. The handcuffs are very tight. Could you loosen them a bit?" I asked.

"You are feeling uncomfortable now, are you? That's good! Why don't you confess? If you confess, the handcuffs will be taken off."

"Can't you loosen them a bit now?"

"Why don't you just confess like the other prisoners? You have brought this on yourself. It's not the fault of the handcuffs."

"Please look at my hands. They are badly swollen."

"I can't do anything about that. If you decide to confess, I will unlock this door and take you out. That's all I can do," the guard said.

"Could you not report to your superior that my hands are very badly swollen?"

"No. If you decide to confess, I will take you out."

It seemed useless to go so on I sat down on the wooden board again.

"Are you going to confess?" he asked me once again. I did not answer. He remained there for a moment longer before going away.

The fact that my hands were badly swollen was no surprise to the guard. Of course he knew the effect of the handcuffs. I could not have been the first person they had done this to. He was probably telling his superior at that moment that I was getting worried and agitated about my hands. From that his superior would think I was nearer to doing what he wanted. They would never loosen the handcuffs to prolong what they would regard as the period of waiting for me to confess. I decided it was useless to ask the guards to loosen the handcuffs. I must just trust God to preserve my hands.

"Come here!" the voice of a female guard said.

I stood up. I was already right by the door. She had turned up rather quickly, I thought.

"I've come to give you some advice," she said in a normal voice, as if she was talking to another guard, not with the harsh tone the guards habitually used to address the prisoners. "You are not a stupid woman. Why don't you do the intelligent thing and confess? Why punish yourself by being stubborn?"

I didn't say anything.

"You are worried about your hands. That's quite right. Hands are very important to everybody, but especially to an intellectual who must write. You should try to protect your hands and not let them be hurt. You can do that easily by just agreeing to confess."

I still did not say anything.

"You know when they said they would never take the hand-cuffs off until you agree to confess, they really meant it. They will do it too. The dictatorship of the proletariat is not something to be trifled with, you know."

I continued to remain silent.

She waited for quite a long time. Then she said, "Well, you think carefully about what I have just said. It's good advice I have given you. I'm sorry for you. Think about what I said."

When I heard her footsteps going away from the door, I sat down again. I was angry with myself for being so stupid. How could I have thought for one moment that they would loosen the hand-cuffs? Now that I had shown them my weakness, they would be glad and think I might indeed succumb to their pressure because of con-cern about my hands. I said to myself, "I'll forget about my hands. If I have to be crippled, then I'll accept being crippled. In this world there are many worthy people with crippled hands or no hands at all." I remembered when my late husband and I were in Holland in 1957, we had bought a painting by a veteran of the Second World War who had lost both his hands. He used his toes to hold the paint brush, I was told. I used to treasure this painting as a symbol of human courage and resourcefulness. It was slashed by the Red Guards when they looted my home. But the thought of this artist whom I had never met inspired me with courage and helped me to become reconciled to the possibility of losing the use of my hands after this ordeal.

The female guard was followed by others. All of them lectured me on the advantage of obeying the dictatorship of the proletariat and confessing. Now that they knew I was suffering discomfort and worrying about my hands, they did not dash away but lingered hopefully outside the door waiting for my answer. After being so long without food and water and not having had much sleep at all, I felt very weak and faint. My intestines were grinding in protest and I had spasms of pain in the abdomen. But I just continued sitting on the board with my head on my knees waiting for the guards to go away.

The day seemed interminable. Patiently I waited for their next move. At last the door was unlocked. A female voice called, "Come out!"

The icy cold fresh air in the courtyard miraculously cleared my head and I felt a surge of life to support my wobbly legs. The guard led me back to the same interrogation room in which they had beaten me up the day before.

The militant female guard and the young male guard who had put the handcuffs on me sat in the place of the interrogator behind the counter. After I had entered the room and bowed to the portrait of Mao, the female guard told me to recite a quotation from memory.

"First, do not fear hardship. Second, do not fear death," I said. It was the first quotation of Mao that came into my head and, under the circumstances, certainly appropriate.

"That quotation is not for the likes of you! Chairman Mao said that to the revolutionary soldiers," the female guard said indignantly.

But they let it pass. They did not ask me to recite another quotation, although I had another one about overcoming ten thousand difficulties to strive for final victory ready to recite if they gave me the opportunity to do so.

"What are you thinking about now?" asked the male guard.

"Nothing very much," I answered.

"Don't pretend to be nonchalant. You are worried about your hands. You would like the handcuffs to be loosened," he said.

I did not say anything.

"What you should think about is why you have to wear them in the first place. It is entirely your own fault. Do we put handcuffs on all the prisoners kept here? Of course not. If you find the handcuffs uncomfortable, you should think why you have to wear them. They can be taken off if you decide to confess. It's up to you entirely," he said.

"Are you going to confess?" asked the female guard.

When she saw that I said nothing, she got angry and shouted, "You deserve all you are getting. You are tired of living, I am sure. I have never seen a prisoner as stubborn and stupid as you!"

"Have you lost all reason? Have you lost the wish to protect yourself? You are being extremely stupid. You are like an egg hitting a rock. You will get smashed," declared the male guard.

A year or two ago, I would have shouted back at them and taken pleasure from doing that. Now I was too ill and too tired. I no longer cared.

They looked at each other and they looked past my shoulder at the small window behind the prisoner's chair. Then they stood up.

"Take her out! Take her out! Let her go to see God with her granite head!" the male guard shouted.

It might seem surprising that a guard in a Communist prison should have spoken of God, but what he said was in fact a quotation from Mao Tze-tung. Referring to political indoctrination and hard labour in labour camps as a means to change the thinking of intellectuals who were supposed to be opposed to the Communist Party, Mao had declared that the purpose of the Communist Party was reform of the enemy rather than annihilation. Then he added, "if some still want to go to see God with their granite heads, it will make no difference."

Since the publication of his remark, "to go to see God with his granite head" was generally used to denote a man refusing to change his mind or accept the point of view of the Party.

A guard flung the door open. Although I felt dizzy, I made an effort to walk steadily and followed him out of the room. The icy air outside was like a knife cutting through my clothes. I shivered violently. The guard led me back to the women's prison and my cell.

When I passed the small room used by the female guards, I saw from their clock that I had been locked in the cement box in the other building for almost twenty-four hours.

The guard unlocked the door of my cell and said to me, "Now you will continue your punishment in here."

When I had been called to the interrogation room the day before, drinking water had just been issued to the prisoners. The water was still in the green enameled mug on the edge of the table where I had hastily placed it. Now I bent over the mug, removed the lid by gripping the knob on top of it with my teeth and placed it on the table. Then I caught the edge of the mug with my teeth, gradually lowered my body to a squatting position and tipped the water into my mouth. By this method, I succeeded in drinking quite a bit of the water. After that, I moved over to the cement toilet, stood with my back to it, lowered my body and removed the lid with my imprisoned hands. I strained my hands to unzip my slacks. I was able to sit on the seat I had made with two towels joined together and to relieve myself. But to strain my hands to one side to unfasten the zip made the handcuffs cut severely into my flesh. It was very painful.

I sat down on the edge of the bed. The cell was very cold and seemed to get progressively colder. But the familiar cell was not as dirty and stuffy as the cement box where I had spent the previous twenty-four hours. When the second meal of the day was delivered to the prisoners, the woman from the kitchen pushed the aluminum container through the small window for me in the usual manner. Even though I was famished, I had to refuse it for I simply did not know how I could eat with my hands tightly tied behind my back.

No one came to ask me if I was going to confess. But I knew I was under observation, for I could hear the guards come to the peephole to look into the cell. At bedtime, the guard called at each cell for prisoners to go to bed. She came to my cell as if nothing unusual had happened and said, "Go to sleep!"

With my back to the bed, I unrolled my quilt and blanket and spread them over the wooden bed. It was slow work and strenuous for one who had not eaten any food for so long. But I managed it.

Then I lay down on the bed. First, I lay on one side with my body weight pressing down on one shoulder and arm. It was extremely uncomfortable; my arm ached. Then I tried to lie on my stomach with my face turned to one side. I found this position impossible on the hard wooden bed because my body weight was on my breasts. After lying like this for a little while I had to give up. In any case, I could not cover myself with the blanket. While I was performing these acrobatics with my hands in handcuffs behind my back, I never stopped shivering. The room was bitterly cold. Finally I decided lying down to sleep was out of the question. I should try to get some sleep sitting up. I sat across the bed with my legs up and my back leaning on the toilet-paper-covered wall. Then I closed my eyes, hoping to doze off.

It was such a cold night that there was ice on the windowpanes and the snow piled against the window did not melt. Inside the cell, the feeble light shone through a haze of cold air. Every breath I took was a puff of white vapour. My body shook with spasms of shivering. My legs and feet were frozen numb. I simply had to get up from time to time to walk around the cell to restore circulation to my limbs. The weight of the handcuffs dragged my hands down so that I had to hold them up with my fingers while walking slowly in the cell. The handcuffs seemed to get tighter and tighter and my hands seemed to be on fire. I tired so easily that after walking round for only a little while I simply had to sit down again. Then I got so cold that I had to walk some more. Perhaps I managed a little sleep from time to time when I sat against the wall with my feet up, but the long night was a night of misery and suffering.

However, it came to an end as everything in life must do, no matter how wonderful or unpleasant. I saw the light of dawn creeping into the room and heard the guard calling outside each cell, "Get up! Get up!"

Soon afterwards the Labour Reform girl pushed the spout of the watering can through the small window to offer me cold water for washing. When she did not see my washbasin, she looked into the cell through the small window. She looked at me inquiringly. I turned my body a little so that she could see my handcuffs. Quickly she closed the small window and went away. In the circumstances, being unwashed was the least of my worries. While I could carry the empty mug to the window to receive the drinking water with my back to it and drink the water by gripping the edge of the mug with my teeth and gradually squatting so that the water would pour into my mouth, my empty stomach protested with spasms of gripping pain which refused to be assuaged by the water. My hands were so hot that I was in a constant state of restless agitation.

On the third day, the pain in my abdomen miraculously stopped. But I felt very weak. My eyes could no longer focus and the usual sound of prison activities seemed to grow fainter and fainter.

That night, I again sat on the bed, leaning against the wall with my hands crossed to hold the handcuffs with my fingers in an effort to reduce their weight. Though I shivered with cold, I no longer had the strength to get up and walk around the room.

After the prisoners had settled down to sleep, the small window was pushed open gently.

I did not hear any sound until a voice that was almost a whisper said through the opening, "Come over!"

I wondered whether it was just another guard trying to urge me to confess. But she had spoken softly, almost stealthily, as if she did not want others in the building to hear her.

With an effort I moved to the small window and saw the face of one of the older guards there. She was bending down to watch my faltering steps through the opening.

From the beginning of my imprisonment I had found this guard the most humane. At first she attracted my attention because she walked in that peculiar way of women whose feet had been crippled with foot-binding, an old custom that lingered into the 1930s in some remote rural areas of China. When the feet of these women were unbound, they were already permanently damaged. This guard was not a native of Shanghai because she spoke with the accent of North China peasants. I thought she must have been one of those country women liberated by the Communist troops as they swept down the plains of North China and she had joined their ranks and become a Party member. I observed that she carried out her duty in a matter of fact manner and did not seem to enjoy shouting at the prisoners as the other guards did. When the weather got cold, if she were on night duty, I often heard her offering to lend bedding from the prison stock to prisoners who did not have sufficient covering. The last time I fainted because of lack of food, it was this guard who took me to the hospital and got the doctor to sign a paper ordering more rice to be given to me. Since it was the Maoists who had reduced my ration to give me pressure on that occasion, I thought she couldn't be one of them.

"Why aren't you eating your meals?" she asked me.

I thought, "What a silly question to ask! Doesn't she know I have got the handcuffs on?"

"They will not remove the handcuffs simply because you won't eat, you know. And if you should starve to death, you would be declared a counter-revolutionary. That's the customary procedure for prisoners who die before their cases are clarified," she added.

"I don't know how to eat without using my hands," I said.

"It's not impossible. Think hard. There is a way. You have a spoon."

She sounded sympathetic and concerned. I decided to ask her to loosen the handcuffs a little, as my tightly imprisoned hands were tormenting me. I was in a constant state of tension because of them. They occupied my mind to the exclusion of all else.

"My hands are swollen and very hot. My whole body feels tormented because of them. Could you please loosen the handcuffs a little bit?" I asked her.

"I haven't got the key to unlock the handcuffs. It is being kept by someone higher up. Just try to eat something tomorrow. You will feel better when you have some food inside you," she said.

A gust of cold wind from the direction of the entrance at the other end of the corridor indicated that the door of the building was being opened and another guard had just entered. She slid the shutter quietly in place and went away.

I returned to the bed and sat there thinking. The guard was right. I should try to eat. To die was nothing to be frightened of. What really frightened me was the possibility that my mind might get so confused that I might sign something without realizing its significance. But how could I handle the food without my hands? The guard said there was a way and told me to think hard. She also mentioned that I had a spoon. My eyes strayed towards the table. First I saw the plastic spoon and then I saw my clean towels neatly folded in a pile. A plan formulated in my mind and I decided to try it when food was offered to me again.

The guard had said that the key to unlock the handcuffs was not kept by the guards but by "someone higher up." There was no hope the handcuffs could be loosened. I must think of some way to reduce the heavy weight of the handcuffs, which were not only dragging my hands down but also pulling my shoulders out of their sockets. With difficulty and very slowly, with my back to the bed, I managed to roll up the quilt. Then I pushed the rolled quilt to the wall. When I sat down in front of the quilt against the wall, I placed my hands on the soft quilt. The weight was lifted and I felt a surge of relief.

To have made plans and thought of some way to overcome difficulty gave me a new lease of life. Although I continued to be cold, hungry and miserable, the long night seemed to pass more quickly.

At daybreak, when the guard called the prisoners to get up, I stood up to stretch my legs. I tried to hold the handcuffs with my fingers, and, to my horror, felt something sticky and wet. Turning to the quilt on which I had rested my hands throughout the night, I saw stains of blood mixed with pus. It seemed the handcuffs had already broken my skin and were cutting into my flesh. I shuddered with a real fear of losing the use of my hands, for I realized I was powerless to prevent disaster.

When the woman from the kitchen offered me the aluminum container of rice through the small window, I went to accept it. I turned my back to the opening and she placed the container in my hands. I took it to the table. With my back to it, I picked up a clean face towel from the pile and spread it on the table. Then I picked up the plastic spoon and tried to loosen the rice from the container with it. The Shanghai rice was glutinous. When it was cooked in the container it stuck to it. I had to dig hard with the plastic spoon to push the rice and cabbage onto the face towel on the table. With each movement of my hands, the handcuffs dug deeper into my flesh. My whole body was racked with pain and tears came into my eyes. I had to rest and take a deep breath. Nevertheless, I persisted with my effort to get the rice out of the container. When I succeeded in getting quite a bit out, I turned round, bent over the towel and ate the rice like an animal.

I repeated this several times. When the woman came to collect the container, she did not immediately open the small window to demand it back but stood outside watching me struggling to get the rice out. Because of the pain and my fear of infection, I stopped after each scoop to take a deep breath. I was very slow. Still the woman said nothing, though normally she was always in a great hurry. As I blinked back tears of pain, I wondered if eating was really worth the effort. But I continued to try, simply because I had decided to stay alive. When I could not carry on any longer and had already got nearly half of the rice onto the towel, I carried the container behind me and pushed it through to her with my wounded hands.

In the afternoon, when rice was given to me again, I found that the woman from the kitchen had already loosened the rice for me. I had only to tip the container and most of the rice fell out onto the towel and bare table.

My being able to consume food seemed to have infuriated the Maoists, for the guards came to the small window again to threaten me. They never mentioned the word "handcuffs," probably because they did not want the other prisoners within hearing to know what they were doing to me. But they continued to urge me to confess. Although the rice I managed to eat each day did in fact make me feel stronger, I was having difficulty walking. For some reason I could not explain, the handcuffs were affecting my feet. Like my hands, they felt hot and painful. My shoes became so tight and unbearable that I had to kick them off. Fortunately they were soft cloth shoes so that I was able to press down the back and wear them as slippers. Now I just staggered about, for my feet could not bear even the reduced weight of my emaciated body. The stains of blood and pus on the quilt where I placed my hands became larger and more numerous as the handcuffs cut through more skin on my wrists and more deeply into the wounds. Either the weather suddenly got a lot warmer or I was feverish; I no longer felt the cold but shivered from pain whenever I had to move my hands or stagger across the room.

One day, when I was at the small window getting drinking water, my imprisoned hands holding the mug trembled so much that half of the water spilled down the back of my padded jacket and slacks.

"Your hands are very bad. The higher ups don't know it. Why don't you wail? As long as you don't cry out, they will not know how bad your hands are," the woman from the kitchen whispered through the opening before hastily closing the shutter.

Though the Chinese people were normally restrained about showing emotion, they did wail to show deep grief at funerals or as a protest against injustice that involved death. The sight of someone wailing had always embarrassed me. It was like seeing someone stripping himself naked. From childhood I had been disciplined never to show emotion. The memory of trying for many years to fight back tears lingered; gradually I came to regard crying as a sign of weakness. Should I wail now just to call attention to the fact that my hands were being crippled? I decided against it. For one thing, I did not think I knew how to emit that prolonged, inarticulate cry that was so primitive and animal-like. For another I did not want to do anything that might be interpreted as asking for mercy. "The man higher up" had ordered the handcuffs put on my wrists so that I would be tormented by them. He believed my suffering would eventually lead to my willingness to give a false confession to save myself. The best way to counterattack was certainly not to show that I could no longer endure suffering. So I ignored the kind advice of the woman from the kitchen.

Several more days passed. The handcuffs were now beginning to affect my mind, probably through their effect on my nervous system. I got muddled periodically and forgot where I was. I no longer remembered how many days ago I was first manacled. Life was just an unending road of acute pain and suffering on which I must trudge along as best I could.

During moments of lucidity, I tried to discipline my mind by doing simple arithmetic. I would repeat to myself, "Two and two makes four, four and four equals eight, eight and eight equals sixteen, sixteen and sixteen equals thirty-two . . ." But after only a little while my ability to concentrate would evaporate and I would get confused again. The guards still came to the locked door. But what they said was just a jumble of words that made no sense to me.

After several more days, I became so weak that I no longer had the strength to stagger to the small window to get rice or water. I tried to refuse when they were offered to me, but whether words came out of my mouth or not I did not know. Perhaps the woman from the kitchen was urging me to take the rice or the drinking water; I did not hear her voice, only sensed that she stood there waiting for something. Most of the time I was so far away that I did not know what was happening around me. After drifting in and out of consciousness like that for some time, I passed out altogether.

When I opened my eyes again, I found myself lying on the dusty floor.

"Get up! Get up!" a man's voice was shouting very near me. "You are feigning death! You won't be allowed to get away with it."

My arms were still bent to my back but they were no longer held together by the handcuffs.

"Get up! Get up!" a female voice joined in.

I pulled myself together and looked up to find the militant female guard and the young man who had put the handcuffs on me standing over me. The cell door was wide open. Dangling in the hands of the female guard was the pair of heavy brass handcuffs they had removed from my wrists. The handcuffs were covered with congealed blood and pus. Probably the guard considered them repulsive, as she was holding them gingerly by the chain by just two fingers.

"Don't think we are finished with you! There are other ways to bring you to your senses. Those who dare to oppose the dictatorship of the proletariat will not be allowed to get away with it," said the man.

The female guard gave my prostrate form a hard kick as they left the cell and locked the door behind them.

I remained on the floor, too exhausted to move. Although the handcuffs were removed, my whole body was aching and hot. Slowly I brought my left arm forward and looked at my hand.

Quickly I closed my eyes again. My hand was too horrible to contemplate. After a moment, I sat up and looked at both hands. They were swollen to enormous size. The swelling extended to my elbows. Around my wrists where the handcuffs had cut into my flesh, blood and pus continued to ooze out of the wounds. My nails were purple in colour and felt as if they were going to fall off. I touched the back of each hand, only to find the skin and flesh numb. I tried to curl up my fingers but could not because they were the size of carrots. I prayed to God to help me recover the use of my hands.

After a while, I tried to get up. But I had to stifle a cry of pain, as my feet could not support my body. As I was very near the bed, I managed to haul myself up to it. The woolen socks were stuck to my feet with dried sticky pus. When I succeeded in peeling the socks off with my numb and swollen fingers, I saw that my feet were also swollen to enormous size. Under each toe was a large blister. I could not take the socks off because some of the blisters had broken and the pus had dried, gluing the socks to my feet. What was making it impossible for me to walk was the fact that some of the blisters had not broken. Obviously I needed a sterile sharp instrument such as a needle to break the blisters so that I could let the fluid out. Also, to prevent infection, I needed bandages and some antiseptic medicine on the wounds on my wrists. I stood up. I almost sat down again immediately because the burning pain in my feet was unbearable. However, I resisted the impulse to sit down and, shuddering, remained standing. I thought that since I had to move about in the cell, the sooner I practised moving about with my swollen feet the better. I moved one foot forward a couple of inches, shifted my weight onto that foot, and moved the other foot a couple of inches. Eventually I arrived at the door. Leaning against it for support, I called the guard on duty.

"Report!" My voice sounded feeble. But almost immediately the shutter on the small window was pushed open. The guard had been right outside the door, watching me through the peephole all the time without my knowledge.

"What do you want?"

"May I see the doctor, please."

"What for?"

"My wrists and feet are wounded. I need some medicine and bandages," I explained.

"The doctor does not give treatment when the prisoner has been punished," declared the guard.

"In that case, perhaps you could just give me some disinfectant ointment or mercurochrome for the wounds?" I knew the guards kept a supply of these in their little room.

"No, not allowed."

"The wounds may become infected."

"That's your business."

"May I just have a roll of bandages to tie the wounds up?"

I lifted my swollen hands to the window to show her the wounds on my wrists but she turned her head the other way and refused to look at them.

"May I have some bandages?" I asked her again.

"No."

I got angry. "So, you do not practise revolutionary humanitarianism in accordance with Chairman Mao's teaching," I said.

"Revolutionary humanitarianism is not for you," she said.

*   *   *

[Nien Cheng was released from prison in March 1973. She returned to Shanghai only to discover after a lengthy investigation that her only daughter, Meiping, had been murdered by the Red Guards during the Cultural Revolution. She left China to emigrate to the United States. Upon her departure from China she wrote, "I wished it was Meiping standing on the deck of this ship, going away to make a new life for herself. After all, it was the law of nature that the old should die first and the young should live on, not the other way round. Also I felt sad because I was leaving forever the country of my birth. It was a break so final it was shattering. God knows how hard I had tried to remain true to my country. But I had failed utterly through no fault of my own."—ED.]

Index

Accusations: among prisoners, 229–230; false, 18, 39, 46, 53, 66–67, 112–127, 133–134, 148–150, 160, 172–173, 177–178, 238, 243–263. *See also* Arrests; Confessions; Denunciations; Informers; Interrogation; Intimidation.

Alapi (quoted), 129–131

Alexia, 51

Alfaro, Luis, 213–216

Almeijeiras, Efigenio, 191–194

"American's Tale, An" (Noble), 42–57

Amnesty for prisoners, 198–199. *See also* Freeing of prisoners for propaganda purposes; Release of prisoners.

Andrassy Street prison, 132

Anti-Americanism, 206

Anti-Communist literature, 4–5, 7–8; gulag literature quoted in, 7–8n; literature criticizing, 10–11. *See also* Gulag literature; *individual titles by name.*

Anti-Communist movement: China, 160; Christians and, 5–6, 8–9, 8n, 60, 89, 92; conservative movement and, 6–7, 9–13; criticism of, 10–11, 217–218; Cuba, 186–187; DAR involvement, 9–10; education programs, 7, 9–11; and foreign policy (U.S.), 12–14; grassroots activities, 5–10, 60; House Committee on Un-American Activities, 58–59; literature, 4–5, 7–8; military circles, 10–11, 188; military issues and, 12–13; post-Soviet, 13; propaganda, 188; United States, 5–14, 59–60, 88–89,

113, 139–140, 142, 159–161, 186–188, 217–219, 239–240; and the Vietnam War, 11–12, 13, 88–89. *See also* Gulag literature.

Anti-Semitic pogroms, 40, 53

Arms control, and the anti-Communist movement, 12–13

Arrests: counterrevolutionaries, 24–25, 38–39, 186–187, 190–195; Doan Van Toai, 220–228; falsified arrests, 20–23, 63, 66–69, 190–195, 236; of government officials, 93–94; of guards, 49–50; intellectuals, 29–30, 52, 125, 154–156, 229, 237–240; Lipper, 18; Martino, 190–194; mistaken identity, 220–228, 235–236; Patrascanu, 93–94, 95; Polish partisans, 40, 53; Prychodko, 58, 63–64; religious crimes, 32–33; Rigney, 163–165; Romania, 92–94; the Ukraine, 61–64; Wurmbrand, 92–97. *See also* Accusations; Confessions; Prisoner categories; Purges; Sentencing.

Asian prisoners in Soviet camps, 40, 53

Bathing in prisons, 49, 64–65, 75, 131, 173, 179, 242, 255–256. *See also* Dirty conditions.

Bayoneting, 199

Beatings: Cuban police stations, 193; deaths by, 40, 238; Hungarian secret police, 116–119; by the NKVD, 64, 67–70, 75, 78; by the PCC, 103–105; prisons, 64, 67–70, 75, 183–185, 210–211, 244–245; soling, 116–117. *See also* Confessions; Torture.

Indifference (*cont.*)
162–163; of prisoners, 124, 243; of
work camp inmates, 23, 79. *See also*
Hopelessness; Insanity; Intimidation;
Psychological methods of
interrogation; Psychological
torture.
Informers, 54–55, 197–198, 215–216,
229–230. *See also* Spying.
Injuries from Cultural Revolution
tactics, 249, 251
Insanity: fear of, 178–180, 257–258. *See
also* Hopelessness; Indifference.
Intellectuals: persecution of, 29–30, 52,
125, 154–156, 229, 237–240; prisoners,
29–30, 52, 66–67, 229; torture of,
237
Interrogation: Calea Rahova, 97–102;
Hungarian police, 113–125; La
Cabaña, 97–102, 201; Martino, 195;
No. 1 Detention House, 241,
243–247, 252–253; psychological
methods, 124–125, 140, 142–150,
155–156, 179, 179n, 180–183; Red
army, 40; Tran Hung Dao Boulevard
prison, 230; Wurmbrand, 97–102.
See also Beatings; Falsified
confessions; Torture.
Intimidation, 153–154, 157–158, 162–163,
164–165; hopelessness, 216; public
accusations, 148–150; public
humiliation, 165; tou cheng, 179,
179n, 180–183. *See also* Confessions;
Interrogation; Psychological
methods of interrogation;
Psychological torture.
Invalid camps, 24; food rations, 24. *See
also* Prisons; Work camps.
Isle of Pines, 198, 213–216; dirty
conditions, 213; education programs,
213–214; informers, 215–216
Isolation: of Katorga prisoners, 36; in
prisons, 131–133, 136, 203, 224–228,
247–249
Ivan, 51

Janssen, Arnold, 172
Japanese prisoners in the Soviet Union,
40
Jianu, Marin, 105
John Birch Society, 6–7

Johnson, Lyndon, Vietnam war
policies, 11–12
Judas, 183–185

Katorga prisoners, 35–36
Kennedy, John F.: assassination of, 188;
Cuban policies, 187–188
Khrushchev, Nikita: denunciation of
Stalin, 4, 59; relations with U.S.,
58–59; testimony against, 58–59;
Ukrainian policies, 59, 61–63
Kiev NKVD prisons, 64–78; beatings,
64, 67–70, 75; boycotting of false
evidence givers, 72; falsified
confessions, 66–67, 72–74, 83;
inmates, 66–67, 82–83; living
conditions, 64–66, 75–76; suicide,
71–72, 74; torture, 70–74
"Kind of Torture, A: A Tale from the
Chinese Cultural Revolution"
(Cheng), 237–263
Kirov, Sergei, 38n
Kolyma, 23–41; clothing, 29–30; cold
conditions, 23–24; fisheries, 28;
food rations, 30, 36–37; gold
mining, 26–31; history, 26–31;
illness, 37; Japanese prisoners, 40;
prisoner-of-war camps, 40;
prostitution in, 39; religious crime
inmates, 32–35; starvation, 30, 37;
suicide, 38; ukazniki, 39; Wallace's
visit to, 19–20
Kravchenko, Victor, 3–5

La Cabaña, 200–206; cold conditions,
203; crowded conditions, 203;
educational programs, 207–212;
interrogation, 97–102, 201; medical
care, 203; riots, 210–211; torture,
201–203; trials, 205
Labor camps. *See* Re-education
centers; Rehabilitation farms; Work
camps.
Lee, 173–174
Lenin, Vladimir Ilich, 95, 96
Life and Death in Shanghai (Cheng),
238–263
Lillian, 23–25
Linder, Roy, 54–55
Lipper, Elinor, 17–20, 58; memoirs,
17–41

A NOTE ON THE EDITORS

Donald T. Critchlow was born in Pasadena, California, and studied at San Francisco State University and the University of California, Berkeley, where he received a Ph.D. in history. He has been a Fulbright Fellow, a Woodrow Wilson Fellow, and a guest scholar at the Brookings Institution, and is now professor of history at Saint Louis University. He is the founding president of the Institute for Political History and editor of the *Journal of Policy History*. He has written and edited eleven books, including *Intended Consequences: Birth Control, Abortion, and the Federal Government*, and *Studebaker: The Life and Death of an American Corporation*.

Agnieszka Critchlow was born in Warsaw, Poland, studied at the University of Kansas, and now teaches in the American Studies program at Charles University in Prague, Czech Republic.